Collecting and Exhibiting Computer-Based Technology

Computer technology has transformed modern society, yet curators wishing to reflect those changes face difficult challenges in terms of both collecting and exhibiting. *Collecting and Exhibiting Computer-Based Technology* examines how curators at the history and technology museums of the Smithsonian Institution have met these challenges.

Focusing on the curatorial process, the book explores the ways in which curators at the institution have approached the accession and display of technological artifacts. Such collections often have comparatively few precedents, and can pose unique dilemmas. In analyzing the Smithsonian's approach, Foti takes in diverse collection case studies ranging from DNA analyzers to Herbie Hancock's music synthesizers, from iPods to born digital photographs, from the laptop used during the filming of the television program *Sex and the City* to "Stanley" the self-driving car. Using her proposed model of "expert curation", she synthesizes her findings into a more universal framework for understanding the curatorial methods associated with computer technology and reflects on what it means to be a curator in a postdigital world.

Collecting and Exhibiting Computer-Based Technology offers a detailed analysis of curatorial practice in a relatively new field that is set to grow exponentially. It will be useful reading for curators, scholars, and students alike.

Petrina Foti is Adjunct Professor in Museum Studies at the Rochester Institute of Technology, USA. She is involved with the Oral History Collection at the Smithsonian Institution Archives, USA.

Routledge Research in Museum Studies

Titles include:

12 **Museums and Photography**
Displaying Death
Edited by Elena Stylianou and Theopisti Stylianou-Lambert

13 **Global Art and the Practice of the University-Museum**
Edited by Jane Chin Davidson and Sandra Esslinger

14 **Museum Storage and Meaning**
Tales from the Crypt
Edited by Mirjam Brusius and Kavita Singh

15 **Museums, Immigrants, and Social Justice**
Sophia Labadi

16 **Academics, Artists, and Museums**
21st-Century Partnerships
Edited by Irina D. Costache and Clare Kunny

17 **Snapshots of Museum Experience**
Understanding Child Visitors Through Photography
Elee Kirk and Will Buckingham

18 **Public Art and Museums in Cultural Districts**
J. Pedro Lorente

19 **Collecting and Exhibiting Computer-Based Technology**
Expert Curation at the Museums of the Smithsonian Institution
Petrina Foti

For a full list of titles please visit www.routledge.com/Routledge-Research-in-Museum-Studies/book-series/RRIMS

Collecting and Exhibiting Computer-Based Technology

Expert Curation at the Museums of the Smithsonian Institution

Petrina Foti

Routledge
Taylor & Francis Group
LONDON AND NEW YORK

First published 2019
by Routledge
2 Park Square, Milton Park, Abingdon, Oxon OX14 4RN

and by Routledge
52 Vanderbilt Avenue, New York, NY 10017

Routledge is an imprint of the Taylor & Francis Group, an informa business

British Library Cataloguing-in-Publication Data
A catalogue record for this book is available from the British Library

Library of Congress Cataloging-in-Publication Data
A catalog record has been requested for this book

ISBN: 978-0-8153-6994-3 (hbk)
ISBN: 978-1-351-17434-3 (ebk)

Typeset in Sabon
by Out of House Publishing

MIX
Paper from responsible sources
FSC
www.fsc.org
FSC® C013056

Printed and bound in Great Britain by
TJ International Ltd, Padstow, Cornwall

For my parents, Andrew and Marian Foti

Contents

Acknowledgments

I am deeply grateful for the access, support, and encouragement I received at the Smithsonian Institution. Everyone I spoke with was more than generous with time and expertise. In particular, I would like to thank the following Smithsonian staff, both past and present: David Allison; Jim Barber; Joyce Bedi; Joshua Bell; Melanie Blanchard; Joan Boudreau; Paul Ceruzzi; Seb Chan; Chris Cottrill; Tom Crouch; Aaron Straup Cope; Alicia Cutler; Michelle Delaney; Corey DiPietro; Barney Finn; Stevan Fisher; Lisa Fthenakis; Anne Goodyear; Frank Goodyear; David Haberstich; Kate Henderson; Pam Henson; Linda Hostetler; Eric Jentsch; Stacey Kluck; Robert Leopold; Peter Liebhold; Bonnie Campbell Lilienfeld; Matilda McQuaid; Vanessa Parés; Sharon Perich; Nancy Proctor; Harry Rubenstein; Ann Seeger; Sarah Stauderman; Carlene Stephens; Hal Wallace; Diane Wendt; Helena Wright; and Cedric Yeh. In addition, I offer a special thank you to those who agreed to be interviewed formally. I would also like to express my gratitude to Smithsonian Institution Archives and especially to Dr. Pamela Henson, for all her advice and support in navigating life post-PhD.

Beyond the Smithsonian, I offer my thanks to Dr. Tilly Blyth, Head of Collections and Principal Curator at Science Museum in London, for finding time in her busy schedule for my project and for her continuous encouragement and generosity. I am also deeply indebted to Computer History Museum in California. In particular, for taking time to meet with me and for all that they did to facilitate my 2018 visit, I would like to thank: David C. Brock, Director of Center for Software History; Hansen Hsu, Curator for the Center for Software History; Dag Spicer, Senior Curator; and Marc Weber, Internet History Program Curatorial Director.

There have been three academic institutions that have had a significant role in the development of this book. First and foremost, I would like to thank the Department of Museum Studies at the University of Leicester for providing the fertile ground of both staff and peers that allowed my PhD thesis to grow and develop. I would especially like to recognize the deep dept that I owe Dr. Ross Parry for his unfailing encouragement and guidance through the difficult process of doctorial research and the road that followed after. I am also grateful to Dr. Timothy Kneeland and the Center for Public History at Nazareth College of Rochester, where I was a fellow in 2017. Finally, I would like to offer my thanks to the Museum Studies Program at the Rochester Institute of Technology for the support I received as I completed my manuscript. I would especially like to express my gratitude to Dr. Tina Lent for her wisdom and encouragement and to my students from my Spring 2018 Cultural Heritage class. You guys inspired me far more than you'll know.

I am also particularly thankful to the organizers of the following five international conferences that allowed me to test my core ideas and develop my thinking: University of Manchester and Newcastle University's joint Researching Digital Cultural Heritage conference (Manchester, UK) in November 2017; the Special Interest Group for Computing, Information and Society (SIGCIS) and Computer History Museum's joint Command Lines: Software, Power and Performance conference (Mountain View, CA) in March 2017; the Museum 2015 Tokyo: Agile Museum conference (Tokyo, Japan) in January 2015; the London Science Museum's Interpreting the Information Age: New Avenues for Research and Display conference (London, UK) in November 2014; and, finally, Loughborough University's Constructing Histories of Computing and Digital Media in Museum Environments symposium (Loughborough, UK) in June 2018.

I am lucky to have a strong support network of family and friends that stretches across the globe. In particular, I would like to thank: Dana Allen-Greil; Paul Aquilino; Amy Barnes; Stephanie Bowry; Katy Bunning; Jenny Chiu; Romina Delia; Ching-yueh Hsieh; Wily Jones; Yon Jai Kim; Elee Kirk; Da Kong; Sarah Kuramochi; Luke Leyh; Lisa Leyh; Priya Lin; Wen-Ling Lin; Sipei (Stephanie) Lu; Cintia Velázquez Marroni; Dawn Mason; Vivi Mazarakis; Darren Milligan; Julie Montgomery; Ryan Nutting; Julia Petrov; Cy Shih; Anne Warnement; Julie Warnement; Gudrun Whitehead; Maya Wilson; Pam Wilson and especially my brothers Mark and Peter Foti for always being there. I do not have the words to convey what you all mean to me.

I would also like to include a few additional words of gratitude, especially relating to this past year. To Maya, Vivi, and Pam, for being my emotional support system and for all the tea and lotus pastries. To Ross, for the constant inspiration and for the reminder "What's next?" To Ching for always being there and for making me laugh, even when I didn't think I could. To Helena, for your wisdom and kindness. To Steph, for always having calm words of advice and encouragement. To Alicia, for always having my back. To Cintia, for reading over my words and for being there when I reached out. To Wily, for the hugs. To Julie and Anne, I'm raising my glass. To Gudrun, my book writing buddy in arms. And a big thank you to Luke for donating his iPod in the first place and to Lisa, both for putting up with him afterward and for just being fabulous in general.

Perhaps most important of all, I would like to thank my mother, Marian Foti, for her unwavering support and encouragement. You are my rock, Mom. Finally, I would like to dedicate this work to the memory of my father, Andrew Foti, and of my grandmother, Mary La Bue.

1 What is computer-based technology?

A familiar technology, an unfamiliar artifact

In February 2008, the Smithsonian Institution's National Museum of American History acquired an iPod for its Computers Collection. The four-year-old iPod was still in good working order and had been used by the owner until a few hours before he donated it. This was the first example of this type of technology to enter the Smithsonian collections and its acquisition prompted a series of e-mail and telephone conversations between the museum's curatorial staff as to how best to classify it for cataloging purposes.[1] The iPod was placed on display for the first time four years later in a major exhibition presenting the "treasured" objects from the museum's collections,[2] with images of the iPod prominently positioned in all promotional and other related material. In the graphic display to mark the contemporary section of the exhibition, the image of the iPod was centrally located among the images of iconic historical figures and objects from the era.

In this one example of computer-based technology, the Smithsonian has collected an object unlike any other in its holdings. Although museum curators had long cared for "machine readable" records and objects related to ephemeral subjects like performance born-digital technology posed new challenges. No objects quite like it had existed before. The curatorial staff were uncertain as to how to classify this particular object, because the standardized vocabulary for how to describe it did not yet exist. Yet despite these uncertainties that come with the state of "newness," the iPod was, nonetheless, acknowledged by the museum to be an iconic object in American history, both by its inclusion in the treasured objects exhibition and as part of the promotion of the exhibit. The Smithsonian's landmark acquisition of its first iPod stands as a vivid illustration as to how the collecting and exhibiting of computer-based technology (a particularly emerging and innovative technology) can disrupt a museum's established patterns and rhythms of collecting.

It was stories such as this that first gave rise to this book, stories with which I had first-hand experience. The iPod first came to the museum during my time as collection manager for the Computers Collection – in part because I had strongly advocated for its acquisition – and, therefore, it was my responsibility to catalog it. I still am able to vividly recall the frustration of not being able to classify this new museum object, even as my own iPod played beside me. This was not the first time that I would find a disconnect between the computer technology I used daily – from computer game programs to web-based social media platforms – and the abilities of the museum to be able to easily record the history of hardware-dependent software and software-dependent hardware. But, as I would glance down the halls to where my fellow curators and collection managers were working on their own collections, I realized that this dilemma extended far beyond the reach of the Computers Collection. It was a problem that the curators in the Photographic History Collection were facing as the rise of digital photography replaced more than one hundred years of film-based photography. It was a question that surely the curators of the Music Collection asked themselves in regard to how they might represent the transformation that internet-based applications, such as iTunes, had on music consumption. However, when I first began my formal study into this problem, I became aware just how quickly curators with no background in computer science and computer history were able to adapt to the challenges that the introduction of computer-based technology-related objects posed to their collections. This was not the rigid behavior that one might expect from a tradition-based institution, such as a museum.

The museum clings to its traditions, not because it knows no other way, because that is the most appropriate response the majority of the time. However, when faced with a set of circumstances for which no precedent easily fits, as is the case with computer-based technology, curators are creative in their approach and prepared to work in new ways to better achieve their objective. This type of curatorial behavior can be dramatic and overt, but often was quiet and subtle in expression. This curatorial knowledge is distributive in where it resides. It does not solely rest on the shoulders of one person, but is shared between dynamic collections of individuals, both museum professionals and non–museum professionals alike. This expertise dispersed across the space of the organization, reaching out to the professional sector and to the very museum visitors that the museum serves. Furthermore, this curatorial practice creates its own legacy when computer-based knowledge is recorded because it represents a greater pattern of curatorial behavior associated with collection stewardship. This type of expertise is shared through time, preserved in the past, and specifically meant to be utilized in the future. This guides what and how curators preserve computer-based technology, since their thoughts are in tune with the needs of their unknown successors as well as their own. This model of expert curatorship – *adaptive, distributive, and transmitted* – offers evidence that, rather than a rigid form of behavior, curatorship is able to be fluid and ever evolving, even in times of uncertainty.

Yet, perhaps even more significantly, this research has captured a moment in time when curatorial precedent is being set. With every iPhone put on exhibit, every computer chip cataloged, every born-digital object acquired for a museum's collection, curators use their adaptive, distributive, and transmitted expertise to establish a working methodology for curating computer-based technology. Through observing these exhibition and collection practices, there is the indication of three distinct expert curatorial methodologies: *documenting*, *operating*, and *representing*. These three methodologies, whether working in tandem or individually, not only form the basis of what might reasonably be understood to be the establishment of a new curatorial tradition that specifically responds to the challenges posed by computer-based technology, but also reveal how we ourselves have begun to comprehend and, dare we say, process what computer-based technology truly is.

Scope and research context

The aim of this book is to uncover Smithsonian curatorial practice by exploring the relationship between staff and their collections. Yet, by investigating this one particular institution, and this specific type of object, this study has also begun to reveal a characteristic of curatorial practice and behavior that might be seen to be more widely applicable. The book will show that, when confronted with an unfamiliar object or type of object, such as those relating to computer-based technology, curatorial staff, specifically those of the Smithsonian Institution, have the expertise to create new curatorial methods. This curatorial expertise is displayed in the documenting, operating, and representing methods employed and through what is preserved in collections and presented on exhibit. The evidence presented is that of an adaptive, distributed, and transmitted model of curatorship, one that has been honed by a long tradition of technology-related collection stewardship and that is fully prepared to answer the challenges posed by computer-based technology by establishing a new curatorial tradition, in a way that is creative and shared, revealing the museum as a trusted source for context and clarity in a rapidly evolving world.

This research represents a mixed method approach, utilizing a combination of semi-structured interviews and archival work with the purpose of understanding the thoughts of the associated curator or collection manager and revealing how the curator views the objects for which he or she is responsible. The field of museum studies has increasingly become more aware of the need to record its history. Some academic studies of contemporary practice include brief histories, such as Philip Hughes' *Exhibition Design*,[3] George E. Hein's *Learning in the Museum*,[4] or Ross Parry's *Recoding the Museum*.[5] These authors each provide invaluable insights (be it on the history of museum education or museum computing), and yet, their histories remain, by design, generalized and condensed. In contrast, other writers have devoted entire theses to historicizing their field, such as Andrea Witcomb's *Re-Imagining the Museum: Beyond the Mausoleum*[6] or

Eilean Hooper-Greenhill's collection interpretation in her book *Museums and the Shaping of Knowledge*.[7] Witcomb examines the museum's role in society, engaging with issues such as museum authority. Her approach is to examine case studies that reveal curatorial practices in order to bring better clarity to theoretical debates, what Witcomb refers to as a "more top down approach."[8] What emerges from her history is a view of the museum, contrary to the image of the staid, unchanging mausoleum, as able to make connections with contemporary audiences and contribute to a growing knowledge base. I employed Witcomb's approach, which emphasizes close analysis of curatorial practice case studies in order to form theoretical conclusions, rather than an application of pre-existing theory.[9]

Hooper-Greenhill's focus is narrower with specific attention given to how museums actively shape knowledge. Hers is a narrative, based on insights from Michel Foucault's work, that investigates how museums developed and for what purpose. The protagonists for Hooper-Greenhill are philosophical rather than practical, a history of ideas perhaps more than a history of acts of accession and documentation. However, Hooper-Greenhill notes a recent shift in the museum's construction of knowledge:

> The lack of knowledge of the work of the curator constituted the visitor as ignorant and the curator as expert in respect of the audience for whom the museum's intellectual products were intended. Now, the closed and private space of the early public museums has begun to open, and the division between private and public has begun to close.[10]

Hooper-Greenhill's observations open new avenues of exploration into museums' relationships with their visitors and how museum expertise is shared. Theoretical examinations of museum history, such as those of Witcomb and Hooper-Greenhill, provide context for how the museum came to be and, perhaps, provide insights into what the museum may yet become.

Perhaps the most influential view of museum practice, Sharon Macdonald's *Behind the Scenes at the Science Museum*[11] takes an anthropological view on the development of a major exhibition for the Science Museum in London, UK. Her study considered "the process involved in 'translating' expert scientific knowledge into knowledge for a lay public,"[12] using an ethnographic methodology that took her into the museum as an embedded observer of the daily activities of the museum staff, in particular the development of the food gallery and the visitor response once the gallery was open. To Macdonald, the dynamic among the Science Museum's staff is a strength, a "magic"[13] that should be respected. Macdonald's seminal work, though tight and situated in context and focus, nonetheless directs us towards the shape and discourse (not to mention the value) that histories of curatorship might usefully take.

In terms of Smithsonian history, recent years have seen an increase in formal, unaffiliated historical studies. In 2013, three books were published that engaged with Smithsonian curatorial history. Robert Post's *Who Owns America's Past? The Smithsonian and the Problem of History*[14] can be seen as a retrospective of the author's time as a Smithsonian curator, whilst Kylie Message's *Museums and Social Activism: Engaged Protest*[15] and William S. Walker's *A Living Exhibition: The Smithsonian and the Transformation of the Universal Museum*[16] provide a comprehensive examination of Smithsonian collecting and exhibiting. The publication of these three books signaled a new interest in examining curatorial history at the Smithsonian, an interest to which this research aims, modestly, to contribute. In particular, Message and Walker's approaches to their research have informed this study's approach. With both books, a broader view of the institution is reflected within their narrow scopes of study. Walker's view of Smithsonian museum development as "part of a longer institutional history" and "an outgrowth of a long process" rather than "a revolutionary transformation"[17] is similar to Witcomb's conclusions that "contemporary museum trends have historical precedents rather than being a radical break with past practices"[18] and is in keeping with the approach this research takes to curatorial history at the Smithsonian.

It should be also noted that the Institution itself has always been conscientious in the recording of its own history, with George Brown Goode (Assistant Secretary of the Smithsonian under Spencer Baird and head of the US National Museum) as one of the first to formally record its history.[19] Within this field, there is a fairly recent tradition of literature where Smithsonian curators, perhaps influenced by the tenants of public history, reflect on museum practice as it relates to the specific instances of particularly challenging collecting efforts or exhibitions. Three such examples from the curators of the National Museum of American History would be Peter Liebhold and Harry R. Rubenstein's "Bringing Sweatshops into the Museum"[20] (which examined navigating the controversy in the process of exhibition development during the "culture wars" of the 1990s), James B. Gardner and Sarah M. Henry's "September 11 and the Mourning After: Reflections on Collecting and Interpreting the History of Tragedy"[21] and David Shayt's "Artifacts of Disaster: Creating the Smithsonian's Katrina Collection."[22] (These latter two works will be examined in more detail in Chapter 2.) All three articles are works of self-reflection with the authors carefully framing their own experiences within the broader sphere of museum practice. Rather than continue in this tradition, I have chosen to focus on case studies with which I was not affiliated.

That is not to say, however, that my time at the Smithsonian did not play a role in shaping this research. I served as collection manager in the Computers Collection at the National Museum of American History from 2006 until 2010 and left the Smithsonian at the end of the following year. Consequently, this position provided me, now as an external researcher, with insight into the structure and culture of the Smithsonian. However, as with any researcher critiquing her own practice or reflecting on her own institution or body of work, with these opportunities come challenges as well, as many of my potential interview subjects were former colleagues.[23] These raised concerns as to the practice of researchers returning to former places of employment. Therefore, this research borrows from autoethnography in that:

> Autoethnographers recognize the innumerable ways personal experience influences the research process... Even though some researchers still assume that research can be done from a neutral, impersonal, and objective stance, most now recognize that such an assumption is not tenable. Consequently, autoethnography is one of the approaches that acknowledges and accommodates subjectivity, emotionality, and the researcher's influence on research, rather than hiding from these matters or assuming they don't exist.[24]

This study acknowledges that my time as a staff member of the Smithsonian Institution has shaped my perceptions and emotions of that institution. Therefore, my approach to conducting research at the Smithsonian has been influenced by my time there. Where appropriate, this study will offer personal testimonials, in keeping with the tenets of autoethnography.

As there was a wealth of relevant potential case studies within the technology-related collections of the Smithsonian, I chose to exclude the majority of objects in the Computers Collection that were acquired, cataloged, or exhibited during my post, focusing instead on the moment when the curator first engaged with computer-based technology, rather than curation after collection policy has been set. While I do not have personal connections to these case studies, this research also holds firm to the philosophy of Richard Evans that through "very scrupulous and careful and self-critical" practice, it is possible to "find out how it happened and reach some tenable though always less than final conclusions about what it all meant."[25]

In terms of how it understands the recording of history by museum practitioners, the approach of this book is aligned to Evans' "modern realist" framing of history after postmodernity. In his key work, *In Defence of History*, Evans presents the forming – or recording, to use a more passive term – of history as something achievable, through careful examination and self-awareness. This is a concept of history that works at two levels for this study. First, it is a philosophy of history that has informed the assumptions made about the past, about the evidence used as historians, and the role this has in assembling a meaningful narrative to our readers and, in the case of museum exhibitions, our visitors. Evans' practice of history allows us still (in a postmodern age) to produce versions of the past that can be evidenced and that can attempt to reflect and resemble a past that did happen. The evidence collected and presented in this book attests to this view. There is a second level, however, at which Evans' view of historiography informs (or at least has resonance) with this book, and that is in the way it might helpfully encapsulate the curatorial drive to evidence the contemporary through acts of collecting. This research works from the assumption that contemporary collecting is a method that curators employ to better assist their future counterparts in their own investigations into "how it happened."

As key information does not always make it into formal archives or even the informal "archives" of individuals' personal papers, oral testimonies are a valuable means of "creating documents to fill a perceived vacuum in the existing record."[26] As a model of conducting such research, I was primarily influenced by the way that the National Museum of American History presented curatorial history on their "September 11: Bearing Witness to History" website,[27] which shall be discussed in more detail in Chapter 2. In an institution as large and as complex as the Smithsonian, it is difficult to stay up-to-date on everything that occurs relating to a given subject. I often relied on "word of mouth" about possible projects and collecting efforts that might relate to my topic. That required a series of informal meetings with various members of staff across the Smithsonian to help identify which curators in which museums had experience in collecting and exhibiting computer-based technology.

In terms of contemporary collecting theory, this book sits between the work of Simon Knell and Owain Rhys, who both explore the concept of collection stewardship. Knell's *Museums and the Future of Collecting*[28] offers a collection of essays from museum practitioners and theorists relating to the challenges and dilemmas faced by current museum collections, with the majority of essays examining issues associated with contemporary collecting. Though similar in scope, the central focus of Rhys' *Contemporary Collecting: Theory and Practice*[29] concerns the reasons for collecting contemporaneously and the practical considerations that come with those decisions. This book builds on Rhys' investigation into museum practice and borrows his rationale as to why contemporary collecting fulfills an important role for the museum. From Knell, it takes the concept of object-based history and the importance of probing collecting practices for meaning and understanding. In Knell's words, "we need museums to remain those object-centered oases in a world of change, but in order to achieve this they too must change."[30]

This research defines the word "curatorial" in the broadest sense to mean those who are responsible for a museum collection, including the curators who interpret, the collection managers who organize, and those who serve in a variety of roles in between. Specifically, this study will focus on collection stewardship, which the American Alliance of Museum defines as:

> the careful, sound and responsible management of that which is entrusted to a museum's care. Possession of collections incurs legal, social and ethical obligations to provide proper physical storage, management and care for the collections and associated documentation, as well as proper intellectual control. Collections are held in trust for the

> public and made accessible for the public's benefit. Effective collections stewardship ensures that the objects the museum owns, borrows, holds in its custody and/or uses are available and accessible to present and future generations. A museum's collections are an important means of advancing its mission and serving the public.[31]

The American Alliance of Museums is the single most influential museum association in the United States and therefore its views on a given museology-related subject can be assumed to be apposite to the American museum sector. This is certainly the case for the museums of the Smithsonian Institution. The Institution's dedication to collection stewardship is subtly revealed in numerous ways. Harold Wallace, for instance, notes:

> We tend to focus on our particular missions. Here at [the National Museum of] American History, our general reason to be is to document and preserve the history of the United States of America. And, in my opinion, our major responsibility is the care and feeding of the national collections and then making those collections accessible to our modern audiences.[32]

Wallace's words on the "the care and feeding of the national collections" provide a humorous way to describe this serious responsibility, and yet, by using terminology associated with living creatures, it also highlights how vitally important he finds this role. Collection stewardship is a central component to the relationship between the curator and the collection for which he or she is responsible. This relationship will be further discussed in Chapter 2.

We should pause here to note the differences in the terms "curation" and "digital curation." The aim of this study is to uncover Smithsonian curatorial practice by exploring the relationship between staff and their collections, rather than to investigate methods of physical or digital conservation. As is true with all forms of conservation, digital conservation is a collaborative effort of conservators, curators, and collection mangers, informed by the most recent technological and scientific advances. This study, therefore, recognizes that "curation" and "digital curation" are two separate terms, as the latter term is increasingly used in the library and archive field to specifically describe the conservation of digital assets and the processes of ensuring those assets are accessible.[33] In contrast, the term "digital heritage" refers more broadly to the use of digital methods in the cultural heritage sector.[34]

With these key terms of "history" and "curator" clarified and defined in this context, it is perhaps also important to be clear on how this work defines "computer-based technology." In this context, "computer-based technology" is understood to mean any electronic device that depends on a computer or related parts (such as a processor chip or a type of software) to perform its assigned function. These can range from GPS devices to digital music players. The consequence of this for the research presented here is that a very diverse range of objects and types of collections will be considered: from the ENIAC, the first electronic general-purpose computer, to the digital images taken with a mobile phone; from an Apple Mac used as music synthesizer to the iPod music player; from the code for a computer app to a large blue Volkswagen car containing software allowing driverless operation. Though diverse, and though perhaps at first sight not a natural set of objects to consider together, these objects do, in fact, all represent "computer-based technology." Indeed, their very diversity and varied format, function, and appearance speak partly to the challenge they present to museums such as those at the Smithsonian Institution. It is for that reason, though the focus of this study remains fully on the Smithsonian, the thoughts and practices of computer history curators from the Science Museum (London) and the Computer History Museum in California will be examined. These curators will offer further examples of museum practitioners whose primary responsibility is the care and interpretation of computer-based technology.

Meet the Smithsonian

For all of its universal qualities, the Smithsonian Institution is unique both in its structure and in its formation. More than just a small collective of museums, the Smithsonian Institution is composed of nineteen museums, nine research facilities, and a zoo. The formal research generated, especially in regard to the scientific contributions of units like the Smithsonian Astrophysical Observatory and the Smithsonian Tropical Research Institute, makes the Institution more comparable to an academic university. To better understand this organization, it is important to first understand its unique and complicated history.

In 1829, James Smithson, a British chemist and mineralogist, bequeathed his fortune to the people of the United States, a country that Smithson had never visited, for the "increase and diffusion of knowledge" for reasons that still have never been fully understood or explained. He never recorded his reasons for doing so in any written form, though many theories exist. The United States government was then left to decide the best method of interpreting his bequest without definite proof or guidance as to Smithson's intentions. After great debate on how the money should best be utilized, the Smithsonian Institution was founded in 1846. In December of that year, the Committee on Organization submitted a report that was included in the first Smithsonian Annual Report. In it, they framed how they – and therefore how the Institution – understood Smithson's wishes:

> "For the increase and diffusion of knowledge among men," were the words of Smithson's will—words used by a man accustomed to the strict nomenclature of exact science. They inform us that a plan of organization to carry into effect the intention of the testator, must embrace two objects: one, the calling forth of new knowledge by original research;

> and the other, the dissemination of knowledge already in existence. Smithson's words, liberal and comprehensive, exclude no branch of human knowledge; nor is there any restrictive clause in the charter under which we act. That charter indicates a few items chiefly relating to one of the above objects, and leave the rest of the plan, under the general provision of the bequest, to the discretion of the board.[35]

Not a school or institution of higher learning, the Smithsonian was designed to be a center for scientific study and public enlightenment, offering support for budding scientists to increase knowledge and understanding of the physical and natural world. The first Annual Report was clear on its objective:

> That it is the intention of the act of Congress establishing the institution, and in accordance with the design of Mr. Smithson, as expressed in his will, that one of the principal modes of executing the act and the trust is the accumulation of collections of specimens and objects of natural history and of elegant art, and the gradual formation of a library of valuable works pertaining to all departments of human knowledge, to the end that a copious storehouse of materials of science, literature, and art may be provided, which shall excite and diffuse the love of learning among men, and shall assist the original investigations and efforts of those who may devote themselves to the pursuit of any branch of knowledge.[36]

In the beginning, journals and the occasional exhibition at the Smithsonian building were the primary means to diffuse the intellectual output of these pursuits.[37] However, in more than a century and a half, the Smithsonian Institution, to better fulfil its mission, developed into a complex series of museums, galleries, archives, libraries, and other types of research centers.

Each museum has developed slightly differently in different time periods and climates with different missions to fulfil. As Harold Wallace, Curator for the Electricity Collection at the National Museum of American History, explains:

> The Smithsonian is very much a conglomeration of disparate organizations that "kinda sorta" operate under the same general rubric. Various administrators and directors have gone out of their way, and in my personal opinion, wasted quite a bit of money coming up with fancy mission statements. Whereas the general Smithsonian mission statement from Smithson's Will, for the increase and diffusion of knowledge, seems to me to be perfectly acceptable.[38]

This "conglomerate," to employ Wallace's terminology, offers many benefits. Carlene Stephens, Curator for the Division of Work and Industry at the

American History Museum, explains: "There are just more resources. There are more audiences. There is more of everything, which should also mean a more complicated, bureaucratic apparatus, but it's good. It's all good."[39] The Smithsonian structure of governance comprises individual units with oversight from a head office. Ultimately, the entire Institution answers to the Office of the Secretary – casually referred to as "The Castle" by Smithsonian staff after the original 1846 Smithsonian building where most of the most senior heads of central administration still have offices.

There are both advantages and disadvantages to this structure. While a museum director normally answers only to his or her board, a Smithsonian museum director answers to the museum's board, the central offices, and the Board of Regents of the Smithsonian Institution. However, the benefits of centralization mean that the burden of cost for building facilities maintenance, including security staff, is shared. Robert Leopold, Deputy Director of the Smithsonian Center for Folklife and Cultural Heritage, notes:

> Looking at it from a museum director's point of view. If a museum director is fundraising for their museum and if they had to share that with other museums? Well, there might be a small revolt! [But] if the individual museums had to pay for their own heating and cooling and guards and parking attendants out of their own funds, there also might be a revolt.[40]

Leopold's example illustrates the costs and the benefits to a centralized form of governance. Not only does the centralization of Smithsonian support services allow, at least theoretically, for a more efficient allocation of resources, but it presents the Smithsonian as one cohesive entity, when reality might be less definitive.

For example, the Smithsonian does not use one specific collection management software system, with each museum and archive making the decision based on what is best for their own unit. However, the Smithsonian's internet-based Collection Search Center aggregates each of these databases into one fully searchable website of all Smithsonian holdings online, regardless of collecting unit, fully accessible to everyone worldwide. For instance, using the Collection Search Center to investigate what items relating to famed baseball player Babe Ruth the Smithsonian has yields close to one hundred results from more than fifteen different record sources, almost all of which have an associated image attached to the record.[41] As the catalogue from the Smithsonian Libraries is included as one of the record sources, there are in the search results multiple records for biographies of Ruth located in a number of the different Smithsonian Library branches. The National Museum of American History offers the records for at least three signed baseballs in the collection and the 1923 ticket booth from Yankee Stadium, where Ruth used to play. The search also reveals that the Smithsonian's National Portrait Gallery has multiple portraits of the baseball legend. While the majority are photographs, there are also a few caricature drawings. Hirshhorn Museum has a record for a painting by Philip Evergood entitled "Early Youth of Babe Ruth (Old North Beach Amusement Park)." The Archives Center, considered to be part of the National Museum of American History, has in its holdings a large collection of sheet music, including at least one specifically about Babe Ruth. The record for this particular piece of music is included in the search results, which might lead a particularly interested researcher to contact the Archives Center in hopes that there might be similar items in the same record unit. Finally, three stamps of Ruth from a lesser-known Smithsonian museum, the National Postal Museum, are intermingled with the rest of the search results. Presented together with no one document source taking precedent over the others, the diversity of these results – for this one random, if iconic example – serves to highlight the depth and breadth of the Smithsonian collections and repositories.

With so many museums with such divergent motives and missions, it is easy for outsiders to wonder if the Smithsonian has truly remained one cohesive entity or is now actually a small swarm of museums that have only a brand name in common. However, for those who work for the Smithsonian Institution, the answer is clear. Wallace notes that the Smithsonian Mission statement "to increase and diffuse knowledge" is applicable to every unit of the Smithsonian, no matter what its individual mission:

> It does apply to every single Smithsonian organization, whether it is American History or one of the art museums, or the Tropical Research Institute: "for the increase and diffusion of knowledge." Once you get past that rubric, we tend to go lots of different ways because, art historians are different from historians of technology, are different from biologists and astronomers and you name it – we do so many different things – but that is one of the very few touchstones that we all have in common. That, and high professional regard for the organization in general.[42]

This shared dedication to the Institution's mission is able to unite the many otherwise different museums, libraries, archives, and research facilities. Concentrating solely on the museums of the Smithsonian, they include art, natural history, cultural heritage, social history, and the history of technology. In size, they range from the Anacostia Community Museum, which has a staff of fewer than thirty people, to the National Museum of Natural History, the National Air and Space Museum, and the National Museum of American History, which are among the most visited museums in the world. Unlike, for example, the Tate Galleries (in the UK), the Smithsonian is manifestly a diverse group of museums; therefore the united sense of identity across the Institution is even more astonishing.[43] Alicia Cutler, Digital Asset Manager at that National Museum of American History's Collections Documentation Service, explains:

> I feel like we are part of something larger, a very varied larger, because there is not that much in common focus-wise between the different units. However, there are a lot of processes within the units that are identical... I always feel like [the National Museum of] American History represents the Smithsonian. It is never just alone.[44]

As Cutler explains, interests and subject matter of these dissimilar museums can often overlap. While the National Museum of American History is clearly dedicated to recounting history of the United States, so too, at least partly, are the National Portrait Gallery (which uses portraiture as a means to explore biography, especially of American figures of history) and the National Museum of African American History and Culture, to name just a few.

It is not surprising that this will often lead the staff from Smithsonian museums with shared interests to collaborate on various projects. Joyce Bedi, Senior Historian at Lemelson Center for Innovation, which is part of the American History Museum, explains:

> There is a difference with every single person you work with because they all have their own personalities. I mean working with [the National Museum of] Air and Space is not the same as working with [the National Museum of] Natural History and you would not want it to be, you know? They all have their primary interests and they all have different personalities of how they like to do things and that is part of the fun of it. I mean if everybody did the same thing we did, the same way we did it, why would we want to do anything with anybody else?[45]

Bedi's words reflect the awareness of the differences between the units, even when their subject interests overlap, and the value that comes from those differences. Eric Jentsch, Deputy Chair and Curator for the Division of Culture and the Arts at the American History Museum, concurs and observes:

> I would say that we have three of the largest museums on the planet here [at the Smithsonian]. Given the size and complexity of each museum, it is difficult to then say we have really strong working relationships with these other organizations, because it is a lot just to keep this place focused and moving. But our sister museums are good in that we are very eager to help each other when the time arises. We share expertise. We share objects. We share intellectual concepts. When there is opportunities for that, we all work together to create the best experiences in each organization.[46]

Jentsch uses the phrase "sister museum" to describe the relationship with other Smithsonian museums, highlighting that there is a common bond shared across the Institution. Sharon Perich, Curator for Photographic History at the American History Museum, further extends the family metaphor to explain the complex relationships between the various Smithsonian units in a more colloquial manner:

> I feel like the Institution itself is like going to a family reunion on a daily basis. You have relatives that you know have been here for a very long time but you have never met them. You have relatives that are characters, with people telling stories about them, and you can't wait to meet them. You have new people always coming on. You have units that are highly reproductive – there are a lot of them – and then you have some that are more sparse. You even have some lines in which they die out. The name doesn't carry on, because that collecting unit gets absorbed or that subject matter gets absorbed, or there's nobody to carry on the Chemistry Collection. And so it's really like this giant family reunion of extended family. And it's dynamic like that. It's always changing like that.[47]

We can see from Perich, Jentsch, Bedi, and Cutler that the diversity of the Smithsonian's museums is something that is celebrated and that there is a shared sense of identity of being part of the Smithsonian Institution. In 2010 nearly 4,000 Smithsonian employees in the Washington, DC, area gathered together for what was believed to be the first group staff photograph. They formed the shape of the sunburst logo. In a visual metaphor, these men, women, and children[48] were from many parts of the institution, but those parts all made up part of the whole. This concept echoes the phrase *E pluribus unum* – "out of many, one" – that appears on the seal of the United States of America and on much of the country's currency. There is understanding among every Smithsonian museum that it is one of nineteen sister museums. These relationships make explicit that the curatorial connections that museum staff create outside the walls of their home institution mirror – as a sort of microcosm – the relationships that form within the museum sector. This, in turn, provides deeper insight to the development of curatorial theory and practice in the American museum sector.

In short, the Smithsonian Institution, while utterly unique in museum terms (and, therefore, an exception in research terms), is also a powerful and useful environment in which to observe curatorial practice. With its complex structural environment, similar subjects and even identical objects have been collected and exhibited in a variety of Smithsonian museums, demonstrating the flexibility of Smithsonian curators and of curatorial practice in general. In the case of contemporary collecting, the Smithsonian offers multiple instances of objects relating to recent events formally being acquisitioned from a variety of academic disciplines. At the National Museum of American History alone, the examples range from political protest materials, household ceramics, costumes and props used during television productions, to the remnants left behind from a natural disaster. Similarly, with respect to our specific case of computer-based technology, the Smithsonian museums offer a wide range of examples, from the traditional mainframe computers of the 1950s and 1960s to today's handheld technology of smartphones and mp3 players. The large holdings of the Smithsonian Institution afford us an opportunity to see the collecting of those particular types of technology objects in a variety of different circumstances, from the slow establishing of collecting policies in the Computers Collection during the 1970s and 1980s to the steep learning curve that curators in the Photographic History faced when the events of September 11 prompted quick collecting decisions in regard to digital photography, as well as how these objects might then be displayed in a meaningful way. Through these many illustrations that the Smithsonian provides, this study begins to trace what it means to curate computer-based technology.

Of the Smithsonian Institution's nineteen museums, the focus of this book is on history museums and not art museums. In particular, this research will primarily concentrate on history museums that contain technology-related collections, specifically the National Museum of American History[49] with additional case studies provided by the Cooper Hewitt, Smithsonian Design Museum,[50] and the National Air and Space Museum.[51] Along with the National Museum of Natural History, the American History Museum and the Air and Space Museum are the most visited Smithsonian museums and are considered to be among the most visited museums in the world.

All three museums (Air and Space, Cooper Hewitt, and American History) have collections that trace their beginnings to the mid to late nineteenth century. Many of the collections at the National Museum of American History (such as numismatics, medicine, textiles, graphic arts, photography, ceramics, and musical instruments) were originally founded as part of the US National Museum. The National Museum of American History building opened in 1964 as a separate museum then known as the National Museum of History and Technology. As the name reveals, there was a strong emphasis on the history of technology. The name was changed in 1980, reflecting an increasing shift towards social history. However, its technology collections remain strong. Perhaps most famous as the repository for the "Star-Spangled Banner" (the flag that inspired the country's national anthem), the museum has approximately 1.7 million objects[52] in its holdings. They are divided into the following curatorial divisions: Culture and Arts, Home and Community Life, Medicine and Science, Armed Forces History, Political History, and Work and Industry. The museum also includes the Archives Center, the Dibner Library, and the Jerome and Dorothy Lemelson Center for the Study of Invention and Innovation.

Like the American History Museum, the National Air and Space Museum can trace its Air Collection to the foundation collections of the US National Museum. It should be noted that when the museum building opened on July 1, 1976, it was during the peak of the country's bicentennial celebrations, a rather apt moment for a museum dedicated (at least partly) to the celebration of American technological progress. A second location, the Steven F. Udvar-Hazy Center, opened in 2003 to allow for the exhibition of larger objects, including the Space Shuttle Discovery. However, such iconic artifacts as the 1903 Wright Flyer and Apollo 11 capsule remain on display at the National Mall location.

The history of the Cooper Hewitt is slightly different. Founded in 1897, the decorative arts museum was meant as a study collection for the Cooper Union for the Advancement of Science and Art. A branch of the Smithsonian since 1967, the museum became the Cooper-Hewitt Museum of Decorative Arts and Design in 1969. It was renamed the Cooper-Hewitt National Design Museum in 1994, reflecting the museum's principal focus, and then again in 2014 to "Cooper Hewitt, Smithsonian Design Museum," emphasizing its ties to the Institution. Located in New York City, Cooper Hewitt is the only Smithsonian museum that does not also have a site in Washington, DC.[53] The museum's collections include more than 217,000 design-related objects and the museum offers a range of educational programs, including an on-site master's degree program with Parsons The New School for Design since 1982, continuing the museum's tradition in education.

Together, these three museums provide the main locations for the research. In approaching the recent history of curatorship at each site, the book will examine both why objects were collected and how curators interpreted those objects once they were then part of the museum's collections. As will be further examined in the next chapter, by focusing on history museums that contain technology-related collections, this research is then framed through the way that these museums understand the challenges of computer-based technology.

Narrative of this book

This chapter has defined key terms and provided context for the narrative to come. Chapter 2 will begin by examining theories and intellectual frameworks around contemporary collecting that are relevant to this study's line of enquiry and then consider the ways in which contemporary collecting might also involve acquiring the unprecedented, and the particular challenges that this can pose to curators. The chapter will then propose that beyond the challenges of recording history contemporaneously, computer-based technology, with its dual nature of hardware-dependent software and software-dependent hardware, poses collecting and exhibiting challenges for which the museum had no precedent. Using the "black box" analogy used by the history of technology field to further illuminate these issues, the chapter then establishes how objects that exist solely in a digital format cannot easily follow the collecting precedent of material objects in the same way that three-dimensional hardware is able. This chapter will suggest how, in terms of the object type, the museum had no completely applicable precedent to follow when dealing with the challenges that digital-format objects present.

Chapter 3 proposes that the patterns of curatorial behavior at the museums of the Smithsonian can be seen as specific characteristics of curatorial expertise. The chapter presents a classification of these into three categories – adaptive expertise (able to meet the unfamiliar with creativity and flexibility); distributive expertise (when expertise is shared between museum professionals, field experts, and museum visitors); and transmitted expertise (preserving knowledge in a way that is beneficial for the next generation of collection stewards) – and examines how this curatorial knowledge is applied. This framework will be used to better understand the case studies in the subsequent chapters.

Chapter 4 begins by examining how curators engaged with the process of collecting computer-based objects or – to extend the computer technology metaphor – the "input" to the museum. This chapter will examine how curators began to collect computer hardware, peripherals, and even the containers for the software (such as the floppy disks) in place of the actual software and how many of the same curators have responded to the acquisition of purely digital objects. Then, in Chapter 5, in contrast to the "input" process, the discussion will turn its attention to the museum's "output," by examining the challenges in displaying very recent examples of computer-based technology on exhibition whilst the full ramification of their impact on society is still developing or remains to be fully revealed.

Chapter 6 synthesizes the patterns of behavior observed in Chapters 4 and 5 and begins to assemble a model of expert curation methodologies, each based on how computer-based technology is understood. With the documenting method, computer-based technology is evidence of technological developments. The operating method is based on the view that computer-based technology – specially software – is action that must be performed to be truly understood by a museum visitor. Finally, the representing method presents computer-based technology as a metaphor for societal change. The chapter will examine both the strengths and weaknesses of each category, as well as how two or more these methods might be utilized simultaneously.

What emerges in Chapter 7 is a revealing look at expert curation of the computer-based technology-related collections at the Smithsonian museums, collections that ranges from computational devices to musical instruments. While computer-based technology continues to evolve at an exponential rate, this study reveals how the museum is able to keep pace. Though the specific technological advances and challenges detailed in this book might soon become obsolete with new developments in the computer industry, the deeper understanding of the internal processes of curatorial practice will remain.

However, to appreciate how curatorial expertise has provided a solution, the problems posed by computer-based technology must first be examined.

Notes

1 National Museum of American History, Accession File 2008.0025, National Museum of American History Computers Collection, Object Records.
2 This exhibition will be discussed in greater detail in Chapter 5.
3 Philip Hughes, *Exhibition Design* (London: Laurence King, 2010).
4 George E. Hein, *Learning in the Museum* (London: Routledge, 1998).
5 Ross Parry, *Recoding the Museum* (London: Routledge, 2007).
6 Andrea Witcomb, *Re-Imagining the Museum: Beyond the Mausoleum* (London: Routledge, 2003).
7 Eilean Hooper-Greenhill, *Museums and the Shaping of Knowledge* (London: Routledge, 1992).
8 Andrea Witcomb, *Re-Imagining the Museum: Beyond the Mausoleum* (London: Routledge, 2003) 3.
9 Andrea Witcomb, *Re-Imagining the Museum: Beyond the Mausoleum* (London: Routledge, 2003) 3.
10 Eilean Hooper-Greenhill, *Museums and the Shaping of Knowledge* (London: Routledge, 1992) 200.
11 Sharon Macdonald, *Behind the Scenes at the Science Museum* (Oxford: Berg, 2002).
12 Sharon Macdonald, *Behind the Scenes at the Science Museum* (Oxford: Berg, 2002) 6.
13 Sharon Macdonald, *Behind the Scenes at the Science Museum* (Oxford: Berg, 2002) 260.
14 Robert C. Post, *Who Owns America's Past? The Smithsonian and the Problem of History* (Baltimore: The Johns Hopkins University Press, 2013).
15 Kylie Message, *Museums and Social Activism: Engaged Protest* (Hoboken, NJ: Routledge, 2013).
16 William S. Walker, *A Living Exhibition: The Smithsonian and the Transformation of the Universal Museum* (Amherst: University of Massachusetts Press, 2013).
17 William S. Walker, *A Living Exhibition: The Smithsonian and the Transformation of the Universal Museum* (Amherst: University of Massachusetts Press, 2013) 1.
18 Andrea Witcomb, *Re-Imagining the Museum: Beyond the Mausoleum* (London: Routledge, 2003) 165.
19 G. Brown Goode, *An Account of the Smithsonian Institution: Its Origin, History, Objects and Achievements* (Washington, DC: Smithsonian, 1895).
20 Peter Liebhold and Harry R. Rubenstein, "Bringing Sweatshops into the Museum," in R. Greenwald and D. Bender (ed.), *Sweatshop USA: The American Sweatshop in Historical and Global Perspective* (New York: Routledge, 2003).
21 James B. Gardner and Sarah M. Henry, "September 11 and the Mourning After: Reflections on Collecting and Interpreting the History of Tragedy," *The Public Historian*, 24, no. 3 (2002): 41.
22 David H. Shayt, "Artifacts of Disaster: Creating the Smithsonian's Katrina Collection," *Technology and Culture*, 47, no. 2 (2006): 357.
23 Acknowledging that this research also makes a contribution to the Smithsonian's own curatorial history, copies of the audio files of all the recorded interviews I conducted during the course of my research were formally donated to the Smithsonian Institution Archives and the materials are now available to the public as part of the Archives holdings.

24 Carolyn Ellis, Tony E. Adams, and Arthur P. Bochner, "Autoethnography: An Overview," *Historical Social Research/Historische Sozialforschung*, 36, no. 4 (138) (2011): 274.

25 Richard Evans, *In Defence of History* (London: Granta Books, 2000) 252–253.

26 Thomas L. Charlton et al., eds., *History of Oral History: Foundations and Methodology* (Lanham, MD: Rowman and Littlefield, 2007) 38.

27 National Museum of American History. "September 11: Bearing Witness to History," Smithsonian Institution, , http://americanhistory.si.edu/september11/2011/collecting.asp (accessed June 5, 2012).

28 Simon J. Knell, *Museums and the Future of Collecting* (Aldershot: Ashgate, 2004).

29 Owain Rhys, *Contemporary Collecting: Theory and Practice* (Edinburgh: Museums Etc, 2011).

30 Simon J. Knell, *Museums and the Future of Collecting* (Aldershot: Ashgate, 2004) 46.

31 American Alliance of Museums, "Collections Stewardship," American Alliance of Museums, www.aam-us.org/resources/ethics-standards-and-best-practices/collections-stewardship (accessed March 10, 2015).

32 Harold Wallace, Smithsonian Institution Archives, Computer Technology and Curation Oral History Interviews, interview with Petrina Foti, August 14, 2013.

33 For further information, please see: Greg Zick, "Digital Collections: History and Perspectives," *Journal of Library Administration*, 49, no. 7 (2009): 687–693.

34 See for example: Ross Parry, ed., *Museums in a Digital Age* (London: Routledge, 2010).

35 Smithsonian Institution, *Annual Report of the Board of Regents of the Smithsonian Institution* (Washington, DC: Smithsonian Institution, 1847) 18.

36 Smithsonian Institution, Annual Report of the Board of Regents of the Smithsonian Institution (Washington, DC: Smithsonian Institution, 1847) 26.

37 Early Smithsonian Reports list the libraries and intuitions worldwide that have received copies of the Smithsonian journals of scientific findings. See: Smithsonian Institution, *Annual Report of the Board of Regents of the Smithsonian Institution* (Washington, DC: Smithsonian Institution, 1847–57).

38 Harold Wallace, Smithsonian Institution Archives, Computer Technology and Curation Oral History Interviews, interview with Petrina Foti, August 14 2013.

39 Carlene Stephens, Smithsonian Institution Archives, Computer Technology and Curation Oral History Interviews, interview with Petrina Foti, September 23, 2013.

40 Robert Leopold, Smithsonian Institution Archives, Computer Technology and Curation Oral History Interviews, interview with Petrina Foti, May 17, 2013.

41 Smithsonian Institution, Collection Search Center, http://collections.si.edu/search/ (accessed March 2014).

42 Harold Wallace, Smithsonian Institution Archives, Computer Technology and Curation Oral History Interviews, interview with Petrina Foti, August 14, 2013.

43 When asked, all my interview subjects expressed, to various degrees, a sense of being connected to the larger concept of the Smithsonian Institution. This corresponds with my own personal experience.

44 Alicia Cutler, Smithsonian Institution Archives, Computer Technology and Curation Oral History Interviews, interview with Petrina Foti, June 3, 2013.

45 Joyce Bedi, Smithsonian Institution Archives, Computer Technology and Curation Oral History Interviews, interview with Petrina Foti, September 13, 2013.

46 Eric Jentsch, Smithsonian Institution Archives, Computer Technology and Curation Oral History Interviews, interview with Petrina Foti, September 10, 2013.
47 Shannon Perich, Smithsonian Institution Archives, Computer Technology and Curation Oral History Interviews, interview with Petrina Foti, September 26, 2013.
48 The children were students at the Smithsonian Early Enrichment Center and therefore considered part of the Smithsonian Institution in their own right, independent of their parents' place of employment.
49 National Museum of American History, "Mission & History," Smithsonian Institution, http://americanhistory.si.edu/museum/mission-history (accessed March 14, 2015).
50 Cooper Hewitt National Design Museum, "About Cooper Hewitt," Smithsonian Institution, /www.cooperhewitt.org/about/ (accessed March 14, 2015).
51 National Air and Space Museum, "History," Smithsonian Institution, http://airandspace.si.edu/about/history/ (accessed March 14, 2015).
52 This astounding number is due, in part, to the large holdings of the numismatics and photographic history collections.
53 The National Museum of the American Indian's George Gustav Heye Center is also located in New York City and predated the location on the National Mall, which opened in 2004.

2 Curating the unprecedented

Introduction

Irrespective of the debates, discussions, and deliberations[1] around what sort of institutions museums are and should be, it is perhaps not too controversial to assert that most museums are built upon their collections. Indeed, to museologists such as Susan Pearce and Simon Knell, the collection remains central to the purpose of the museum, perhaps even to its detriment. Knell observes:

> Given the history of museums – the one with the warts rather than simply the heroics – it is no wonder that the profession is deeply protective of collections. Indeed, the profession swears to a creed which makes the collection a god over it. As disciples of this god, museum professionals are indoctrinated with arguments which support growth and retention, and, using well-chosen examples, justification is simple and the collection remains largely unchallenged, if not entirely understood.[2]

To Knell, the role of the collection is so central to the museum that it appears to be sacred. Yet, this is not a sanctity that should remain unexamined and unquestioned. Collections are essential to the museum for specific reasons and to better understand those is to better understand the purpose of the museum itself. Pearce notes that there is a value in the authentic that museums are able to provide.[3] Museum collections offer tangible evidence to support insubstantial words. As the authors of *Museums in Motion: An Introduction to the History and Functions of Museums* note:

> Most museums collect because of the belief that objects are important and evocative survivals of human civilization worthy of careful study and with powerful educational impact. Whether aesthetic, documentary, or scientific, objects tell much about the universe, nature, the human heritage, and the human condition. Museums thus carefully study and preserve their holdings so as to transmit important information to the present generation and to posterity.[4]

Though some museums choose not to extend their holdings beyond their founding collections, most do so to fulfill their missions. The question, therefore, is not whether museums should collect, but on which categories and subject classifications they should focus their attention. As Paul Ceruzzi, curator of Aerospace Electronics and Computing at the Smithsonian's National Air and Space Museum, explains:

> The classic definition of a machine is that it does one thing and it does it well. Engineers spend all their time doing that thing better and better. Along comes the computer and that whole definition is thrown out the window. Because a computer can do anything that you can program it to do... For a museum, this presents a huge dilemma. Because museums are organized usually according to what these things do.[5]

As Ceruzzi notes, the challenges of computer-based technology are not limited to a specific discipline or field. And yet, furthermore, computer-based technology itself also offers unique challenges as a consequence of its combined format of being both hardware and software. With computer-based technology, the museum is confronted with a new challenge not just in terms of what specifically to collect, but also how the museum staff ought to approach the accommodation of what might be an unprecedented type of object

There are multiple motivations that drive museums to collect in a given subject area. In the same manner, there are multiple situations that lead curators to collect from a given subject while the history of that subject is still being written. Traditionally, curators and museologists have focused on collecting objects representing non-contemporaneous subjects, since the past at least affords the opportunity to evaluate what might offer a legacy. However, as museology grows as a discipline, there has been an increasing discussion of whether there is also a value in recording events and trends in society at large as they are happening. With computer-based technology, there is often little choice given the rapid rate that it continues to develop and transform. Much the same way as the industrial revolution transformed manufacturing and consumption, so too has the computer industry transformed communication, information management, and entertainment.[6] Jan van Dijk in his seminal work *The Network Society* notes:

> A new lifeline is being added to all the ones we already had. Today, we no longer only depend on roads, electricity cables, water pipes, gas lines, sewers, post-boxes, telephone wires and cable television to conduct our daily lives and manage our households. We now also need networks of electronic communication... This dependence does not only apply for individuals. It also goes for organizations and society at large.[7]

We can see with van Dijk's words just how pervasive and vital this technology has become. As the technology is able to do more, users begin to test and push the limits of these new capabilities. This brings to light new avenues to be developed, which, in turn, increase what these machines are able to do, all in the space of the curator's own lifetime. As Knell, in the introductory chapter of his book *Museums and the Future of Collecting*, explains:

> So while some museum workers have been at pains to distinguish contemporary collecting from history collecting, the fact is that all collecting is inevitably contemporary collecting, even if we are collecting things which are valued because of their association with the past. Contemporary collecting is one of the most difficult of practices because of its overwhelming and multifaceted nature, and because we are collecting things that reflect our own society, which we know to be complex. Collecting historical material only seems easier because there is less of it, we know it less well, and because historians have constructed narratives which value one thing above another.[8]

Knell's framing of all museum collecting as contemporary reminds us that the act of recording history, whether it is currently occurring or the subject of ages past, is not a neutral action. The curators or collectors are actively shaping knowledge by what they choose to preserve. Apocryphally, most museum curators are themselves collectors, independent of their chosen profession, which makes a museum in reality an organization of collectors who have agreed to a certain set of rules and goals. The main challenge of computer-based technology is that these objects often come with a set of circumstances where these agreed rules and goals no longer provide guidance. However, as this study will examine, the museum regularly encounters instances of collecting with no precedent to follow, which then create a precedent for the future. It could even be argued that there is a precedent to follow when dealing with unprecedented situations.

This chapter will examine the ways in which contemporary collecting – which, for the purposes of this study, shall be defined as collecting objects related to subjects that occurred within a curator's own lifetime – might involve acquiring the unprecedented and consider the ramifications that this poses to the curatorial staff at the Smithsonian. First, how computer technology has an innate duality in its structure will be explored. It is at once both hardware-dependent software and software-dependent hardware – each with its individual set of challenges, exacerbated by the rapid rate of computer technology development. With that understanding the chapter will present how objects that exist solely in a digital format cannot easily follow the collecting precedent of material objects in the same way that three-dimensional hardware is able. This suggests how, in terms of the object type, the museum has no ready precedent to follow when dealing with the challenges that digital-format objects present. Therefore, computer hardware can be seen as (to use the words of some of the Smithsonian curatorial staff) a "black box," its internal processes remaining hidden.

Contemporary collecting at the Smithsonian Museums

In many ways, contemporary collecting distills and emphasizes the museum's role as a bridge to the past. As Owain Rhys has noted in his study of contemporary collecting:

> The failure of museums to collect contemporaneous material in the past has resulted in significant gaps in the collections – these gaps mean that certain aspects of history cannot be told today. Contemporary collecting helps to fill those gaps, but can also create a dialogue between past and present objects, especially if museums base their collecting on the strengths of current collections.[9]

Non-contemporary collecting is a more passive form of history recording, by allowing outside factors to determine both the historical narrative and what is preserved for the future. Though it may be considered a less perilous method, Rhys reminds us that there is a cost with this approach. Museum practice of actively "filling these gaps" has led to the rise of new theories and policies to support accepting this form of history documenting. By reviewing Smithsonian curators' annual reports,[10] it is clear that the museums at the Smithsonian have, indeed, had a long tradition with contemporary collecting in many fields and disciplines. Stacy Kluck, chair for the Division of Culture and the Arts at the American History Museum, explains:

> The goal, to me, of the collections, is how do we show how people were engaging with technologies in the past, but also what technologies they are engaging with now, and try to guess at their meaning. Some things will be obvious and some things we might miss, because we just do not know what is important right now.[11]

Kluck's observations are evidence of Smithsonian curators' careful contemplation when they choose to collect contemporaneously. Contemporary collecting can be seen as a continuing contribution to the greater tradition of collection stewardship in which curators and collection managers actively and contentiously participate. Museum collections are meant to last beyond the span of a human lifetime, which means that one collection will have its own history of curatorial staff responsible for it. These staff members, in turn, understand that they are part of a tradition that will continue after their time at the institution. Contemporary collecting offers the opportunity for current curators and historians to assist their future counterparts.

The Division of Political History at the American History Museum has had a long tradition of contemporary collecting starting in the 1960s.

During this time period, the division was attempting to collect the history of the country's political process, as the United States was in the middle of a very turbulent political environment, including the civil rights movement and the Vietnam War protests. Since Washington is the political center of the country and many of these protests were taking place in the museum's figurative back yard, the Political History curators naturally began to collect what was happening around them. Former curator Keith Melder later recalled that the early collecting of the 1960s – which resulted in some of the rarest artifacts of the movement to be preserved – was done "almost by accident,"[12] rather than the more systematic field collecting that would happen later in the decade and continue through to today. The division's former chair, Harry Rubenstein, explains:

> This division had a model that was easy to follow. If you are doing American politics, clearly you see what is going on. You know the history of your collection. You say: "why am I waiting to fill certain holes after the fact when it is so much easier to do it now." And that leads to other kinds of contemporary collecting as well, because you see sort of major protest movements taking place and you have seen how it works for the campaign collection, you can see how it works for the contemporary collection. So, it was very natural for this division to always have been engaged in contemporary collecting. How aggressive it should be is a limit of budget and staff resources.[13]

While the original collecting impulse might have been motivated by a number of outside factors, the division continues to collect because of the successful precedent set. The result is a collection rich in material culture that no longer exists anywhere else.[14] However, when collecting is dependent on the interest of one person, it cannot be independently sustained should that person lose impetus. For example, Melder, in an American Association of Museums Centennial Interview, recounted a story from his days as a curator for the Division of Political History at the National Museum of American History that highlights the risks with contemporary collecting. After the assassination of Dr. Martin Luther King Jr., Melder and his colleagues collected memorial items and put many on exhibit. In days before high-security displays of objects, someone was able to take a torch to one of the handmade memorial banners on display. The perpetrator was never caught. The remains of the banner were preserved, but that lone act of terrorism had a much greater negative effect on the museum's collection. The combination of grief for King and anger at the destruction of museum property prompted Melder to discontinue actively collecting such material, not out of fear, but from the disappointment that future generations with a distance of time might be more immune.[15] Had there been no other curators in the Political History Division at the American History Museum to continue on with the model of collecting already established, it is conceivable that the collection would have stagnated, having returned to a passive collecting model. Contemporary collecting is dependent on the curator and therefore subject to his or her strengths and weaknesses. This can be an unnerving proposition for a curator when he or she must collect with no precedent to follow.

While contemporary collecting at the Smithsonian is normally left to the judgment of the curator, the historical evidence indicates that there are occasionally events or movements that spur museum staff to coordinate an initiative that would involve the entire unit and even the entire Institution. One of the most powerful examples of this would be the collecting undertaken by the curators at the National Museum of American History after the September 11 terrorist attacks in 2001 in New York City and Washington, DC. The historic significance of the attacks, the deadliest on US soil to date, was clear even to those who were not in the history field. In the months that followed, staff at the American History Museum discussed how best to record the events and their aftermath. Shelly Foote, then Assistant Chair to the Division of Social History, explains:

> It's a little difficult for the people who are collecting because you're very close to it, especially living in a city that was one of the cities that was affected. You have your own viewpoint and you have to kind of set that aside and think of it as a curator – what you should be saving for the future.[16]

Yet it is likely that this closeness is what motivated the curators in the first place. Relying on earlier precedents, such as when curators from the Division of Political History at the National Museum of American History were simultaneously collecting and experiencing the American civil rights movement of the 1960s, the curators at the American History Museum used their own skills as museum professionals to understand and explain what was happening around them. Just as amateur and professional photographers alike almost unconsciously reached for their cameras to document what they were seeing, the curators at the National Museum of American History were driven to collect and preserve when faced with events that were almost beyond their comprehension. This motivation to preserve what was occurring around them was best explained by David Shayt, one of the collecting curators:

> The most important function of the collection is preservation, in and of itself – the fundamental purpose of the museum. Preservation for posterity, whose uses we can't even, or ought to imagine. It could be a grandchild of one of the deceased who will come here one day in her wheelchair to see what her great grandfather went through. That will justify everything we've done, with one visit.[17]

The collecting for those in the future gave the curators a mission that they could fulfill. It could also be argued that preserving artifacts from the present offered a sense of comfort since it would mean that, even if the events of the day were incomprehensible now, that would not always be the case.

It was not only the curators as museum professionals who felt it was their responsibility to preserve what they could for future generations. In December 2011, Congress declared that the National Museum of American History would be an official government repository for September 11–related material. This national recognition validated the curators' drive to collect what was happening around them. However, the public's desire for the historical preservation also served as a further challenge. In a journal article written less than a year after the attacks, authors James B. Gardner and Sarah M. Henry[18] explain the difficulties in collecting in the midst of national grief:

> History museums and the historians who work in them thus find themselves in the unaccustomed and in many ways uncomfortable position of working at the intersection of grief and history. In addition to doing our usual work of collecting, preserving, and interpreting history, we are also filling a new emotional need for the public: the need to understand what it means to be living in a moment of historic proportions. Historians' priorities are objects that tell stories, that evoke moments and lives, not simply fragments or relics of more emotional than historical value. But although we may see a clear difference there, the public does not.[19]

Gardner, then Associate Director for Curatorial Affairs, spearheaded the collecting efforts at the American History Museum. After long consultations, the museum decided that the majority of the accessioning should happen at the collection level, with a few curators tasked with the role of following the overarching timeline of events.[20] The point was not to interpret, but to gather as much material culture from the events as they could. Gardner and Henry note that

> every historian knows that the inadvertent or unconscious evidence embedded in the historic record can be the most interesting and revealing material for understanding the past. What those will be in this instance we cannot say, but a broad-based collecting effort has the best chance at including the rich evidence that will support the broadest historical understanding in the future.[21]

Indeed, the two exhibits related to September 11 that the American History Museum has displayed, the 2002 *September 11: Bearing Witness to History* and the 10th anniversary *September 11: Remembrance and Reflection*, owed perhaps more to a sense of reverence, memorialization and publicly shared grief than they did to historical interpretation. One assumes that the curators have decided that there is no need to explain the circumstances of the day to an audience who had witnessed those events for themselves. The sense here, perhaps, is that it is only when the public becomes more removed from these events that it becomes necessary to provide this context. The curators at the American History Museum were actively seeking a way to record the physical and emotional impact of the events of September 11 so that they might be better studied and understood. With the burden of interpretation mainly a consideration for future curators, the team's main task was to make decisions based on what would provide the most information for generations yet to come.

It was this tradition of museum practice that led the exhibit team for the 2002 exhibition to engage in another unusual and somewhat unprecedented form of collecting. In addition to object histories, eyewitness accounts, and historic images, curators recorded their own thoughts and experiences. Not only would future generations have a wealth of material culture to examine, they would be able to understand the thought processes that led to these objects' accessioning. It also contributed to a legacy that was the complete opposite of passive collecting (accepting objects into the collection as they are offered, rather than actively soliciting donations).

Though there was no way of telling what would be important to the future, the curators knew what past and current visitors found relevant and therefore could assume that visitors would respond in a similar way in the future. Social history had been practiced in the museum for decades, allowing curators to understand the weight and value of material culture on a personal level. Memorial museums like the United States Holocaust Museum or the Hiroshima Peace Memorial Museum in Japan served as evidence that "sometimes the most seemingly ordinary or unremarkable objects are the ones that speak most eloquently about the human experience of tragedy."[22] The events of September 11 may have been unprecedented, but years of museum practice allowed curators to understand what would make a strong foundation for a museum collection, even if it was being formed without the benefit of mental distance.

The collecting that was carried out after September 11 in turn served as a model for other collecting initiatives at the American History Museum that pivoted around key events, such as David Shayt's contemporary collecting after Hurricane Katrina. The decisions made during the process of collection around the events of September 11 provided the theoretical framework and the precedent for future collecting initiatives after other disasters. Shayt observed in the journal article "Artifacts of Disaster: Creating the Smithsonian's Katrina Collection":

> The idea of museum collections built from disasters, natural or man-made, can be unsettling. Yet collections are the basis of everything that history museums do. This explains why in the weeks after 9/11 the Smithsonian Institution gathered artifacts from the World Trade Center,

> the Pentagon, and the field in Pennsylvania where Flight 93 crashed to earth in an effort to capture something of the material record of what happened that day. And it explains why shortly after Katrina collided with the Gulf Coast the curatorial staff of the National Museum of American History met to consider the problem of collecting artifacts to support future museum exhibitions, public programs, websites, and publications concerning this exceptional hurricane and its aftermath.[23]

Like the September 11 collecting initiative, the resulting collecting effort after Hurricane Katrina led to the acquisition of objects that would likely be difficult or even impossible to find if the museum were to attempt to collect years later. For example, given the devastation of the flooding, it is reasonable to assume that someone might choose to save a portion of the breached levee, if only in commemoration. However, the window valance that Shayt found in the abandoned home in the flooded Ninth Ward would likely be discarded by anyone other than a museum professional looking for objects that would best describe the devastation that had happened in New Orleans after the Level 5 hurricane had made landfall. The valance was stained with muddy water that left only the few top inches closest to the ceiling untouched and stands in mute testament to the depth of the flooding. In that same collecting trip, Shayt was able to locate the owner of the home in a relief center. Not only did this ensure proper transfer of legal title, but Shayt was able to interview the owner about his family's experience. Shayt was even able to recover some of the beloved toys that the owner's young daughter was forced to leave behind when the family was evacuated. In an earlier draft of that article, Shayt reflected on the act of contemporary collecting after a disaster:

> Disaster collecting shall always remain an inexact science, producing a fragmentary record unique to each collector. Few rules apply, beyond a good sense of museum ethics, a zeal for collecting the most authentic object possible, and a commitment to professional standards of museum care and collections documentation. Potential concerns that such collecting so soon after a disaster is inappropriate are relieved by the knowledge that the immediacy of such a response maximizes authenticity. Doubts also are quenched by the gratitude of victims and other donors who realize that their experiences might be remembered by generations to come.[24]

Shayt articulates both the difficulties in contemporary collecting and his own personal motivations for recording the history of disasters shortly after they have occurred. As Shayt's collecting efforts after Hurricane Katrina and the museumwide efforts after September 11 remind us, collecting can often feel intimate and emotional for the curators involved.

Collecting without precedent

There are many difficulties that come with recording history as it is occurring. While the curatorial staff involved with the overall narrative associated with September 11 had to sort through a mountain of potential accessions,[25] those who were responsible for individual museum collections had the additional task of acquiring objects that would follow the needs and constraints of their collections' subject histories. Meanwhile for some, such as those who worked in Political History, previous contemporary collecting efforts could serve as a model. However, that was not the case for all. As Curator of Graphic Arts at the American History Museum Helena Wright reflected on the museum's website:

> As historians we normally have a period of reflection when we evaluate what's happening. We're not really involved in current events – it's rather contradictory to what historians do. Usually some time elapses before we can evaluate and determine what's to be brought into a collection. So in that sense the immediacy of this situation is quite unusual. It does feel different. There is a kind of rush to make sure that we actually do capture and acquire what we need to before it's either destroyed or disappears.[26]

Michelle Delaney, then Collections Manager in the Photographic History Collection, equally had no precedent to follow she noted that

> collecting for September 11 has probably been the most important thing that I've done during my 12 years here at the museum. As soon as the events occurred, I started wondering what this would mean to the history of photography. I was worried about people I knew, thinking about the events that were occurring and thinking about my job, because I knew I would, over the next months – no matter what happened – be thinking about how to collect and who to collect, what to collect, would there be equipment to collect.[27]

We can see that both Wright and Delaney were aware of the significance of their actions and proceeded with great care and deliberation when they committed to collecting with no firm precedent or guidelines to follow. The risk was high that they either would collect something that would ultimately prove to be meaningless or would miss something important.

Though flattering, the public perception that a museum is consistently dependable can spark serious ramifications when an inevitable miscalculation occurs. While an individual collector is likely only seeking to please him- or herself, a museum's mission to preserve the past for the future builds the expectation that anything that is collected for the general public must therefore be of great significance, but that assumption may not actually prove to be the case. Many of the essays in Bruce Altshuler's *Collecting the New* examine and challenge this concept of the museum as an infallible institution. Howard H. Fox notes in the chapter "The Right to Be Wrong" that the perception of the infallible museum has the potential to be damaging to both the museum and the subject the museum hopes to preserve through collections. Fox further observes:

> Collecting the past, the traditional job of museums, is itself a fraught enterprise that challenges curators and institutions to uphold their integrity and standards. When museums, or their curators, misstep, implications about professional expertise and public confidence rumble like distant thunder.[28]

The unspoken authority that a museum has and the inadvertent endorsement that occurs when museums accept objects into their collections have far deeper ramifications than just resource expenses. Altshuler reflects in his introduction that art museums, perhaps, have a far more rigid role within the development of art history narratives than other types of museums.[29] Ironically, when an art museum accepts a contemporary work into their collection they risk changing the narrative of art history by instantly providing endorsement to that artist or movement, which, in turn, might unintentionally influence the art market. In contrast, history and technology museums are not as closely tied to a particular economic marketplace. When a history museum accepts an object that later proves to have very little historical relevance, for example, collecting an item from pop culture prematurely, there are not deeper economic ramifications, though the cost of collecting in terms of conservation and storage concerns still looms. Despite this, their acquisitions can also be seen as certification that this particular object or subject is significant. Bernard Finn, Curator Emeritus for the American History Museum's Electricity Collection, explains that there are those who would seek the possible economic benefits from their donation:

> We have a lot of instances where an inventor will come in here and say "Gee, I thought you'd like this. It's wonderful: and so forth." They have their reasons for presenting this and usually they are pretty transparent. They want to be able to go out and say "My object's in the Smithsonian Institution and it must be important" and use it for advertising and whatever else. This is fairly clear and we are concerned about that. Even if they say they are not going to do anything, we are concerned that we are putting [a certification] here on this when we should not. But I think we are pretty good at trying to take care of that in at least telling the donor that this is not any sort of certification, that we are making no representations about the value of this thing. We are taking it whether it is successful or not and maybe we will take competitors' as well. We are

> looking at technology from a broad point of view and not just at all the guys who were successful.[30]

Finn demonstrates how museums that present the history of technology are able to frame their collecting behavior to mitigate the possible economic impact that their acquisitions might have. This suggests that history and technology museums might more easily transform their image from that of a repository to part of a current dialogue.

The National Museum of American History (originally called the National Museum of History and Technology) and the National Air and Space Museum were both founded with the concept of presenting American technological progress to the public. However, the start of the science- and technology-related collections at the Smithsonian stretches even further back to the Institution's earliest days. This emphasis on what Steven Lubar refers to as the "gospel of progress"[31] creates an environment that lends itself to contemporary collecting. Often, if a particularly significant technological breakthrough is not collected contemporarily, it is because examples only become available after the technology becomes obsolete. This can be seen in 2012 when the NASA Space Shuttle Discovery was accepted into the collections of the National Air and Space Museum, replacing the prototype Space Shuttle Enterprise, which had previously been the only noncommissioned model available for display. In many ways, focus on technological innovation and science discovery provides a more impartial collecting standard than impact on society. While the public's interest is appreciated (and even sought), it is not necessary to wait for future generations to provide a more historical perspective. Bernard Finn notes:

> Sometimes it is as well not to have historical perspective and we sometimes use that argument in saying that "I don't care if this thing is successful or not." Lack of success is just as important as success if you get down to interpretation.[32]

Finn reminds us that with technological and scientific research, there is always the risk of failures and setbacks. Even technological success can prove to be a marketing failure. Examples of these failures are often difficult to collect at a later time, providing even more impetus for curators to collect contemporaneously. However, though it is easier to collect artifacts representing scientific and technological milestones as they are occurring, there are no guarantees that recognized technological triumphs will always be as valued by future generations. Take, for example, the 1847 "life car" invented by Joseph Francis, the founder of the U.S. Life-Saving Service. This boat was used to rescue shipwreck passengers, as many as 199 during the wreck of the *Ayrshire* in 1850. Lubar notes that "it was one of the most popular exhibits on display at the turn of the century and included on every list of Smithsonian treasures. But as maritime disasters became less common, Francis's fame diminished and the life car was moved into a smaller exhibit area on disasters at sea."[33] It is not unreasonable to think that this could occur with the familiar, even arguably ubiquitous computer-based technology objects of today such as the iPod. However, even if its technological impact and public interest have faded, that does not negate an object's value or importance. As Knell's words at the opening of this chapter remind, the fact that these objects were collected at all gives more significance to a period of history in which they were collected. The "life car" serves to illuminate the worries of a seafaring society to one that now primarily relies on alternative mentions of transportation in the American History Museum exhibition *On the Water: Stories from Maritime America* (opened May 22, 2009). There are specific challenges and unknowns that come with collecting without the guidance of an established historical narrative. Contemporary collecting in particular poses questions in terms of what should be collected and how it might be understood in the future, especially in circumstances that have no previous models of collecting that the curator might easily follow. In addition to these challenges of the unprecedented, computer-based technology (as a set of potentially collectible objects) offers a particularly difficult set of circumstances both for its prevalence and for its complexity.

"Everything becoming ones and zeroes"

No matter what formal discipline they might be from, the curators who record the history of computer-based technology are faced with a longstanding problem – inherited from the history of computation machines – of trying to collect and exhibit hardware-dependent software and software-dependent hardware when only one of these two is tangible. Paul Ceruzzi, in addition to being a noted scholar of computer technology history, has been, for many years, Curator of Aerospace Electronics and Computing at the National Air and Space Museum at the Smithsonian Institution. The influence of and the insight provided by that role are in direct evidence when he speculates what the rising dominance of software and cyberculture might mean in *A History of Modern Computing*:

> The history of computing, as a separate subject, may itself become irrelevant. There is no shortage of evidence to suggest this. For example, when the financial press refers to "technology" stocks, it no longer means the computer industry represented by companies like IBM or even Intel, but increasingly Internet and telecommunications firms. In my work as a museum curator, I have had to grapple with issues of how to present the story of computing, using artifacts, to a public. It was hard enough when the problem was that computers were rectangular "black boxes" that revealed little of their function; now the story seems to be all about "cyberspace," which by definition has no tangible nature to it.[34]

David Allison, who had been Curator for the Computers Collection at the American History Museum for more than twenty years, acknowledges that

> one of the biggest challenges is how we collect software as well as hardware. Traditionally, we have focused on hardware collections – physical objects – rather than the software that goes along with them. So that latter is the greater challenge than collecting the hardware.[35]

Alicia Cutler, Collection Manager for the American History Museum's Computers Collection during the 1990s and currently Digital Asset Manager for the museum, agrees:

> There has been more focus on the physical aspect and not on the information contained. Everybody knows it is an issue. Across the Smithsonian, I have spoken to other curatorial staff and very few actually deal with an object that is computer-based alone. The majority still deal with these very physical objects. Nothing that combines a physical format and a digital format.[36]

Ceruzzi, Allison, and Cutler show us that software, or objects that solely exist in a digital format, cannot easily follow the collecting precedent of material objects in the same way that three-dimensional hardware is able. The challenges that digital-format objects present would therefore be unfamiliar to the museum.

Though not a curator, Nancy Proctor, former Head of Mobile Strategy & Initiatives for the Smithsonian and current Director of the Peale Center for Baltimore History and Architecture, is very familiar with digital format objects and conjectures that

> there are a lot of challenges in collecting technology and perhaps software-based technologies maybe more so than others... The rate at which the components, if we can call them that, of digital "objects" change is so fast, perhaps compared to analogue and non-computer based technologies that keeping operating systems up-to-date, abreast of the languages used to create any software and I am sure there are issues around networking technology and all of that. I am not the expert, but I would guess it is very difficult.[37]

Proctor reminds us that, without materiality, software can be modified, effectively creating a newer model without having to adapt its hardware "container." The challenge of software might therefore be framed as one where the balance between software-dependent hardware and hardware-dependent software has shifted. Marc Weber, the Curatorial Director for the Internet History Program at the Computer History, explains:

> I think from the beginning, software has always been the most elusive... When there are objects, they are easier to get than software. The things that people preserve are whatever the user experiences. They will preserve the terminal, not the server. They will preserve the phone, not the phone system. So, it is whatever the user has and therefore kind of imprints on. We all know what our phones look like. Do you have any idea if they have changed the entire network that supports it? No, you don't. Even people that are engineers in these sorts of things, there is still this natural kind of tendency to save the part that you touch and feel. It's the same reason that browsers get a lot more attention than servers when it comes to the web.[38]

Software no longer depends on advances in hardware technology as drastically as it has in previous years and therefore can continue to develop at an unchecked rate. As a result, two examples of the same computer-based technology might look identical, as mass-produced objects do, but have entirely different software, making them two distinctly different objects. Aaron Straup Cope, former Senior Digital Engineer for the Cooper Hewitt, Smithsonian Design Museum, notes:

> Right now, we have this problem where, for perfectly good reasons, software does not track with hardware and operating systems. I mean that is the luxury that we give the private sector to iterate and move as fast as they can make their technology move. But from an archiving perspective, we are going to collect these things that just will not work.[39]

As Cope shows us, the museum does not have the resources to keep pace with the rapid technological development of the private sector. This is a concern for Michelle Delaney, both as a curator and as an administrator:

> I think that technology within museums, from my twenty-year perspective, has always been lagging. So, when you bring in new technology and try to exhibit, or even maintain it behind the scenes in the collection, how do you keep up? You would think that a large institution like the Smithsonian would be the cutting edge. Well, we are trying... I continue to worry about how museums in this economic time can keep ahead of the learning curve to present the computer. I definitely think that it should be collected across all subjects, as it applies. But, specifically, with photography and the visual arts culture, how do we bring a level of knowledge up to speed for the curators in their positions?[40]

We see from Delaney's words that a specific knowledge base is required to understand computer-based technology, since the museum must understand what it hopes to preserve.

However, as digital format objects and applications are increasingly incorporated into society, there is a pressing need for the museum not only to understand, but also to respond. This need is further heightened by computer-based technology's rapid development. Shannon Perich, Curator of Photography at the American History Museum, observes:

> The way that the light-bulb changed was not radical from year to year in the same way that computer technology is radically different from year to year… To collect computer technology, you have to have somebody who is contemporary and in the moment, as well as [somebody who] has the capacity to follow it and collect for it.[41]

Perich reminds us that rapidly evolving technology also means a rapidly evolving historical narrative. Sebastian Chan, former Director of Digital & Emerging Media for the Cooper Hewitt, Smithsonian Design Museum, concurs and explains:

> I think it is much easier as an institution to collect with the distance of twenty years than it is to collect with the distance of twenty minutes, but I think these things are moving very fast, and have been for pretty much all of our lives. We have grown up, being the ages that we are, of these things never being settled. So, this sort of sense that you could collect historically is a little ridiculous to us.[42]

Certainly, the technological innovation of computer development can (and indeed does) play a large role in marking major moments of the history of computer-based technology. What is also of note here is that, owing to the particularly rapid rate of change, in the case of computer technology there appears to be a particular issue for curators in identifying landmark moments. David Brock, Director of the Center for Software History at the Computer History Museum, explains that at his museum

> we are interested in the problem of the potentials and perils for trying to collect and preserve the history of software of the twentieth-first century, because with the increased use of networking and how software is delivered and how software functions, it is much more tied, through computer networking to commercial providers and platforms. The mobile telephone and the smartphone have become the overwhelmingly predominate form of computing that people interact with. Without a network and without all sorts of valid credentials, none of the software on these devices will function. So, that really raises a lot of questions, in terms of executable software, about what we do. What can we collect from that? What do you collect when the software is being modified by its maker remotely all the time [through] patches and updates? That kind of issue of versioning is already around in software that used to

> come to you on some sort of medium, but now, when it is delivered over a network, it is a different problem.[43]

Hansen Hsu, Curator for the Computer History Museum's Center for Software History, concurs, noting that

> software is no longer deployed in ".0" increments. There is a lot of continuous deployment. So, it is a continuum now. And so, where do you take snapshots? There is not a discreet set of milestones. You have to decide when you want to take a snapshot, because it is constantly changing.[44]

Dag Spicer, Senior Curator for the Computer History Museum, echoing the words of Hsu and Brock, explains that

> the agile development methodology has created continuous updating as the norm. So, what are you really capturing? Even if you could take a snapshot of the code, there are so many other dependencies on other code snippets and Facebook's own little weird ways of doing things.[45]

Spicer's example of the nearly ubiquitous social media platform Facebook serves as a reminder that computer-based technology constantly poses new challenges for the museum even as that technology grows in popularity to the point it has begun to transform society. As Brock observes, "To preserve something like Facebook, you would need to replicate Facebook, which clearly we are not going to do, so what are we going to do?"[46] This brings to mind the words of Simon Knell that contemporary collecting "is one of the most difficult of practices because of its overwhelming and multifaceted nature, and because we are collecting things that reflect our own society, which we know to be complex."[47] The concerns of Spicer and Brock illustrate how understanding the complexity of social media sites such as Facebook does not necessarily mean that a solution will be readily available.

Collecting and exhibiting websites, such as Facebook, in a way that is understandable and meaningful is one of the main areas of concern[48] for Weber. He explains the difficulty of collecting software and internet applications:

> In the museum we have a huge amount of shrink-wrapped software, but that is disappearing, because it is no longer being made the way it was... There is just less and less [chance] that there is any reasonable path that [software] could get to us. Or that even if we had it, that we could reconstruct to do anything with, because it tends to get more knitted together to various other software, running over lots and lots of servers. It becomes a whole eco system... Even if a company would give you the contents of a few particular set of hard disks in their server farm – the

> servers themselves, the blades – it is not something that would be useable in anyway by itself.[49]

With such complexities as those posed by software, it is understandable that, even as the museum struggles to comprehend computer-based technology in order to better collect and exhibit it, the larger question of "how" looms. Ross Parry, in the landmark digital heritage reader *Museums in a Digital Age*, observes:

> Historically, museums have been about material things. After several centuries of collecting and displaying physical objects, curatorial practice has largely been predisposed to the solidity of collections and exhibitions. Up to the digital age, the museum was ostensibly a project in practically apprehending and spatially rendering cultural heritage. Consequently, digitality presented something of an anomaly to the profession; at once in tune with the institution's instinct to research and accrue information and to present knowledge compellingly; yet, a departure from the tangibility that had defined the venue, visit and vocation of the museum.[50]

Parry here refers to the digital as a potential new "venue" for the museum, in terms of virtual exhibitions and new media outreach. Yet, this new venue is also the reason that curators are now faced with the potential proposition of collecting digital-format materials as museum objects when the museum itself is far more comfortable with the "solidity" of the objects in its collections. Tilly Blyth, Head of Collections and Principal Curator for the Science Museum (London), notes that

> museums are brilliant at acquiring and preserving material culture. The artefacts, the objects. We are less brilliant at thinking about digital technology because it is more recent. It is hard to think about actually how you preserve electronics in the longer term. We are very used to paper. We are great at wood. We are brilliant at brass and glass. But, actually, plastics and electronics... They are full of PCBs. They are full of other issues. So, the longer term preservation of that type of material is difficult. But also, on top of that, with a computer, you are not just thinking of the physically artifact. Obviously, you are thinking about the software and the program that runs on that machine. And in the age that we are in now, actually, it is less and less about the physical and more and more just that the software itself *is* a machine![51]

Blyth, who prior to her current role had served as the museum's Curator of Computing and Information and the Lead Curator for the Science Museum's *Information Age* exhibit (October 2014 to present), sees the role that computer-based technology currently plays in everyday life as a particular challenge for museums, not only in terms of collecting, but during exhibition development as well. She explains:

> We are in this weird transition, where actually our worlds are becoming less and less "artifact-ual," less and less material, and more and more digital, for want of a better term. And that poses a set of really, really big challenges for museums, both in terms of how you curate that and also in terms of how you preserve it in the longer term. And then, how do you present it to visitors? What is it to show a program that may have run in the 1980s that actually most visitors will not engage with because it looks fairly basic and fairly uninteresting? So, trying to present the bigger context around computing, rather than just the material object is a real challenge for us.[52]

In a sense, the greatest difficulty of digital-format objects is that curators do not know what the greatest difficulties might actually prove to be since the technology is still developing. Aaron Straup Cope, who served in computer engineering roles before and since his post at the Cooper Hewitt, notes:

> I think it is difficult, because it is uncharted territory for everybody. To the extent that there are museums like the Computer Museum, which by its nature, is in a better place than most. They just understand the issues. They understand what it is they are trying to collect, even if they do not know how. That is the problem, because no one knows quite how. There was all that rhetoric in the 1980s particularly about everything becoming 1s and 0s. It did not happen the way it was being talked about, and I think people sort of just decided it was "buzzword bingo." The problem is that somewhere between now and then it started happening, and people are a little bit adrift.[53]

Blyth and Cope's observations illustrate that it is digital-format objects' very unfamiliarity that makes them so challenging. For this reason, the difficulties that curators face when collecting without precedent directly apply to computer-based technology. Stacy Kluck, Chair for the American History Museum's Culture and the Arts Division and one of the curators affiliated with its Music Collection, explains:

> I think it is easier to describe the technology when you have something physical that you can actually show, but when the physical thing is actually a computer file, then it changes how we exhibit these things to our public. So, it is finding a balance telling the story, but now how can we show it because we are a museum. We are about physical things; we are about stuff. When that stuff becomes out in the ether-world, how do we

display that? I think that is going to be a challenge, for certainly future generations and for museums in the future.[54]

Kluck frames the primary challenge in terms of exhibit display, which is a concern for many museums, not just the American History Museum. Tilly Blyth in *Information Age: Six Networks That Changed Our World*, an edited volume published to coincide with the opening of the exhibition with the same name, observes that

> museums acquire material culture as evidence, as tangible proof of technological change. But information – the bits and data – is insubstantial. When the machines are turned off, the messages cease to flow, information disappears. It is the machines, the hardware, that lives on, providing the only proof of the form of change and the lives previously touched through information and communication technology. The material culture of information – floppy discs, CDs, Morse tapes, punched tap – can all be displayed, but the information they contain is invisible, sometimes undecodable, lost to history like momentary thought.[55]

Though computer technology has an associated material culture, the software, which has no physical presence, is often the critical part of the story that the museum wishes to tell. At Cooper Hewitt, Chan notes:

> I think it is also a challenge, because, unlike libraries and archives which are perhaps better placed to deal with it conceptually, museum collecting at the moment is very driven by the need to exhibit things, particularly here because we are running out of physical space. There is always a "Well, if we acquire this, how are we going to show it?" And sometimes you need to acquire things when you do not know how you are going to show them, because you cannot acquire them at any other time. I think libraries and archives are a little bit better at accommodating that. We were talking about a bunch of stuff the other day and the first question I got asked by someone on our board was "How would you exhibit that?" and I was like "Well, that's kind of like the second order question." It is not "we should acquire this first and then figure that out" rather than only acquire things that are exhibit-able, because otherwise we will not acquire the things that matter.[56]

Chan's observations suggest that, more than mere repositories, museums are places of exhibition and display and that digital-based objects do not lend themselves easily to that form of output. It is for this reason, as will be seen in Chapter 4, museums like American History are more likely to exhibit computer hardware than deal with the complications of the digital. However, collecting and exhibiting computer hardware alone are not without their own challenges.

The inscrutability of black boxes

While, in comparison to digital-format objects, computer hardware might seem straightforward, one need only examine the constraints of exhibition to see that this is not necessarily true. Roger Bridgman, in a formal critique of the American History Museum's *Information Age: People, Information and Technology* exhibit (May 9, 1990–September 4, 2006), notes the difficulty that comes with using computers as objects and primary evidence (rather than as interpretive medium and interactive) within an exhibit:

> The idea that you can use artefacts to tell a story enjoys widespread currency. But there are at least two obstacles in the way of those who, equipped with a storehouse and impassioned by the knowledge of their history, would use the artefacts to communicate the passion. The first of these obstacles is the invisibility of unfamiliar artefacts, or at least the unfamiliar parts of unfamiliar artefacts: people find it difficult to see what they have never seen before. The second is that, even if an artefact is clearly seen, to use it in a story you have to use it as a sign … and the meaning of any sign is socially determined. Neither of these obstacles exists for artefacts in common circulation; but these are the very artefacts that museums, as repositories of the exotic or the forgotten, tend to exclude.[57]

While museology might challenge Bridgman's assessment on the effectiveness of object-driven exhibits in general, there is a certain truth when applied to exhibits dealing with computer-based technology. The visual is an important tool used in museum exhibitions, but it is not one that easily lends itself to the internal process of computer technology. As Ceruzzi notes, "It is difficult because it is hard to display [computers] and because they do not look that interesting to a visitor. Visitors who own these devices at home do not understand what the historical context is."[58] While Ceruzzi's words partially echo Bridgman's concerns, Ceruzzi reminds us that computer technology is highly familiar to museum visitors, though perhaps not within the context that the museum is attempting to present.

This is further complicated by the computer technology in question providing no visual clues to assist the museum visitors in better understanding this context. For some visitors, however, this does not pose much of a problem. The Computer History Museum, for example, is located in "Silicon Valley." This area of northern California has continued to serve as the global center of computer technology for decades and therefore the museum attracts a large number of visitors who work in the computer industry. Senior Curator Dag Spicer notes that

> if your audience was a technical audience, they probably could be quite satisfied with the hardware. For example, we used to have "Visible

> Storage" at the museum and there were, as is common with that display technique, no graphics and minimal interpretation. Just simple labels and artifacts, cheek by jowl, stuffed into this big room. The techies loved it! Since these guys had this built in understanding, most of them did not even read the labels.[59]

However, the museum recognizes that not all of its visitors arrive with the specialized knowledge. In fact, the museum actively seeks to attract a more general audience. That requires a more complex form of exhibition than visible storage. Spicer explains:

> What we discovered was, however, that if you wanted to broaden the audience for that you really have to look at the computer as an enabler of other things. And, sure, it is a beautiful object in itself. That is celebrated and we literally put them on pedestals. But what we are really trying to get at, in [the Computer History Museum's permanent exhibition] *Revolution*, and in a proper exhibit, are the stories of how this impacted the world and people around it. And, specifically, what problems were they trying to solve at the time.[60]

However, beyond the interpretation, the computer technology remains difficult objects to exhibit. Stevan Fisher, whose job as Senior Exhibit Designer for the American History Museum allows for deeper insights into what makes a successful exhibit, notes that

> there are difficulties in computer technology in trying to present it to the public when it is not plugged in or working. Software displays tend to not be interactive for that reason or, if they are, are very limited in timeframe... How do you show what it actually does? On the device itself, it is often not possible. As a device that is part of an exhibition [interpretation], then it is not actually the technology on display; it is just another means of getting information to the visitor.[61]

Computer-based technology, due to its size and design, is not immediately intuitive, even with an accompanying explanation. Curator of Electricity Harold Wallace notes that, when it comes to exhibiting computer-based technology,

> in some respects, [it is not difficult] because you do have the physical objects, whether it is a PC, laptop, external hard drive, or peripheral. So, you do have objects there that you can put in a showcase that people can look at and relate to, especially if it is something that they remember from when they were a kid. In another way, it is difficult because as opposed to a steam engine where you can see how the piston moves and how the connecting rods hook up. You could see physically how these things

> would work. With the computers, you open them up and show a little microchip. You cannot see the electrons running around and the ones and zeroes flopping back and forth. So, how easy is it for a visitor to intuitively begin to understand how the computer works and what is going on in there? You have to, ironically, resort to analogy to explain this digital technology. So, in some ways it is no more difficult than any other technology and in some ways it is. And that is not even mentioning software.[62]

What Wallace shows us is that computer technology hardware itself is complex and therefore difficult to parse. Joyce Bedi, Historian for the American History Museum's Lemelson Center of Invention, concurs:

> I think exhibiting [computer-based technology] is a challenge because it is not easy to see what it is and what it can do. Mechanical machines where you can see the gears and the belts or at least follow it through a diagram, but showing someone a circuit diagram of what is inside or what is on a motherboard is not going to help any more than just showing them the box.[63]

Computer History Museum Curator Marc Weber concurs, noting that

> seeing a non-working steam locomotive or a stationary engine, sure that may be very dull compared to seeing it work, but anybody can see it and, at least, understand, these parts move and these parts do not. With computers, even if the cover is off or transparent, it does not do anything visible when it is operating, for the most part. You cannot see the electricity going through it the way you can see wheels move and gears turn. That is just the nature of the technology that there is no simple solution to that.[64]

Weber, Wallace, and Bedi offer explanations as to why the complexity of computers cannot be easily visualized, beyond their familiar plastic casings. Ceruzzi was quoted preciously as acknowledging: "It was hard enough when the problem was that computers were rectangular 'black boxes' that revealed little of their function."[65] Ceruzzi's use of the term "black box" was not poetic or accidental. It is a familiar terminology for history of technology practitioners and it has often been used to describe the very problem that Bedi and Wallace have identified. Helena Wright, Curator of Graphic Arts at the American History Museum, recalled:

> Back in the 1980s and 1990s, there was a lot of talk, within the Society for the History of Technology about the so-called "black box conundrum" of comprehending – studying – new technologies. Within that organization, museum people were especially struggling with what to collect and how to exhibit these new technologies because they were

> so obscured by the "black box." There was nothing to see. There were no moving parts. It was not something that could easily be explained.[66]

Wright shows us both the long association between the history of technology and museum curators and how this trait of computer technology might provide a challenge for the museum. David Allison explains:

> There are a number of challenges [to exhibiting computer technology]. One of course is having something the public understands. Computer technology tends to be the quintessential "black box" – that is, what it looks like does not necessarily represent what it is. On an automobile, you can look at it, see the wheels, see the steering wheel, and get a sense of what it does. A computer, which is a general-purpose machine rather than a special purpose machine, is something very difficult to understand the significance just by looking at the object itself – particularly older computers where people are long distant from how they operated in society. So, making the technology interesting, making it relevant, I think that is very challenging.[67]

Again, a Smithsonian curator uses the term "black box" as a way to explain the visual challenge that computer technology presents. Bernard Finn, Curator Emeritus for the American History Museum's Electricity Collection, concurs with both Wright and Allison:

> I think we all have a problem with recent technology, period. It is the old "black box" argument. You cannot understand easily what is going on inside the device. It is more difficult to exhibit than nineteenth-century technologies simply because what is happening is not visible. You cannot grab a hold of it and explain it as easily.[68]

It should not be surprising that Wallace, Bedi, Ceruzzi, Wright, Allison, and Finn should use the same terms and concepts when discussing the exhibition of computer-based technology. As curators long associated with the history of technology, they would be driven to explain how technology works to a general audience. As Tilly Blyth notes:

> We live in a world where we are repeatedly told that the relationship between humans and technology is changing in an unprecedented way and at an unprecedented rate. Each week we are sold the "next big thing": we are informed that access to data on the move "transforms everything", that our data live in "the cloud", that we are moving towards a "quantified self" surrounded by connected machines that can talk to each other through an "internet of things." But our experience of change brought by new technology is actually remarkably similar to our information age ancestors. For the Victorians time take to send and

receive a message across the Atlantic reduced from weeks to minutes. This transformed everything, from international trade, to access to news and personal communications.[69]

Blyth's linking of the computer-based technology to the telegraph demonstrates how the principles associated with the history of technology provide the context that curators use to understand a new technology, even if those principles do not innately provide solutions to the challenges that computer technology poses.

Conclusion

Building upon the insight into contemporary collecting theory and practice at the Smithsonian Institution, this chapter has attempted to examine the challenges specifically associated with the collecting and exhibiting of computer-based technology, specifically the difficulty of representing software in a meaningful way and of presenting hardware that visually reveals very little of its function. Digital-format objects cannot easily follow the collecting precedent of material objects in the same way that three-dimensional hardware is able while computer hardware can be seen as a "black box" as its internal processes remain hidden. Computer-based technology presents the museum with a series of dilemmas. It is both hardware and software – making it hard to determine what specifically is being collected. It is today within a moment of exponential change and development – rendering the decision on specifically when and what to collect difficult. Furthermore, it is part of its own history of computation while also wired into so many other contemporary histories. This presents the museum with a challenge of how to categorize it within the existing classifications and departments of the institution.

Yet, it is not just the history of technology curators' collections that are now engaging with these types of objects. Smithsonian curators who are more closely associated with social history, design, or art history (to name just a few) also have different collection parameters based on the principles of their own individual disciplines, which, as will be explored in Chapters 4 and 5, can lead them to sometimes quite different solutions to the difficulties in collecting and exhibiting computer-based technology. Chapter 3 will examine the expertise that these curators employ when they establish solutions to the challenges posed by computer-based technology.

Notes

1 See for example Simon J. Knell, Sheila E. R. Watson, and Suzanne Macleod, *Museum Revolutions: How Museums Change and Are Changed* (Abingdon, Oxon; New York: Routledge, 2007).
2 Simon J. Knell, "Altered Values: Searching for a New Collecting" in S. Knell (ed.), *Museums and the Future of Collecting* (Aldershot: Ashgate, 2004) 15.

3 Susan Pearce, *Museums, Objects and Collections: A Cultural Study* (Leicester: Leicester University Press, 1992) 4.
4 Edward P. Alexander et al., *Museums in Motion: An Introduction to the History and Functions of Museums*. (Lanham, MD: AltaMira Press, 2008) 188.
5 Paul Ceruzzi, Smithsonian Institution Archives, Computer Technology and Curation Oral History Interviews, interview with Petrina Foti, June 1, 2017.
6 For a deeper look into the relationship between modern communication and the economy, please see Manuel Castells, *Communication Power*, 2nd ed (Oxford: Oxford University Press, 2013).
7 Jan van Dijk, *The Network Society*, 3rd ed. (London: Sage, 2012) 1–2.
8 Simon J. Knell, "Altered Values: Searching for a New Collecting" in S. Knell (ed.), *Museums and the Future of Collecting* (Aldershot: Ashgate, 2004) 33–34.
9 Owain Rhys, *Contemporary Collecting: Theory and Practice* (Edinburgh: Museums Etc, 2011) 17.
10 Smithsonian Institution Archives, Record Unit 158, United States National Museum, Curators' Annual Reports.
11 Stacy Kluck, Smithsonian Institution Archives, Computer Technology and Curation Oral History Interviews, interview with Petrina Foti, August 21, 2013.
12 Keith Melder, Smithsonian Institution Archives, American Association of Museums Centennial Interviews, 2006.
13 Harry Rubenstein, Smithsonian Institution Archives, Computer Technology and Curation Oral History Interviews, interview with Petrina Foti, April 12, 2012.
14 For further reading on the contemporary collecting efforts of the Division of Political History, please see: Kylie Message, *Museums and Social Activism: Engaged Protest* (Hoboken, NJ: Routledge, 2013).
15 Keith Melder, American Association of Museums Centennial Interviews, 2006.
16 National Museum of American History, "September 11: Bearing Witness to History," Smithsonian Institution, accessed June 5, 2012, http://americanhistory.si.edu/september11/collection/curators.asp.
17 National Museum of American History. "September 11: Bearing Witness to History," Smithsonian Institution, accessed June 5, 2012, http://americanhistory.si.edu/september11/collection/curators.asp.
18 Gardner and Henry were senior management for the National Museum of American History and the Museum of the City of New York, respectively.
19 James B. Gardner and Sarah M. Henry, "September 11 and the Mourning After: Reflections on Collecting and Interpreting the History of Tragedy," *The Public Historian*, 24, no. 3 (2002), 41.
20 National Museum of American History, "September 11: Bearing Witness to History," Smithsonian Institution, accessed June 5, 2012, http://americanhistory.si.edu/september11/2011/collecting.asp.
21 James B. Gardner and Sarah M. Henry, "September 11 and the Mourning After: Reflections on Collecting and Interpreting the History of Tragedy," *The Public Historian*, 24, no. 3 (2002), 43.
22 James B. Gardner and Sarah M. Henry, "September 11 and the Mourning After: Reflections on Collecting and Interpreting the History of Tragedy," *The Public Historian*, 24, no. 3 (2002), 45.
23 David H. Shayt, "Artifacts of Disaster: Creating the Smithsonian's Katrina Collection," Technology and Culture, 47, no. 2 (2006), 357.

24 David H. Shayt. "Collecting Katrina: The Museum Challenge," March 10, 2006 draft. I would like to thank Peter Liebhold, then Chair and Curator for the Division of Work and Industry at the National Museum of American History, for providing access to documents relating to David Shayt's collecting efforts surrounding Hurricane Katrina during my doctorial research.

25 I do not use this imagery lightly. Curators were often presented with large piles of wreckage, photographs, and personal effects. The emotional and physical toll of looking through relic after relic should not be underestimated. On the National Museum of American History's website, Peter Liebhold recounted one of the most extreme of these collecting trips: "One of the longest-lasting efforts was the quest for artifacts from Flight 93. After several years of discussions with company representatives and a myriad of attorneys, we finally gained access to the wreckage of the plane. When we arived at the small airport where the material was stored, we found the airplane wreckage was in 20' long ocean-going shipping containers. When the doors were opened we saw the debris was in amazingly small pieces. David [Shayt] worked the front of the piles while I climbed into the container, wriggling over the top of the pile, trying not to get cut by the sharp fragments of fuselage." National Museum of American History, "September 11: Bearing Witness to History," Smithsonian Institution, accessed June 5, 2012, http://americanhistory.si.edu/september11/2011/collecting.asp.

26 National Museum of American History, "September 11: Bearing Witness to History," Smithsonian Institution, accessed June 5, 2012, http://americanhistory.si.edu/september11/collection/curators.asp.

27 National Museum of American History, "September 11: Bearing Witness to History," Smithsonian Institution, accessed June 5, 2012, http://americanhistory.si.edu/september11/collection/curators.asp.

28 Howard Fox, "The Right to Be Wrong," in Bruce Altshuler, *Collecting the New* (Princeton, NJ: Princeton University Press, 2005) 15.

29 Bruce Altshuler, *Collecting the New* (Princeton, NJ: Princeton University Press, 2005) 2.

30 Bernard S. Finn, Smithsonian Institution Archives, Computer Technology and Curation Oral History Interviews, interview with Petrina Foti, August 14, 2013.

31 Steven D. Lubar et al., *Legacies: Collecting America's History at the Smithsonian* (Washington, DC: Smithsonian Institution Press, 2001) 123.

32 Bernard S. Finn, Smithsonian Institution Archives, Computer Technology and Curation Oral History Interviews, interview with Petrina Foti, August 14, 2013.

33 Steven D. Lubar et al., *Legacies: Collecting America's History at the Smithsonian* (Washington, DC: Smithsonian Institution Press, 2001) 25.

34 Paul Ceruzzi, *The History of Modern Computing* (Cambridge, MA: MIT Press, 2003) x.

35 David Allison, Smithsonian Institution Archives, Computer Technology and Curation Oral History Interviews, interview with Petrina Foti, August 12, 2013.

36 Alicia Cutler, Smithsonian Institution Archives, Computer Technology and Curation Oral History Interviews, interview with Petrina Foti, June 3, 2013.

37 Nancy Proctor, Smithsonian Institution Archives, Computer Technology and Curation Oral History Interviews, interview with Petrina Foti, August 15, 2013.

38 Marc Weber, interview with Petrina Foti, March 15, 2017.

39 Sebastian Chan and Aaron Straup Cope, Smithsonian Institution Archives, Computer Technology and Curation Oral History Interviews, interview with Petrina Foti, September 26, 2013.
40 Michelle Delaney, Smithsonian Institution Archives, Computer Technology and Curation Oral History Interviews, interview with Petrina Foti, September 5, 2013.
41 Shannon Perich, Smithsonian Institution Archives, Computer Technology and Curation Oral History Interviews, interview with Petrina Foti, September 26, 2013.
42 Sebastian Chan and Aaron Straup Cope, Smithsonian Institution Archives, Computer Technology and Curation Oral History Interviews, interview with Petrina Foti, September 26, 2013.
43 David Brock, Smithsonian Institution Archives, Computer Technology and Curation Oral History Interviews, interview with Petrina Foti, March 16, 2018.
44 Hansen Hsu, Smithsonian Institution Archives, Computer Technology and Curation Oral History Interviews, interview with Petrina Foti, March 16, 2018.
45 Dag Spicer, interview with Petrina Foti, March 28, 2018.
46 David Brock, Smithsonian Institution Archives, Computer Technology and Curation Oral History Interviews, interview with Petrina Foti, March 16, 2018.
47 Simon J. Knell, "Altered Values: Searching for a New Collecting," in S. Knell (ed.), *Museums and the Future of Collecting* (Aldershot: Ashgate, 2004) 33–34.
48 Marc Weber, "Exhibiting the Online World: A Case Study" in A. Tatnall, T. Blyth, and R. Johnson (eds.), *Making the History of Computing Relevant. IFIP Advances in Information and Communication Technology*, vol. 416 (Berlin: Springer, 2013).
49 Marc Weber, Smithsonian Institution Archives, Computer Technology and Curation Oral History Interviews, interview with Petrina Foti, March 15, 2017.
50 Ross Parry, "Introduction to Part Five," in R. Parry (ed.), *Museums in a Digital Age* (London: Routledge, 2010) 294.
51 Tilly Blyth, Smithsonian Institution Archives, Computer Technology and Curation Oral History Interviews, interview with Petrina Foti, December 7, 2017.
52 Tilly Blyth, Smithsonian Institution Archives, Computer Technology and Curation Oral History Interviews, interview with Petrina Foti, December 7, 2017.
53 Sebastian Chan and Aaron Straup Cope, Smithsonian Institution Archives, Computer Technology and Curation Oral History Interviews, interview with Petrina Foti, September 26, 2013.
54 Stacy Kluck, Smithsonian Institution Archives, Computer Technology and Curation Oral History Interviews, interview with Petrina Foti, August 21, 2013.
55 Tilly Blyth, ed., *Information Age: Six Networks That Changed Our World* (London: Scala Arts, 2014) 15.
56 Sebastian Chan and Aaron Straup Cope, interview with Petrina Foti, September 26, 2013.
57 Roger Bridgman, "Information Age – a Critique," in B. Finn (ed.), *Exposing Electronics* (Amsterdam: Harwood Academic, 2000) 143.
58 Paul Ceruzzi, Smithsonian Institution Archives, Computer Technology and Curation Oral History Interviews, interview with Petrina Foti, July 24, 2013.
59 Dag Spicer, interview with Petrina Foti, March 28, 2018.
60 Dag Spicer, interview with Petrina Foti, March 28, 2018.

61 Stevan Fisher, Smithsonian Institution Archives, Computer Technology and Curation Oral History Interviews, interview with Petrina Foti, August 5, 2013.
62 Harold Wallace, Smithsonian Institution Archives, Computer Technology and Curation Oral History Interviews, interview with Petrina Foti, August 14, 2013.
63 Joyce Bedi, Smithsonian Institution Archives, Computer Technology and Curation Oral History Interviews, interview with Petrina Foti, September 13, 2013.
64 Marc Weber, Smithsonian Institution Archives, Computer Technology and Curation Oral History Interviews, interview with Petrina Foti, March 15, 2017.
65 Paul Ceruzzi, *The History of Modern Computing* (Cambridge, MA: MIT Press, 2003), x.
66 Helena Wright, Smithsonian Institution Archives, Computer Technology and Curation Oral History Interviews, interview with Petrina Foti, August 5, 2013.
67 David Allison, Smithsonian Institution Archives, Computer Technology and Curation Oral History Interviews, interview with Petrina Foti, August 12, 2013.
68 Bernard S. Finn, Smithsonian Institution Archives, Computer Technology and Curation Oral History Interviews, interview with Petrina Foti, August 14, 2013.
69 Tilly Blyth, ed., *Information Age: Six Networks That Changed Our World* (London: Scala Arts, 2014) 10.

3 Adaptive, distributed, and transmitted

The expert curation in action

Introduction

As examined in the last chapter, the challenges that computer-based technology has posed for museums, owing to its lack of alignment with established collecting traditions, were examined. To curators such as Helena Wright from the American History Museum's Graphic Arts Collection, the challenge of collecting computer-based technology is not the challenge it was twenty years ago, but instead has increasingly "become more part of the mainstream of everything in life, so therefore it has to be part of what museums collect."[1] Wright's words serve as evidence as to why it is so important for museums to engage with collecting computer-based technology, despite the innate difficulties. Because computer technology has been so adopted into contemporary life, museums are motivated to collect and exhibit these technologies to better reflect a true picture of their world. And as they do so they also establish a precedent for collecting a type of object that was previously unknown. Robert Leopold, Deputy Director of the Smithsonian Center for Folklife and Cultural Heritage and former Director of the National Anthropological Archives, notes: "I believe that it is not only easy to collect computer-based technology, I think [museums] do it all the time. I think that there is no way to stop museums from collecting."[2] Leopold further explains that

> computer technology is not new. We are finding it new to have to deal with some of the repercussions of it in practices like archiving that developed a century and a half ago... They are unfamiliar challenges, is what they are. Again, the opportunity is that they give us the chance to rethink business as usual and to think "Wow, what would be unusual? What can we do that is greater, that is better, that is more useful than things we have done in the past?"[3]

Leopold reframes the difficulties that computer-based technology often presents into new opportunities for the museum to develop and expand beyond its existing parameters. Wright and Leopold's observations serve as illustrations of how museum practice has begun to transform the unknowns of computer-based technology into a tradition with its own rich evidence.

Curators who engage with computer-based technology in their practice exhibit a series of traits that have facilitated this transformation and this ability to accommodate the unknown and assimilate the new. As will be seen in Chapter 5, in the exhibit *Time and Navigation*, Curators Carlene Stephens and Paul Ceruzzi found creative ways to present their non-traditional-appearing computer-based technology. It is therefore not so surprising that Stephens does not find recording the history of computer-based technology difficult:

> I think that there are any number of imaginative ways to collect computer technologies – users, makers, inventors – and it is the same kind of imaginative work that pertains to just about any object or subject. If people have imagination and the will to collect, it can be done.[4]

Stephens' words remind us that, rather than being paralyzed by a lack of precedent, curators who engage with computer-based technology display the ability to meet the challenge of the unknown creatively. This study proposes that there are specific traits associated with this skill as characteristics of curatorial expertise. These traits might be further categorized into discrete types: *adaptive*, *distributive,* and *transmitted*.

First, how curators are able to react quickly and flexibly when they seek solutions to accessioning, interpreting, and exhibiting new types of museum objects might reasonably be classified as an "adaptive" type of curatorial expertise. In each case the curator's dilemma and actions demonstrated a willingness to be agile and flexible, to be willing to adapt established work processes or to consider the application of an alternative approach in order to accommodate and manage the anomaly that appeared to be presented by computer-based technology. Second, shared expertise between curatorial staff, experts in the field, and even museum visitors themselves – a common thread that will be followed in Chapters 4 and 5 –highlights an expertise that is not only "adaptive," but also "distributive." In other words, in the work (and reflections) of the Smithsonian Institution curators considered here, there is a willingness and openness to acknowledge a wider and distributed network of expertise. As the Smithsonian is further examined, there are examples of expertise being seen as something collective that could be shared (rather than something individual and personal), and something that could extend beyond the institution (rather than remain internal). Finally, in these acts of collecting and display, examples of curatorial expertise are also knowingly "transmitted" – that is, collecting that is recorded in a way to be passed down through generations of curatorial staff. This can be expressed when a curator chooses to collect on a given contemporary topic, mindful of how incomplete the accessioning might be, but acknowledging that this accession might only mark the beginning (rather than the totality) of an act of knowledge capture. It too was a recognition of "transmitted expertise" that was present in the reaction of the curators at the American History Museum to the events of September 11, when their introspection revealed how difficult the moment of contemporary collecting might be, and how it would be for future curators at the institution to make a more contextualized judgment on the value the object might have.

This chapter will examine these three types of expertise (adaptive, distributive, and transmitted) and, in doing so, this study will begin to trace a larger emerging pattern of what might usefully be called "expert curation." This term is not meant to refer to the academic area that the curator has specialized in, but to reflect that the man or woman in question is an expert in the museum practice that we refer to as "curation." This chapter will consider each of these cultures of expertise and how they provide a structure and environment for engaging with unprecedented collecting and suggest that expertise can frequently operate in these active, complex, and nuanced ways. The unusual challenges posed by computer-based technology, combined with the unique environment of the Smithsonian, help us perhaps to see a much more ordinary facet of curatorial practice that might otherwise be obscured by its very ubiquity. In short, by seeing how the museums of the Smithsonian respond with agility to extraordinary and unprecedented objects, it demonstrates the inherent capacity the Institution and, indeed, all museums, have for change and adaptive practice in the face of a rapidly evolving world.

Adaptive expertise

Adaptive curation can be seen in practice with how the American History Museum's Division of Art and Culture has recorded the impact of the internet on American entertainment consumption. As illustrated in Chapter 2, the rise of the digital and the difficulty in representing this shift do not easily adapt to traditional museum patterns of collecting. Eric Jentsch, Deputy Chair of Art and Culture, concurs and explains how this impacts the collections in his division:

> The types of modern technology you are talking about impacts our work as well. You have the production of Monday Night Football. You have the creation of CGI effects. You have the recording of music. All of those things that we are going to have to address and try to find ways to collect that will represent those stories in a way that people can understand and connect with. I do not think our role in this division is to collect all the technologies to show the change in time over every type of way music was recorded.[5]

Jentsch illustrates the depth in which computer technology has been adopted by society so that even entertainment has been transformed.

However, in keeping with the focus of the division, he deliberately chooses to focus on the social history, rather than attempt to record the history of technology.

The division's Entertainment Collection includes examples of sets, props, and costumes from theater, movies, and television productions. There are many examples of contemporary collecting, specifically objects acquired in response to an external event or, in this case, contribution to popular culture. However, as seen in Chapter 2 with the once-popular 1847 life car – a type of lifeboat technology that faded from public awareness and interest once society became less maritime-centric – the risk of landmark collecting is that the significance of the contribution can fade from popular consciousness. The names of the most famous vaudeville stars are barely remembered nearly a hundred years later and their costumes, collected during the height of their popularity, are now only of passing interest to modern museum visitors more interested in the ruby slippers from *The Wizard of Oz* or Jim Henson's Kermit the Frog. Jentsch notes that

> if you just look at some of our collections from the past, would they collect an entire *Barney Miller* set today? Perhaps not. And nothing against *Barney Miller* [a late 1970s situational comedy program], but what now in the long run differentiates that show from all the others? But we are happy to have it because we can tell certain stories. So in terms of collecting technologies in the future, it is really hard to get away from the three-dimensional aspect in terms of our process. That does not mean I do not think it is of value to collect digital realms, but to me it is more of an accentuation.[6]

As Jentsch reminds us, there are multiple ways to record and represent history. It is up to the curator to decide how that might best be done. The collecting precedent of the Entertainment Collection is based on the three-dimensional props, scripts, and costumes that are regularly generated in the entertainment field and continue to allow movies and television shows to be represented in a meaningful way for museum staff and visitors alike. Yet to continue to honor these collecting principles, the curatorial staff of the Entertainment Collection must seek creative solutions when computer-based technology becomes a large part of the story.

In the past twenty years, the music and entertainment fields have undergone a massive transformation with the development of DVDs and streaming services such as Netflix, which has led to, as Jentsch terms it, a "golden age of adult drama, long form stories that involve very mature themes."[7] Thanks to advances in technology, it is now possible for fans to watch any episode they wish of their favorite programs. Unlike in years past, modern American television serials are currently being developed with the expectation that all but the most casual of viewers will watch the series in its entirety. Jentsch notes that

> the actual props and content of a series would not only say what this series represents, but also that the series exists because of these technological changes. So, they can be used to tell that story as well… You could now watch *Game of Thrones*, or even *The Sopranos*, all at once. This changes the types of stories you can tell because you know that your audiences could follow it based on their maturity level but also on their ability to watch it whenever they want.[8]

We can now see from Jentsch's words that the familiar Entertainment Collection practice of collecting props and costumes is actually functioning on a more complex level, serving as a representation of concept: the rise of long-form narrative storytelling in early twenty-first-century American television. By representing a larger story in American popular culture, this, in turn, serves as a method to ensure that these acquisitions stay relevant even after the interest in their represented productions has faded. This illustrates a thoughtful and agile curatorial response to emerging social and technological patterns and structures.

We can see this same agility at play in the early plans[9] of Jentsch and his colleagues to record the rise of Netflix, a company that does not have specifically associated representational hardware or software. The American company began in 1999 as a subscription service that offered DVD rentals by mail and in 2007 introduced streaming services, which would allow subscribers to watch movies and television shows on their computers via the internet.[10] In recent years, Netflix began to offer original content exclusively as part of their streaming packages. Jentsch notes:

> They furthered [streaming television shows] and now they are actually a producer of content. That shows the power of and plasticity of the technology in that they went from taking a hard product and sending it through the mail where you could watch a movie, to actually creating content and presenting it in a new way. Instead of just being a delivery system, they are actually a producer of entertainment. So, they are almost like a network on themselves, which changes the whole paradigm of who owns the production of content.[11]

Here are objects that do not contain computer technology being collected to represent a social change prompted by computer-based technology. This reflexive response is indicative perhaps of how expert curation navigates through a rigid set of circumstances. The computer technology – while essential to the rise of streaming services and therefore partly responsible for the shift toward long-form storytelling – is not central to the representational needs of the museum when it seeks to collect this phenomenon and therefore the museum need not directly address the "black box."

What is interesting about this adaptive representation of computer-based technology is that it can be applied to already-existing museum holdings, such as the laptop used as a prop during the television show *Sex and the City*.[12] The program, which ran from 1998 until 2004 and was then followed by two feature films in 2008 and 2010, examined the lives of four women living in New York City. As the series celebrated high fashion and explored issues pertaining to romantic and sexual relationships, it might seem rather surprising that the museum's sole representation takes the form of computer technology. It is interesting to note that the web label for the laptop reflects this possible disconnect:

> Manhattan newspaper columnist Carrie Bradshaw, played by Sarah Jessica Parker used this laptop to record her observations on modern relationships in the risqué comedy series *Sex and the City* (HBO, 1998–2004). Frank, witty, and often outrageous, the Emmy Award-winning cable show won millions of loyal fans with its depiction of four women friends and their romantic urban escapades. It also established cable TV as a competitive producer of original programming. *Sex and the City* set fashion trends, from Manolo Blahnik shoes to cosmopolitan cocktails, and provoked cultural debates about sex, relationships, and gender roles.[13]

What is not reflected in the web label is the larger curatorial motivation for the laptop's selection. Since the main character and narrator Carrie Bradshaw, played by Sarah Jessica Parker, was a columnist for a fictional newspaper who worked from home rather than in a central office building, the laptop, accessioned in 2004, was collected in part to represent the social movement of the home office. However, the laptop can also be interpreted in terms of its use within the show and how that might be connected to current internet-based social communication. Jentsch notes:

> It is not just using it as a plot device. It is also a way to explain her character as being this modern woman that people can relate to, especially in the use of her technology… I would say that the character of Carrie Bradshaw is someone who represents that figure for a lot of people. Instead of being a journalist or writing letters to her friends, or some other plot device they might have used in the past, she is writing a blog, for a general audience, all about herself.[14]

By virtue of their multifunctionality, computers and computer-based technology pose difficulties for museums when attempting to isolate an individual capability of the technology.

While computers are multipurpose machines, this particular computer, by virtue of being a prop, is associated with a particular computer application: internet communication. Therefore, it can represent that application. Jentsch explains:

> The main thing for me is how much is the same or different in terms of content produced on these devices. It goes back to the telegraphs. How did people interact and what kind of messages did they have? The internet when it came out, [it was] like "this is the information superhighway, and we can learn anything." Well, what did people want to do? Talk about themselves. That is the human element. They want to see themselves in technology. They want to use it for their own life and their own psychological reasons.[15]

Jentsch has taken an existing museum object – one that is still quite contemporary – and reinterpreted it in the context of the current understanding of technology. Helena Wright of the Graphic Arts Collection notes the same process of assessment and reassessment when working with her own collection that Jentsch exemplified:

> I am continually trying to make the collection relevant and part of that is understanding what is here and unpacking what is here, figuring out why it was collected, when it was collected, and then what do we want to add to that from our perspective that will build on what they have done.[16]

Wright explains in general the curatorial thought process that Jentsch illustrated in the specific. Therefore, this ability can be understood to respond to and reframe existing knowledge to be a central trait of adaptive curation and one that provides great assistance to curators engaging existing knowledge.

This tradition of responding to developments in society by reframing existing collections also serves as a reminder that the collections of the Smithsonian, even those that were primarily composed through contemporary collecting, are long-established when even the youngest collections can measure their history in decades. Many, such as the American History Museum's Physical Science Collections (from which the Electricity Collection originated), the Graphic Arts Collection, and the Photographic History Collection, were founded during the latter half of the nineteenth century, before their current parent museum, which opened in 1964, was even planned or proposed. Therefore, this process of revaluation can be understood to be a curatorial technique honed over a long period of time and one that would then naturally be applied to computer-based technology as a pattern of curation that is familiar and well tested. Adaptive curatorial expertise offers a precedent of curatorial practice for the challenges of the unprecedented, whether in terms of scope, as seen with the September 11 collecting in Chapter 2, or subject-specific matters, as will be explored with computer-based technology in Chapters 4 and 5.

Yet, in this observation of "adaptive expertise" around computer-based technology, it is possible to see implications for museum practice more widely. These were curators over multiple generations at one institution who were confronted with a series of objects without precedent. These were museum professionals making judgments on collecting object types for the first time, but then working within departmental structures and processes of collections management not (on the surface at least) suited to the anomalies presented to them. However, in these powerful examples, the Smithsonian Institution is able, as it were, to flex its expertise and show a willingness to readdress its processes in order to collect and incorporate the "black box" into its holdings. This says much about the Smithsonian Institution itself, and how it has been able to find precedents for being adaptive by looking back on previous examples from a span of decades of collecting the unprecedented. These examples may also speak to a more embedded characteristic of museum curation more generally. Computers at the Smithsonian constitute, of course, a very specific case of a localized culture of museum practice. Yet, this expert curatorial response might also serve as an illustration of a trait of curatorship that might be encountered with other types of contemporary objects in other types of institution worldwide. What has been detected here, in short, may be a responsiveness and agility of modern curatorial expertise, rather than just exclusively a character of Smithsonian professional life.

Transmitted expertise

A further consequence of long-established collections with histories that exceed the length of human life spans is the number of curators who are therefore affiliated with those collections, creating a curatorial "genealogy," so to speak. Chapter 2 examined the concept of collection stewardship, in which a central tenet is the understanding that the ramifications of any curatorial decisions will be inherited by future generations of museum practitioners. This is illustrated with Wright's drive to make relevant the work of her predecessors by "understanding what is here and unpacking what is here" to carefully and thoughtfully "build on what they have done."[17] Like links in a chain, curators look backward to the examples set by their predecessors while reaching forward to provide their successors with the same assistance

The Computers Collection is a history of technology-based collection with many of the artifacts collected while similar examples were still being used, or, in the case of more unique computers such as ENIAC or the IAS Machine, shortly after they were decommissioned,[18] similar to the acquisition of the Space Shuttle Discovery, as seen in Chapter 2. Therefore, the vast majority of objects in that collection can be classified as examples of contemporary collecting, with the technological impact of a given example of computer technology providing the impetus for collecting. The early history of computer technology is closely associated with the history of computation and mathematics. It therefore is not surprising that the Computers Collection at the National Museum of American History is closely tied to the Mathematics Collection, with a single curator initially responsible for both collections. Though the Computers Collection has been considered a separate collection for decades, many connections between the two collections still remain. For example, the collections continue to share a storage space.

The collection has been largely shaped by three curators: Uta Merzback, Jon Eklund, and David Allison. While the three did work together for many years, the informal stewardship was slightly more linear, starting with Merzbach and ending with Allison after Eklund's retirement. This curatorial lineage can be seen in the evolution of collecting patterns. Allison, now Senior Scholar in the museum's Office of Director, served as curator for the Computers Collection for more than twenty years and observes:

> Uta Merzbach – who was really not a curator of computing – she got into that field because she was a curator of mathematics primarily. She treated computers as much as anything as mathematical tools and mostly collected some of the early and large computers in the collection. She was not as interested in the social side of the story as we became interested later. Jon Eklund, her successor, was primarily interested in personal computers. So, his interest was much more the recent history of computing, although he did collect some earlier mainframes as well. He was primarily a historian of chemistry and so he picked this up on the side. But again he was more interested in the technological side of computing than the social side. I felt like, coming in, I tried to be more balanced in the things that I was collecting, as interested in the personal stories and in the social context as in the computing technology. I also believe that the limitations of the Computer Collection at the Smithsonian should be collecting not so much for the history of the discipline itself, but how computing fits into the larger history of the United States and try to collect things that had connections to other parts of our collection rather than just the internal history of computing.[19]

Allison's personal perspective on his and his predecessors' collecting behaviors demonstrates a clear understanding of how the Computers Collection formed and the legacy that they have left for their successors. Merzbach's focus on computers as computational machines – and how her interest shifted away completely once the collection had found an engaged collection steward in Eklund – makes sense within the context of her academic interests. In contrast, Eklund's experience with personal computers motivated him to become more involved with the collection on a professional level. Yet, Allison's recollections also reveal a shift in the collection's collecting mission to incorporate more social history, which in turn reflects a larger shift that was taking place across the museum.

In addition to Merzbach, Eklund, and Allison, the Computers Collection has often had a Collection Manager, whose responsibility it was to process new accessions and to maintain object storage and the catalog.[20] During the 1980s, Ann Seeger served in this role. She recollects:

> Jon was always interested in personal computing. He was one of the first people here to have a desktop computer – a TRS-80 – and got the director into it. So, when the *Information Age* exhibit was just in the planning stages – just still in people's heads – Jon really wanted to be involved, because of his interest in computing... They brought in David Allison to head the division and then Jon moved into the Computing Collection, also maintaining his responsibilities in the Chemistry Collection. So, of course, he had to bring his technician specialist – whatever I was at the time – with him. So, I ended up having the two responsibilities.[21]

Seeger's memories of Eklund reveal how his personal interest in computer technology influenced his professional career. However, while Eklund was an avid user of computer technology, Seeger was not. She explains:

> [Eklund] taught me how to use personal computers, but I knew nothing about the history of computing. Jon was spending his time working with people on planning *Information Age* and working out what he wanted to collect, because there were no personal computers in the collection when he joined the division. Uta Merzbach had concentrated on mainframe computers, the various kinds of storage devices and the smaller, like IBM350s, those kinds of computers. There were no smaller [desktop] computers. So, he was working on that and I was working on trying to familiarise myself with the whole subject. I actually did a little mini-inventory of the computer section, just so I could sort of know what was there. Then I had to start working with Peggy [Kidwell] who was there as the specialist in the Math Collection and working out how we were going to divide up the space and getting some additional storage units for all these computers. I did not really have any say in what was collected. My role was more making sure everything was properly accessioned and stored.[22]

Seeger's recollections serve as an example of how museum curatorial staff are able to become experts in subject matters for which they might not originally have been formally trained. When Seeger says she was trying to familiarize herself with the whole subject, it is striking not only in the efforts she made on her own behalf but also that her efforts were focused on what would benefit the collection. Seeger understood that the collection had the subject-specific expertise in the form of Eklund, Merzbach, and later Allison. What she could offer was her collection management expertise. Seeger's "mini-inventory" reveals a practical approach to understanding her new collection. Seeger's words also remind us that there are specific concerns that come with the structure and organization of new collections, especially one consisting of unfamiliar and still rapidly developing technology.

These collection management concerns can include the classification system used in cataloging. For example, upon surveying the collection's cataloging records,[23] the following terms can be seen to be employed: mainframe, minicomputer, and microcomputer. These machines are never identified merely as a "computer." Further extended examination of the museum's cataloging records reveals that when the term "computer" is used in the classification field without a modifier, it is for a stray example of computer technology associated with another collection.[24] Alicia Cutler, Seeger's successor in the role of Collection Manager, explains that such specification of language is used in cataloging because "it cannot be that generic" as "it is a computer collection," where "everything within that collection, you already understand at that level is a computer or related to a computer – so you have to break it down."[25] This echoes the explanation that Cutler provided me with during my training as Collection Manager. The classification system that was first employed during Seeger's tenure was the same means I, who was as unfamiliar with computer history or computer science at the onset of my post as Seeger initially was, used to understand the collection. This level of curatorial practice reveals how curatorial staff approach and organize an unknown subject or technology through classification and identification in a way that will be understood by future generations of curators and collection managers.

The decisions made by previous collection stewards establish a general curatorial precedent that subsequent curators are then able (with agility) to mold and adapt to unfamiliar situations – such as when collecting computer-based technology for the first time. The curators employ the knowledge that they gained from their predecessors, whether directly through personal contact or correspondence or indirectly in the form of collection "rules" and traditions. For an example from my personal experience, I directly benefited during my training as Collection Manager of the Computers Collection from having access to my predecessors Alicia Cutler and Ann Seeger, who were able to explain the rationale behind past decisions and convey stories from their own tenure on which I was later able to draw when making similar challenging decisions.

When curators actively collect, they are building holdings for the future, even if that future time might be after they have left or retired. As can be seen in Chapter 2 with Rhys, contemporary collecting is one of the methods that curators use to fill gaps in collections, not just for themselves but for their successors. This could especially be seen with the American History Museum's September 11 collecting. While the Museum's current use of the collection could be classified as memorialization, the collections were built with the understanding that future generations of museum staff would use these holdings to explain and contextualize the events for future generations of museum visitors. In this manner, through contemporary collecting, curators are able to fill any potential gaps in their collections while it is still easy to do so, allowing their successors to concentrate on other areas. For example, the American History Museum's Harold Wallace explains that decisions made by previous curators affiliated with the Electricity and Physical Science Collections – including those of George Maynard, who came to the Institution in 1885 – have implications for Wallace's priorities today:

> What they have collected tends to be things that I no longer have to worry so much about. Maynard brought in a lot of very good telephone materials and telegraph materials and then Barney Finn brought in the Western Union Museum. So, it is not often that I collect any telegraph-related materials.[26]

The telegraph material, it should be noted, still generates interest from the public a century later even though the technology has long since been replaced by internet communication. However, as a technology becomes obsolete, related materials, once commonplace, become scarce and difficult to find. Wallace and Finn would not be able to recreate the wealth of material that was easily accessible to Maynard. Through contemporary collecting, curators, in addition to seeking to provide themselves with the materials they need to complete their research, provide for the needs and concerns of those who will follow. This can sometimes take surprising forms, as can be seen in the American History Museum's Graphic Arts Collection. Curators Helena Wright and Joan Boudreau actively sought a donation from Hewlett-Packard for computer paper, still in its original packaging, along with related trade literature for the Graphic Arts Collection. Wright explains:

> We had the idea that we should be collecting the materials that went along with this revolution in printing technique, so paper of course was a big part of that. The packaging for that paper tells us something about the marketing as well. So, we were learning about specific papers for specific digital output uses and that is why we wanted a sort of a time capsule of those papers. We have a strong collection of paper-making that goes back to paper made by hand that came with Dard Hunter in the 1920s and he had collected material from the sixteenth and seventeenth centuries forward: Asian handmade papers, European handmade papers, watermarked collections. We have a tradition of a subsection within the collection of paper-making and this is part of that.[27]

Just as with George Maynard and the telegraph materials, Wright and Boudreau, through collecting patterns established by their predecessors, were able to understand that while computer paper might be abundant today, that would not always be the case. Though there is no way for museum curators to predict what precisely their successors might need, their own experience and expertise in general museum curation serve as guidance. This process can be thought of almost as a dialogue between the past and the present, though the linear rules of time and space make it rather one-sided. With such a tradition, it is easier to understand how today's curators are motivated to ensure that this conversation is continued with the next generation of curatorial staff, and how this motivation might serve as guidance when confronting the unknowns of computer-based technology.

Stepping back, a survey across the Smithsonian's collecting and display of computer-based technology reveals a mindfulness toward continuous legacy of transmitted knowledge. When confronted with the complexities (and opacities) of the "black box" of computing, the curatorial staff not only responded with a willingness to adapt and adjust practice to accommodate new forms of objects, but also remain aware of how this practice would need to make sense to generations of curators to follow. The double challenge they worked through was not only to justify these acts of contemporary collecting to themselves, but also to consider the vantage point of the future as well. In this way, again, a trait of modern curatorship that extends beyond the Smithsonian can be seen. This study might indeed evidence what might be called "transmitted expertise" at the Smithsonian Institution (a form of expert curatorship that is processing something entirely new, while also considering how this act will be perceived and understood in the future), but it also might be helping us to see a quality, more generally, of modern curatorship.

Distributive expertise

Sociologist Eliot Freidson, considered to be one of the leading contributors of his time to sociology of professions, in his book *Professional Powers: A Study of the Institutionalization of Formal Knowledge* stated that

> down at the level of everyday human experience, in schools, prisons, scientific laboratories, factories, government agencies, hospitals, and the like, formal knowledge is transformed and modified by the activities of those participating in its use. Thus the paradox that, while institutionalization of knowledge is a prerequisite for the possibility of its connection to power, institutionalization itself requires the transformation of knowledge by those who employ it. The analysis of scientific and scholarly texts can be no substitute for the analysis of the human interaction that creates them and that transforms them in the course of using them in a practical enterprise.[28]

Freidson sees the relationship between knowledge and professionalism as a fluid social dynamic. So, it is only reasonable that if museum curatorial staff feel they do not have the specific knowledge needed on a given topic, they will expand their resources beyond the limitations of formal institutional structures to include other experts in the field, regardless of their past experience in curation or museums. During the course of this study, curatorial staff at the Smithsonian have exemplified this behavior. An interesting example of distributive expertise can be seen in an exhibition currently in development at the Smithsonian's National Museum of Natural History, a somewhat surprising location for an exhibition about cell phones and mobile technology. The exhibition, alongside scholarly articles and academic publications,[29] is the product of a long-term project with multiple partners, both external academic institutions and internal Smithsonian units. (This exhibit will be discussed further in Chapter 6.) Project Director and Curator of Globalization Joshua Bell explains:

> The thread that runs through my research is the role of objects technology in our society and how people deploy that in their everyday life… Cell phones are remarkable and, as we tend to pitch in exhibits [proposals] and as any historian of technology knows, there is a window when a technology comes onto the scene in which the media ideologies and just the anxieties about that device gets worked out. Right now, with smartphones, we are working that out. So, as long as that is still something that people are working out, I think that, as an anthropologist, I have to study it. I do not know when that will stop because the device itself is changing through the app so much that we'll see.[30]

Bell further notes:

> My goal there is to push people to think that technology is not outside of us, but it is part of what we conceive of as our nature… Not only untangling the way in which we separate technology from humanity and natural thing, the cell phone *is* a product of our environment and so brining that out.[31]

Bell's words reveal that he is interpreting computer-based technology though his own discipline of anthropology, not history of technology, like the curators in the Computers Collection at the American History Museum. By using a different perspective, familiar subjects, such as computer-based technology, can be seen in new light.

Distributive expertise is an acknowledgment that no one person is necessarily the exclusive repository of knowledge on any given subject. Often, as is evidently the case with computer-based technology, the result is that one historical narrative might be told through multiple collections, as can be seen with the American History Museum's video game holdings. The Museum's recording of the history of video games, for example, might be classified as "passive," with no one curator or collection leading collecting efforts and with the majority of accessions in this area entering the museum as unsolicited donations. As Alicia Cutler, former Collection Manager for the

Computers Collection and current Digital Assets Manager for the American History Museum, notes:

> The museum has not focused at all on video games. It has been sort of incidental. Somebody calls and wants to donate something and it just so happens that video games are a part of it: "I want to donate this computer and all the software I had with it." The software will often – unless it was for business – include video games because almost everybody who had a computer at home had some sort of game.[32]

Cutler provides a vivid example of how curatorial interest – or lack thereof – shapes what history is being recorded. Since curators did not actively seek to record video game history, the history that was recorded was dependent on the interest and motivation of potential donors. Cutler observes:

> I think that goes across the board with all curatorial staff. As a curator, you have an interest in something and obviously you have some sort of interest in collecting and documenting the past, if you are working in a museum. You do not just happen into a museum job because you just decided you were going to do it. So, I think every curator has their biases. Their specialties. In the 1990s, the specialties of the curators [in the Computers Collection] really were just dealing with the machines. It was not necessarily dealing with the culture of the machines. Except for the whole "Homebrew" culture... But because video games were part of your everyday life, everybody from my age on would consider that an important part of history and not sort of this side thing.[33]

Culter's observations illustrate how collecting can often be directly related to personal experience. Cutler explains: "I think for the curators, they all came before the video game age. To them, video games were not part of your everyday life. For me, it was."[34] Like Cutler, video games were part of my "everyday life" since my childhood. So, like Cutler, I saw the importance of recording the history of video games and, since I left the American History Museum, other museum staff born in the age of video games have been actively working to ensure this part of history is represented within the museum collections. In fact, despite the overall passive interest in collecting, early video game history was well represented in the museum's collection by the time that I joined the museum in 2006. Under Cutler's guidance, a Game Boy was collected in the Computers Collection. In the Electricity Collection, there are two arcade games: *Pong* and *Pac-Man*. In addition, there is a small collection of computer games from the early 1980s in the Division of Home and Community Life as part of their larger Toy and Game Collection. From a public standpoint, the formal collection with which each of these objects is affiliated makes little difference, but, from a curatorial perspective, it exemplifies the ability for multiple voices to be viewed as expert.

Even the Ralph Baer accession,[35] which is arguably the museum's most high- profile collecting effort in recording video game history, has a distributive narrative, being shared by the Computers Collection and the museum's Archive Center. Ralph Baer, who is considered by many to be the Father of the Video Game, had approached the museum with an offer to donate his early video game console prototypes from the 1960s and early 1970s, including the famed 1968 "Brown Box."[36] David Allison, who led the collecting effort, explains:

> It was a great story from many different perspectives. The so-called "Brown Box" is a really terrific visual object that helps people understand something complex. Almost everybody that comes through this museum either knows about or has played videogames, some people as part of their growing up. To see something that was the beginning, to see that it was just a box covered with contact paper and open it up, unlike the videogames today, where the internal components of it are mostly chips, this has a lot of wires and early electronics. You can see the circuitry in it, the way the "Brown Box" works, with switches and handwritten instructions about whether you are playing "Chase" or whether you are playing "Ping-Pong" or playing something else. It makes it really feel like a prototype device in ways that are endearing, are interesting, and are visual. Things that are hard in the technological sphere to illustrate, this object can illustrate. So, it was already an interesting story. It became more interesting because of the three-dimensional objects that went along with it, the personality of the man who had done it, his motivations, and his personal story. It had many aspects that make a good and powerful museum object and collection.[37]

The materials themselves are distributed with the prototypes residing in the Computers Collection and Baer's extensive paperwork documenting his invention process in the Archives Center. A member of the collecting team, Joyce Bedi, Senior Historian for the American History Museum's Lemelson Center for the Study of Invention and Innovation, notes:

> It is one story, and the materials are cared for where they are best cared for. So, the documents are in the Archive Center because they can take care of that, and the artifacts are up in Computer Collections because they can take care of that.[38]

With the Ralph Baer accession, museum expertise itself is distributed, with specific members of staff offering specific skill sets tailored to particular needs. Archives are equipped to handle documentation en masse with curatorial collections providing for the needs of three-dimensional objects. Therefore, it can be understood how, like subject-specific expertise, general museum expertise is also distributive, with individual curatorial staff offering unique perspectives into a given topic.

Significantly, this concept of distributed expertise, especially in regard to computer-based technology, can also be extended to include museum visitors. As will be seen in Chapter 5, exhibit labels often reflect this, offering to augment the visitor's existing knowledge rather than assuming that everything relating to computer-based technology needs to be explained. This awareness of a shared knowledge extends beyond exhibit walls, to the way that curators understand and explain their collection, as can be seen with Wallace and the telegraph-related objects in the Electricity Collection. Wallace explains:

> When I either give a tour of the collections storage area or do a lecture about Morse's telegraph and its dots and dashes, [I describe it as] a binary system. Especially for younger visitors today – who resonate immediately with computers – the ones who have any technical knowledge about computers' work, you say "binary" and they immediately get it: "Oh, okay, this is what's going on." It is just a different form of binary coding than they are used to thinking about, but that is basically what it is.[39]

Wallace can both explain and understand his collection in terms of modern computer technology equivalents and recognizes that the general public will be able to do the same. As previously noted, Jentsch has reflected back on the use of the telegraph in his understanding of how society responded to internet communication. This too can be seen as an example of distributive expertise, as Jentsch has never formally been affiliated with the Electricity Collection. However, he is able to understand and interpret the telegraphy objects in a way that is meaningful and connected to themes that relate to objects under his stewardship. This agility of thought displays how curatorial expertise often crosses formal internal boundaries in ways that might be surprising, but are completely rational.

More broadly, this distributive expertise can be seen at work across the Smithsonian. As evidenced in the Smithsonian Collection Search Center,[40] near-identical computers, smartphones, and other similar examples of computer technology have been collected by a number of different Smithsonian museums. This reflects a view that knowledge and expertise is not the exclusive purview of the few, but shared by many, with no group or individual experiencing privilege over others. Yet even as the many ways that the structure of the Smithsonian Institution has fostered and encouraged this open, distributive environment can be observed, we might recognize that this environment of collaboration exists outside the Smithsonian as well. What this study evidenced as "distributive expertise" at the Smithsonian might well be an indication of a far more widespread practice of modern museum expertise worldwide.

Expert curation

This study has proposed three aspects of curatorial expertise at play in the Smithsonian Institution: namely, expertise that is adaptive, distributive, and transmitted. Adaptive expertise is displayed in Smithsonian curators' ability to meet the unfamiliar with flexibility and creative solutions. Adaptive acts are those in which the institution, after noting changes in perceptions or values, is prepared to modify already-established museum traditions accordingly. Transmitted expertise allows this generation of collection stewards to preserve knowledge in a way that is beneficial for their successors, as they are, in turn, reliant on the work of their predecessors. Transmitted expertise is expertise that is mindful of future practice and dependent on past traditions. Finally, a further curatorial culture at the Smithsonian, in which expertise is distributed among museum professionals, field experts, and museum visitors, has been evidenced. By acknowledging an idea of distributed expertise, the institution increases its knowledge base when making acquisition decisions and can confront complex topics on the exhibition floor, which, as has previously been noted, are crucial to its accommodation of new and unprecedented objects such as computer-based technology. More significantly perhaps, together, these cultures of expertise, these patterns of working, represent a mode of practice that might usefully be understood as "expert curatorship." This is a culture of curatorship shared by museums across the globe that is willing to challenge the complex, that is comfortable in finding new ways to represent and present, but that also shows a sensibility to current communities of expertise in all of their many expressions, but also to future communities of expertise and the ways in which they might, in turn, carry on the traditions of curatorial practice.

However, another important characteristic of "expert curatorship" that has been detected from this Smithsonian example, at least, is its ability to learn from the past. The ability of being adaptive and distributive speaks much more to a method of working with flexibility and efficiency, and yet it is one that values and is shaped by previous practice. Significantly, the examples of expert curatorship examined here included those moments when the knowledge that the curatorial staff employed was informed and guided by earlier precedents that, while not identical, could be applied to current circumstances. There was precedent for dealing with the unprecedented. It seems important, therefore, to also note that the qualities of expertise in museum practice at the Smithsonian and more widely in the sector are not static and beholden to traditions of collecting and collections that extend back a century or more, but can, in fact, employ those traditions as a form of inspiration in the process of evolutionary change.

Conclusion

This chapter has offered examples of curators from different subject matters and disciplines, each employing these types of expertise in practice when collecting and exhibiting computer-based technology. This evidence indicates that, even though the Smithsonian museums may not have previously encountered this form of technology, the Institution has had a model of curatorial practice and expertise in place that can respond and react to the challenges posed by computer-based technology. Smithsonian curators engage with the challenges of hardware-dependent software and software-dependent hardware, not by applying an already preformulated response, but by careful examination and relying on a honed curatorial skill set. Through these actions, what was once unprecedented for the museum has been transformed into established museum practice. Together, these examples offer evidence of how museum curation subtly, but ever steadily, evolves.

It is, therefore, to how specifically the museum deals with these myriad challenges that we now turn. Chapters 4 and 5 consider in turn how the curators of the National Museum of American History, the National Air and Space Museum, and the Cooper Hewitt, Smithsonian Design Museum have engaged with collecting and exhibiting computer-based technology. Taking the challenges highlighted in this chapter as their focus, and informed by the conceptual framework of Chapter 2, our next two chapters look, in turn, at the ways in which one institution has productively responded to the "black box conundrum," which, as has been seen, can be a shared response among many curators and disciplines or very tailored to one individual collection. With the Smithsonian Institution's collective response, examples of how to accommodate the unprecedented can be observed. This offers insight into a much wider theme of how expertise works within not just this institution, but, perhaps, the sector more widely.

Notes

1 Helena Wright, Smithsonian Institution Archives, Computer Technology and Curation Oral History Interviews, interview with Petrina Foti, August 5, 2013.
2 Robert Leopold, Smithsonian Institution Archives, Computer Technology and Curation Oral History Interviews, interview with Petrina Foti, May 17, 2013.
3 Robert Leopold, Smithsonian Institution Archives, Computer Technology and Curation Oral History Interviews, interview with Petrina Foti, May 17, 2013.
4 Carlene Stephens, Smithsonian Institution Archives, Computer Technology and Curation Oral History Interviews, interview with Petrina Foti, September 23, 2013
5 Eric Jentsch, Smithsonian Institution Archives, Computer Technology and Curation Oral History Interviews, interview with Petrina Foti, September 10, 2013.
6 Eric Jentsch, Smithsonian Institution Archives, Computer Technology and Curation Oral History Interviews, interview with Petrina Foti, September 10, 2013.
7 Eric Jentsch, Smithsonian Institution Archives, Computer Technology and Curation Oral History Interviews, interview with Petrina Foti, September 10, 2013.
8 Eric Jentsch, Smithsonian Institution Archives, Computer Technology and Curation Oral History Interviews, interview with Petrina Foti, September 10, 2013.

9 To date, these remain merely plans that may or may not come to fruition in the near future depending on a numerous set of outside circumstances. However, it is important to recognize that these early thoughts (which are rarely recorded) can be used to illuminate the curatorial process.
10 Netflix Media Center, "A Brief History of the Company That Revolutionized Watching of Movies and TV Shows," Netflix, accessed February 20, 2015, https://pr.netflix.com/WebClient/loginPageSalesNetWorksAction.do?contentGroupId=10477.
11 Eric Jentsch, Smithsonian Institution Archives, Computer Technology and Curation Oral History Interviews, interview with Petrina Foti, September 10, 2013.
12 National Museum of American History, Accession File 2004.0163, National Museum of American History Entertainment Collection, Object Records.
13 National Museum of American History, Accession File 2004.0163, National Museum of American History Entertainment Collection, Object Records.
14 Eric Jentsch, Smithsonian Institution Archives, Computer Technology and Curation Oral History Interviews, interview with Petrina Foti, September 10, 2013.
15 Eric Jentsch, Smithsonian Institution Archives, Computer Technology and Curation Oral History Interviews, interview with Petrina Foti, September 10, 2013.
16 Helena Wright, Smithsonian Institution Archives, Computer Technology and Curation Oral History Interviews, interview with Petrina Foti, August 5, 2013.
17 Helena Wright, Smithsonian Institution Archives, Computer Technology and Curation Oral History Interviews, interview with Petrina Foti, August 5, 2013.
18 Peggy Kidwell and Paul Ceruzzi, *Landmarks in Digital Computing: A Smithsonian Pictorial History* (Washington, DC: Smithsonian Institution Press, 1994).
19 David Allison, Smithsonian Institution Archives, Computer Technology and Curation Oral History Interviews, interview with Petrina Foti, August 12, 2013.
20 As previously mentioned in Chapter 1, I served in this role in the Computers Collection from 2006 until 2011. Therefore, this study will only discuss the history of the collection prior to that time.
21 Ann Seeger, Smithsonian Institution Archives, Computer Technology and Curation Oral History Interviews, interview with Petrina Foti, September 24, 2013.
22 Ann Seeger, Smithsonian Institution Archives, Computer Technology and Curation Oral History Interviews, interview with Petrina Foti, September 24, 2013.
23 National Museum of American History, Mimsy XG Database, Object Records (accessed July 2013).
24 National Museum of American History, Mimsy XG Database, Object Records (accessed July 2013).
25 Alicia Cutler, Smithsonian Institution Archives, Computer Technology and Curation Oral History Interviews, interview with Petrina Foti, June 3, 2013.
26 Harold Wallace, Smithsonian Institution Archives, Computer Technology and Curation Oral History Interviews, interview with Petrina Foti, August 14, 2013.
27 Helena Wright, Smithsonian Institution Archives, Computer Technology and Curation Oral History Interviews, interview with Petrina Foti, August 5, 2013.

28 Eliot Freidson, *Professional Powers: A Study of the Institutionalization of Formal Knowledge* (Chicago: University of Chicago Press, 1986) xi.
29 Please see: Joshua Bell and Joel Kuipers (eds.), *Linguistic and Material Intimacies of Cell Phones* (London: Routledge Press, 2018).
30 Joshua Bell, Smithsonian Institution Archives, Computer Technology and Curation Oral History Interviews, interview with Petrina Foti, November 2, 2017.
31 Joshua Bell, Smithsonian Institution Archives, Computer Technology and Curation Oral History Interviews, interview with Petrina Foti, November 2, 2017.
32 Alicia Cutler, Smithsonian Institution Archives, Computer Technology and Curation Oral History Interviews, interview with Petrina Foti, June 3, 2013.
33 Alicia Cutler, Smithsonian Institution Archives, Computer Technology and Curation Oral History Interviews, interview with Petrina Foti, June 3, 2013.
34 Alicia Cutler, Smithsonian Institution Archives, Computer Technology and Curation Oral History Interviews, interview with Petrina Foti, June 3, 2013.
35 National Museum of American History, Accession File 2006.0102, National Museum of American History Computers Collection, Object Records.
36 Originally called "TV Game Unit #7," the "Brown Box" was so nicknamed in regard to the brown wood-grained, self-adhesive vinyl that was used for decorative purposes, rather than as a reference to the term "black box."
37 David Allison, Smithsonian Institution Archives, Computer Technology and Curation Oral History Interviews, interview with Petrina Foti, August 12, 2013.
38 Joyce Bedi, Smithsonian Institution Archives, Computer Technology and Curation Oral History Interviews, interview with Petrina Foti, September 13, 2013.
39 Harold Wallace, Smithsonian Institution Archives, Computer Technology and Curation Oral History Interviews, interview with Petrina Foti, August 14, 2013.
40 Smithsonian Institution, Collection Search Center (accessed March 2014), http://collections.si.edu/search/.

4 Dealing with the digital

Computer technology in the collection

Introduction

As has been previously examined, there are specific issues that can surround collecting computer-based technology, relating to its dual nature of hardware-dependent software and software-dependent hardware. Digital-format objects do not easily fit the constraints of long-established precedents of three-dimensional collections and, yet without them, computer hardware is an inscrutable "black box." Dag Spicer, Senior Curator for the Computer History Museum, has more than twenty years' experience with collecting and exhibiting computer technology. He notes that

> from a historical point of view, software is pretty opaque. My approach has always been to record the user experience and not worry about the code so much, because that just presents a whole host of problems. Even if you have the code ready to go, there are still deep technical and interpretive problems. You need the original platform or want to do it under emulation. You know, all sorts of things. That, I think, is the number one challenge of our time on the software preservation front, namely that software is simply so evanescent, so ephemeral, that it is almost impossible to nail down. It is just not distributed anymore in a way that is conducive to preservation.[1]

Digital objects raise interesting questions about what is real. In an analysis of digitizing museum collections (making records of museum objects available online), Simon Knell notes that

> what is interesting about these developments is that the fundamental drive to collect and engage with "real things" (even if digitised) remains. The computer scientists who now lead the "digital heritage" revolution, like many museum practitioners and the early founders of our museums, retain a firm belief in both the inherent factuality of the object and the ease with which it can be gathered up.[2]

As Knell reminds us, when an object is digitized, the original "real thing" still exists for museum visitors and professionals if they should wish to engage with it. A digital-format object has no such counterpart. The question then becomes one of how this object is best collected. Susan Pearce notes that

> museum collections embody an important part of the discipline-based intellectual inheritance by which we understand the world, and they transmit the aspirations of collectors from one generation to another, but they have a third, equally significant, characteristic which may be labelled their museological nature. Museum material does not come in bland pre-packaged form, like crates of baked beans arriving at a supermarket. Quite the contrary: the material comes in fits and starts.[3]

To Pearce, museum collections are not static, easily classified building blocks. They are something much more complex and evolving. Computer-based technology serves as a practical illustration of how a collection might form in what Pearce terms as "fits and starts." Marc Weber, Internet History Program Curatorial Director at the Computer History Museum, notes that

> you end up with ten objects to every document, basically. Or ever photo that someone has bothered to save, much less software. And software is the most elusive. And getting more elusive because as it goes to the cloud, there's really nothing that individuals can give you. Or very very little. Potentially, people save copies of a few thing on their own machines, but the problems of networking software and the web twenty years ago, has now spread to basically everything.[4]

This illustrates why curators who wish to collect computer-based technology choose not to wait passively to accept objects into the collection as they are offered, but rather actively seek to collect contemporaneously.

With the aim of identifying trends in curatorial thought and practice, this chapter attempts to present how the curators at the Smithsonian Institution have collected software in their collections, whether it be digital-format objects, the process that computer technology has replaced, or the actual computer code itself. Curators at the Smithsonian have responded in a manner most appropriate to their particular collections, whether it is to focus primarily on computer hardware or to directly engage with digital-based objects. When presented with a desktop computer or a digital photograph, looking back over twenty years of collecting software and digital computer-based technology, curators have been accessioning objects in a way that is thoughtful and agile.

"For physical looks alone"

The influence that exhibition development for the National Museum of American History's *Information Age: People, Information and Technology* exhibit (May 9, 1990–September 4, 2006) had in the formation of the Computers Collection should not be underestimated. As seen in the last chapter, Anne Seeger, his collection manager, noted that Jon Eklund, the second curator to be affiliated with the collection, "was spending his time working with people on planning *Information Age* and working out what he wanted to collect."[5] Seeger's words reveal that the development of the American History Museum's *Information Age* exhibition (1990–2006) played a large role in how the collection was formed and can further speculate how influential exhibit development might have been to the history of the National Museum of American History. Allison considers exhibitions to have played a large role in his own personal career, noting:

> In my own career here, almost from the beginning really up until the present, it is rare that I have not been involved in some exhibition development, it is rare when I have spent all my time just as a curator than if I was not – and often an administrator too – because when I finished *Information Age* and soon thereafter was involved in another major exhibition, but then I became a Department Chair. So, I was dividing my time between curating a collection and doing administrative work. I would say [collecting] is determined in large part by what the activities of the curator are. If the person is working on major exhibitions, they are probably collecting as one end of that in addition to just picking up other things.[6]

As can be seen from both Allison and Seeger's recollections, Eklund and Allison were often curators for the Computers Collection and curators for major exhibitions simultaneously. This recalls the words of Owain Rhys in Chapter 2 about how contemporary collecting can help fill perceived gaps in the collection. One of the ways that these perceived gaps might be identified would be through exhibition development. This illustrates that exhibition development might drive collecting.

One of the ramifications of this focus on exhibition was an emphasis on display in terms of how computer technology was collected. As will be seen in the next chapter, exhibit curators must have been keenly aware that what they collected must have strong visuals to lead an exhibition and must address the specific issues of the "black box." This is particularly difficult with computer-based technology, which often is visually unappealing. As Marc Weber notes, "There's no correspondence between importance and visual interest."[7] During our examination during Chapter 2 of why computer hardware is difficult to represent on the floor in an exhibition, Allison identified software as more challenging to collect than hardware. He further explains:

> We have tended to collect software as physically displayable objects – that is, collecting the media as opposed to collecting the coding itself and have done that in conjunction with the three-dimensional objects that

> we're collecting. So, for example, in early PCs we have often collected cassette tapes, 8" disk, 5 1/4" disks, that contain representations of the software, rather than collecting the code and trying, for example, as some museums do, to simulate that or run it on a machine or make it something that you can research and use in our electronics collection. So by and large it has been software media that has been the focus, that relates to the three-dimensional objects, rather than the software itself.[8]

As Allison demonstrates, by focusing on what can be placed in a display case, curators had a criterion they could employ. The visual of the "software media" could be utilized in an exhibition in a clear, easily identifiable way. This philosophy can be seen at play in the 2001 accession of Microsoft Windows NT OS/2 Design Workbook,[9] which contains the original design specifications for Windows NT, the first version of Microsoft's current line of operating systems. Rather than an attempt to collect the code, the binder is a tangible way of presenting the story of the operating system's development. While one could argue that a simple black binder is not the most visually appealing object, it highlights the work and planning that are required in software design. It is interesting to note that this accession follows decades of similar patterns of documenting software within the collection, serving as an example of how museum curators are able to create curatorial precedent where none previously existed.

Yet, an unfortunate result of this indirect approach to recording the history of computer software was that the actual software itself was often ignored. Cutler recalls that "I did have the occasional thought, when we would bring something in, what was the point? Did we just bring it in for physical looks alone? And yes, indeed, this museum did focus on that."[10] Computer software is an integral part of what makes a computer, a computer and, as Cutler illustrates, one might reasonably question if the purpose for collecting if the software is then ignored. A survey of the cataloguing records[11] shows that rarely does the record include notation on the computer language, operating system or specific software application examples that might have been used. This is partly due to the fact that the records – including the ones I created – take a strong collection management stance with an emphasis on physical descriptions and partly because these systems were not meant to run. These arguably negative effects should be viewed in the context of the period of time of computer development when those policies were formed. As Cutler notes "memory back then was really expensive. So, you could not just pull off the information from the disks and store it somewhere."[12] Collecting "software media" was a practical, thoughtful response to a given set of limitations. However even at the time, this solution seemed inadequate. Seeger explains:

> The software, now that, that has always been a much thornier issue. I mean Jon obviously collected software. He would even donate some of

> his old software besides collecting it. So, we have it in all kinds of forms, all the various floppy discs and the tapes and then the hard discs, all that. I guess the problem always was what good is this down the road if the instruments that are used to read the software become totally obsolete? What does this software say? I never really had those discussions with Jon. I just used to tear my hair out because he would bring so much of it in… That question, I am not really sure if anyone here in the museum working with the Computer Collection ever really addressed it to anyone's satisfaction.[13]

As Seeger's words reveal, solutions are constantly being re-evaluated, an expression of adaptable expertise. In my own experience, David Allison and I would have this conversation approximately once a year, with no progress made, current capabilities of technology being the most limiting factor. The collections stewards of the Computers Collection worked with the understanding that the solutions of today do not necessarily mean a better solution cannot be discovered tomorrow. This is one of the reasons that all "software media" in the Computers Collection has been designated as "non-accession" status.[14] Unlike the more formal accessioning process, the non-accession status is considered less permanent and therefore easier to deaccession. This allows a certain degree of flexibility in regard to how curators respond to "software media," both now and in the future. For example, should a time come when technical capabilities would allow for the actual code to be preserved separate from its container, then the current collection steward would be able to make the assessment as to what would be the best method to process this without necessarily being constricted to preserve the "software media" container. What can also see from this example is how transmitted expertise can work in tandem with adaptive expertise, as curators chose the best method for their own needs while allowing the possibility that their successors might require a different approach.

Beyond the Computers Collections

However, it can be argued that the most profound impact of computer machines has had much less to do with mathematics (which, as was seen in Chapter 3, was the discipline with which the Computers Collection was and remains the most closely affiliated), and much more with its application into other fields. Starting with the information sciences, computer technology was adopted and adapted into other fields and disciplines. As Paul Ceruzzi, Curator of Aerospace Electronics and Computing at the Air and Space Museum, observed:

> As far as the public face is concerned, "computing" is the least important thing that computers do. But it was to solve equations that the electronic digital computer was invented… The story of the computer illustrates

> that. It is not that the computer ended up not being used for calculation – it is used for calculation by most practicing scientists and engineers today. That much, at least, the computer's inventors predicted. But people found ways to get the invention to do a lot more.[15]

What Ceruzzi argues in his history is not that computers as computation machines are less significant, but rather that this technology proved to be a powerful tool that could be adapted to suit a variety of needs and purposes. Ceruzzi noted at the start of Chapter 2 that "a computer can do anything that you can program it to do" and how that poses a challenge for museum since they are "organized usually according to what these things do."[16] Communications and information processing was one of the earliest fields to adapt computer machines, which in turn meant that computers could be viewed as information technology devices, the same as telephones, telegraphs, typewriters and television. This history of technology narrative can be seen in Steven Lubar's *InfoCulture*[17], written in conjunction with the *Information Age: People, Information and Technology* exhibit (May 9, 1990–September 4, 2006) at the American History Museum. While the narrative of mainframe computer to hand-held is preserved, both the exhibition and accompanying book presented computers not only as mathematical devices but as part of a larger narrative of how people process and understand information and communicate with one another.[18] A more recent example would be the Science Museum's *Information Age* gallery – which opened in November 2014 – divided into six sections: Cable (telegraph), Exchange (telephone), Broadcast (radio and television), Constellation (satellite technology), Web (the internet and other computer networking) and Mobile (mobile technology). The design narrative of the Science Museum's *Information Age* reminds us that areas of communication that have been transformed by computer technology continue to expand.

Once computers are adopted into new fields of study, so they also become assimilated into the history of those fields, such as the incorporation of computers into the historical narrative of communications history, as could be seen in the American History Museum's *Information Age*. A good way to illustrate this is through a consideration of digital cameras and how they gained such dominance in the field of photography. Any curator who intends to record photographic history after the mid-2000s will, inevitably, be writing the history of the digital camera. In this way, the same curator is writing the history of computer-based technology, regardless of his or her background in computation machines. In Chapter 2, Paul Ceruzzi mused in his *A History of Modern Computing* that "the history of computing, as a separate subject, may itself become irrelevant. There is no shortage of evidence to suggest this."[19] Indeed, Ceruzzi himself, curates a collection where the primary focus is not to tell the history of computing. He explains:

> The Air and Space Museum obviously does not collect computers as computers, but computers are very important components of aircraft and spacecraft. It is important to document how, over the history of aviation and space, that computer has contributed in various ways.[20]

Here, at with this particular collection, at this particular museum, computer-based technology and its application are used to tell the history of a different field of study.

This raises interesting questions about the possible ramifications this might have in a museum whose holdings are organized by academic traditions in regard to classification and collection scope, especially in light of a subject-specific Computers Collection. Allison explains:

> I do not know that we have fully understood or embraced as an institution the degree to which some kind of computing technology is embedded in just about everything around you, whether that is a washing machine or an automobile, a printer or camera. It is very rare that you pick up a piece of modern technology that does not have some kind of computer intelligence in it. We still tend to think of the computer collection as those things that are stand-alone computing devices. The degree to which everything has some computing in it has not meant that we have said "everything belongs to us." ... Collecting is not a science and the collections here are not wholly dependent upon rational decisions. A lot of things can end up in one division or another dependent upon the personality, on how much space, on how much interest people have.[21]

Allison's words suggest collecting is often influenced by many factors and that the lines between collections can be fluid. Harold Wallace, Curator of Electricity for the American History Museum, notes that:

> Since the museum has the Computers and Math collections, we in Electricity tend not to collect computers and peripherals and that kind of thing, because it is not within our collecting purview. It makes no sense to duplicate collections. That having been said, we do have the extensive collection of microelectronics and computer chips. Which when viewed in the context of the development of the Electricity Collection makes perfect sense.[22]

Another example of this development context in which computer-based technology naturally fell into the Electricity Collection's "collecting purview" would be how the collection's Alexander Graham Bell prototypes led to larger collecting efforts in telephone-related technology, including mobile devices. This, in turn, has led to examples of smartphone and other similar PDA technology entering the collection. This overlap between Electricity and Computers is not unique and is becoming increasingly more commonplace as computer-based technology begins to influence other disciplines.

The computer-based technology is often so seamlessly a part of Electricity Collection accessions that the computer-development aspect is only apparent to an informed observer, as can be seen with the objects collected as part of the solid state electronic ballast program or the LED prototype donations by Color Kinetics Incorporated. The solid state electronic ballast objects are of particular note since Wallace collected those, in part for their demonstration capabilities. Wallace explains how these devices – which used to limit the amount of current into an electronic circuit – were more than "just black boxes":

> [Department of Energy's Lee] Anderson had been demonstrating this technology to various manufacturers at trade shows; the demonstration devices were made to be seen, so he could demonstrate this expensive technology. In bringing that into the collections here, that allows us to demonstrate more easily to our visitors: "Okay, here's what's going on. It's not just a black metal box. Here's what's going on inside there." That is one example of the convergence of computer technology and lighting technology that I realized was important to bring into the collections, because documenting the history of the late 20th century in lighting technology, the growing influence of automation – of computer technology – is part of that story and has to be reflected in the collections.[23]

Wallace uses the parameters of his discipline to frame the collecting of computer-based technology. Like with the Air and Space Museum, these objects are not collected for their contribution to the development of the field of computer technology, but for how they shaped and changed the lighting technology, whether the objects in question are demonstration prototypes, lighting software or even computer chips.

Just as Wallace has responded in a way specific to his discipline and the needs of his collection, so too have other curators responded in a way that is appropriate to their discipline. In the museum's Photography Collection, this same philosophy is at play. The development of digital photography, which is itself an example of computer-based technology, changed how photographs were created and processed. Unlike with scanned images, born-digital photographs are created using digital recording devices from the onset with no initial physical form. Everything is software-based. Shannon Perich, Curator for the collection, recalled one of the first times she engaged with the practicalities of born-digital photographs, and how that suddenly made clear the difficulties of this new medium in terms of both collecting and exhibiting:

> [The] photograph actually was never physical until we printed it here. It was transmitted digitally. It was taken digitally. It resided on [the

> photographer's] computer. When I received it, it was one of the first photographs that I received digitally and I did not know what to do with it. I did not know where to put it. How could I possibly collect this? There was even the question of where do I put this so that the [exhibit] designer can have access to it. Everything I had ever done before had a physical place to be. This did not have a physical place to be. That one was a real eye opener.[24]

This recalls Knell's words at the start of the chapter regarding "the inherent factuality of the object and the ease with which it can be gathered up."[25] Perich's memories of her confusion and uncertainty vividly illustrate the difficulties when the traits of tangibility that contributed to this previous ease are no longer applicable. This, in turn, illustrates not only how computer-based technology is unprecedented collecting, as identified in Chapter 2, but also how computer-based technology has the potential to transform previously established curatorial traditions into something unfamiliar and new. In the case of the Photographic History Collection at the American History museum, this is further exacerbated by the collection's collecting scope.

It is an important distinction that the collection is very focused on the history of the technology, which includes documenting the process, not just the end product. This is a different concern to those held by the photography collections of the Smithsonian's art museums. Lisa Hostetler (Curator of Photography for the Smithsonian American Art Museum at the time of interview and current Curator in Charge for the Department of Photography at the George Eastman Museum), notes that at the American Art Museum "the final object is what we collect" and adds that, in contrast to the American History Museum's Photographic History Collection, "there is not a tradition of collecting negatives and contact sheets and things like that."[26] With its broader collecting mission, the holdings of the Photographic History Collection include not only the final photographic print, but negatives, contact sheets, the cameras used and even the photographic experiments with the purpose of documenting how the technology developed and was used.

As the collection's curatorial staff have begun to collect digital photography, these principles seem to have remain guidelines in how best to record this technology, as can be seen with the accession of John Paul Caponigro's "digital darkroom."[27] Caponigro had previously made donations to the collection and this long professional relationship allows a level of trust to build, which facilitates documenting the personal process of creation and experimentation. Collecting Curator Shannon Perich explains:

> One of the things that we miss in collecting, one of the things that gets lost in the digital, are the mistakes, are the decision makings, are the contact prints. So, I asked him, "Do you have notes? Do you have physical ephemera, do you have samples of what your work looks like before

> it gets to the finished product" because so much decision-making is happening, and you cannot track those changes in Photoshop. So, what we wound up with, shockingly, were things like pastel colors, because he was trying to match the colors to an existing physical palette, and see what the relationship balance was, because he was trying to see what they were going to look like when they were printed, not when they were on the computer... We collected his digital cameras. So, in the same way that we would have collected a darkroom historically with collecting an enlarger, the printing, the printing trays, the chemistry, with Caponigro we collected the comparable set of tools.[28]

Perich is following collecting principles set by her predecessors as a guide for how to navigate the documenting process. Using previous precedents allowed Perich to know what types of objects would best serve the needs of the collection and Caponigro would then be able to supply what he used in an equivalent way. Among the items collected were the Photoshop CD that he used and his iPhone. Much like the Computer Collection's "software media," Perich has collected the container, rather than attempting to preserve the code.

> The Photoshop CD is representative, because it green and it says Photoshop 2.0 on it, and it is the disk, but "what Photoshop is" is really the code. So, we did not collect the code, but only as the code resides on the CD. That is the opposite of how we collected for the September 11 images... In some ways it is comparable to the library collecting the manuals. It is a tool and it is a representative tool, so you would put this on exhibit and say, "here's a printer, here's the CD that was used to facilitate this particular activity." It is not the code. We have collected a couple of other CDs of Photoshop, but it is as a tool.[29]

Perich's words reveal her thought process and mental system of classification for her collection. Perich identified that the role the Photoshop CD was to play in the collection was as a physical representation of a process and then proceeded to collect accordingly. This representation classification holds true for the iPhone as well. Perich notes that:

> This is really interesting again, because we collected it as a representative container of the thing. We did not even turn it on. I do not know if the apps are still on it. We collected the iPhone and he used it to make postcards. So, he did all of the manipulation, all of the image making, on the iPhone, and then downloaded it to print it. So, he sent me a set of prints through the mail, because they were postcards and then he sent me a pristine set. It is just like the camera or the computer or the printer. It is all embedded in that tiny little object. We know what apps he used to manage those images, but we did not collect the app itself and

> we would not probably. Even if we exhibited the iPhone, we would not exhibit it constantly on to show what apps are on that phone.[30]

Perich has echoed the collection rationale behind the "software media" in the Computers Collection, with display qualities as a criterion for collecting. While it is possible that collecting priorities for the Photographic History Collection were influenced by the precedent set in the Computers Collection – indeed both collections were part of the same division for decades – it is clear from Perich's words that this collecting rationale was formed with consideration as to what would best suit the collection utilizing her adaptive curatorial expertise. That is not to say that all collections at the National Museum of American History would make the same assessment.

One needs only to look to the American History Museum's Music Collection to find a different rationale used for engaging with computer-based technology and therefore a different collecting conclusion. In terms of collecting music-related software, Stacy Kluck, one of the Music Collection curators as well as chair for the Culture and the Arts Division notes:

> I think it depends on how we would use the collections and what stories we would want to tell. As far as telling the story of MP3s, it is very different. What is basically the hard copy that you have? It is very easy to tell the story of a 78 rpm – a shellac record – because you can physically show something. Whereas, when you have a digital copy of something, how do you show that? How do you represent that to the public? We can talk about how things have changed, how the technology has changed as far as how people experience that music or experience that digital file. But to represent that in a different way would be challenging to do. So, the story is continuing. We definitely want to talk about how people experience the music, but I think that is going to be a challenge as far as what contemporary things do we collect.[31]

Though the subject has remained theoretical to date, the flexibility in Kluck's thoughts on how computer technology might impact his collection, a hallmark of adaptive expertise, is demonstrated. As Kluck observed in Chapter 2: "I think it is easier to describe the technology when you have something physical that you can actually show, but when the physical thing is actually a computer file, then it changes how we exhibit these things to our public."[32] His view is even more understandable when the priority that his colleagues in both the Photographic History Collection and the Computer Collection have placed on exhibition display is considered. This evidence reveals that exhibit display is a guiding principle at the National Museum of American History, regardless of the collection with which a curator is associated. However, for Kluck, that does not mean that collecting the software container would necessarily be the answer as it was for his colleagues:

> Floppy disks or whatnot, I do not see being very purposeful for the work, as I see it, which is mostly using objects to help researchers and visitors understand the history of our country. But it does have a purpose for people interested in a more focused: how does technology work, how did it change and that might be more of an archival.[33]

In this instance, the method of "software media" is not the most appropriate form of documentation for a collection whose focus is Music History. In fact, Kluck and his fellow curators already have a different model of curation to follow.

In the Music Collection, there is a long tradition at the Museum of documenting how new technology has been adopted in the traditional musical instruments, from electronic guitars to music box technology used in player pianos. Kluck explains:

> We certainly have instruments that really have not changed that much. Maybe they have been electrified. For example, the violin has not really changed that much and looks about the same. Certainly, there have been some improvements with the newer violins that are electrified, but they are more specific, made for a specific purpose. So not only can we talk about the technology, but also why was this technology developed, where was it used. If you want the sound of a violin, if you are in a big arena and you have got a ton of drums, guitars, and all these other instruments, how is that instrument going to be heard? And so, the instrument has to adapt. The technology has to change to accommodate new styles of music, or just changing types of music.[34]

Kluck expresses a certain level of adaptability on the collection level to changes and incorporations of new technologies. This curatorial expertise is exhibited vividly with the accession of Herbie Hancock's synthesizer and computerized musical instruments.[35] Multi-award winning American jazz musician and composer Hancock might arguably be most famous for his 1983 mainstream hit "Rockit" and its music video featuring automatons. The computerized instruments acquired by the Music Collection were used by Hancock during this time period. Building on the established tradition of collecting new musical technology, Kluck explains that:

> It is looking at the technology first of all. This [accession] is mostly artifacts that date from the 1980s, so we are far enough removed from that that we can tell the story about the development of this but also about how it relates to us now. We can look at how these were used. I think that synthesizer, the Yamaha, was actually used on tour. So, it is very different than using it in a recording studio. A much different story there, but, nonetheless, it still demonstrates the three instruments – the synthesizers, the Yamaha and the Fairlight, and

> then the MemoryMoog – all were used in different ways by Herbie Hancock, some in the studio, some on tour. It also captures his changing style of music, experimenting with different sounds and different things. He was certainly well known as a jazz musician and then branching off into pop and rock music, but using the new tools to do that, rather than using the older instruments, taking advantage of this new technology and turning around and doing something different with it.[36]

In other words, to Kluck these instruments would work as representational objects, much like the Caponigro iPhone. In this instance, the instruments' significance is that they were owned and used by Hancock, a jazz musician and composer famous for his innovation and pioneering work, rather than as an example of the technology. Furthermore, Hancock was well documented during the 1980s using his Fairlight, MemoryMoog and other computer technology in composing and playing his Yamaha in concert. Therefore, using the criteria for musical performance that Kluck outlined above – which in this instance involves running computer software – it is evident that the software component is not a concern for this particular accession. There is already a plethora of examples of how these instruments were used and how they sounded and these videos and these audio sources reside in a multiplicity of other publicly accessible repositories. The Music collection therefore need only concern itself with the preservation of Hancock's actual objects.

As seen with the Caponigro accession, collecting a personal story is often an easier method of recording technological change, which one might speculate is due to a more limited scope. Similar to how Perich looked to collect the digital equivalent to the photographer's darkroom, Kluck and his colleagues in the Music Collection used their previous curatorial experience to decide how to approach the computerized instruments:

> John [Hasse] took the lead on this. This was actually collected as part of Jazz Appreciation Month because of Herbie's jazz background. I had a few conversations with John about some of the things that were being offered and having a conversation about what stories can we tell with these. Not only technology. How are they used, how do these objects impact on the future of this music, and how did it change. One interesting thing with Herbie Hancock is the fact that MTV was also a really important part of the story, because not only taking this new music, but also having a video of it. It opened Herbie to a completely new audience who probably would never have heard of Herbie Hancock had it not been for MTV and "Rockit."[37]

In addition to presenting the collection rationale, Kluck's words highlight the collaborative environment of the curatorial staff of the Music Collection. Kluck explains:

> At least in our division, no one works in a bubble. People do talk to each other and we talk about not only these objects, while important, but how do they relate to what we have, how do they relate to what else is in the museum, and so. Having that broader story is really important. Certainly, I think as we develop the collections, having acquired these led or inspired us to look at other types of objects. For example, what else was going on during that time, or around the same time. We recently acquired a Kurzweil synthesizer, from about the same time period [as the Herbie Hancock artifacts], and so, looking around at the bigger stories that we can tell. It is interesting, because once again we are far enough away that we are not necessarily validating that this technology is the best thing ever, but we are saying: "Okay, look at the stories we can tell" and how these objects and everything that surrounds them influence what we are doing today.[38]

Kluck demonstrates for us the flexibility of thought that he and his colleagues utilize when they plan the future of their shared collection. The curators of the Music Collection are preparing for how potential technological advances in computer technology might impact music history and beginning to form an appropriate response. In addition, the adaptive process by which collecting precedent is set is demonstrated in how Kluck and his colleagues utilize transmitted expertise by looking for connections both within their existing holdings and with potential future accessions. Objects that are selected for acquisition are framed within existing patterns within the collection and evaluated for their potential to create new connections. The Hancock accession has now served as a gateway for a new narrative of computerized music creation.

The Kurzweil accession that Kluck refers to is a very recent addition to the computerized music creation narrative. Rather than an internationally known artist such as Hancock, this synthesizer was owned by a musician who was only known at a local level and represents how the average musician in the late 1980s might experiment with computerized music creation. It is also interesting to note that the Kurzweil synthesizer is an Apple Mac. Though they were aware that there were at least two Apple Macs[39] from the same period of time in the Computers Collection, the curatorial staff in the Music Collection decided that in this particular instance, those computers could not be used as a substitute. The Kurzweil synthesizer was the central focus of the story, so it is incidental that there were other Apple Macs in the Museum's collections. This is in keeping with Perich's views on the Caponigro iPhone:

> We know that there are other phones in the museum, so we collected [the iPhone] specifically because it was associated with a photographer, used for photography, that it would reside in Photography because that is its contextual relationship. Technically it could exist anywhere and

> there are other iPhones in the building. That is the curatorial part of collecting the technology. It is the intent of the technology and keeping it physically located – at least textually linked to – how it was used, why it was used, who it was used by, and all of that curatorial data, to give significance to that particular object. And the same thing goes with the laptops that we have collected.[40]

Perich's words remind us that, while an individual example of mass-produced computer technology might not be unique, it is the meaning that the particular object represents that is significant. Whether there are many identical objects in the collection or none at all is often not a factor when a curator decides if an object should be accessioned or not. Far more important is the role that object plays in the story the curator is attempting to record. What evidenced here is distributive expertise at work as curators interpreting computer-based technology using the knowledge of their own discipline to offer a broader perspective into how the history of computer-based technology is recorded.

As seen with the Electricity, Music, and Photographic History collections, the decision on how to approach the "black box" conundrum of collecting computer-based technology often depends on many factors. The question is often what best represents the specific history that the curator is seeking to record. In an example from a history of science collection, for instance, Terry Sherrer collected a DNA analyzer[41] from the National Cancer Institute's Lab of Pathology for the Health Services Collection. Ann Seeger, who at the time was serving as Acting Chair for the Department of Medicine and Science, was confronted with a dilemma of what to do when an example of a type of desktop computer typically used with the analyzer arrived with the other items selected. Ultimately, she decided against accessioning the computer, as her 2006 memo indicates:

> The computer is not strictly a part of the machine; the analyzer was linked to a computer when in operation but it wasn't necessarily this computer. Consequently, I did not accession the computer. It will be retained in the division as an unaccessioned accessory.[42]

In a later interview, she explains the rationale she employed to make this decision:

> First of all, we are not planning to ever operate these instruments. So, collecting the computer which is necessary for the operation is kind of crazy, because they take up so much space. I mean we did – I did accession the one and now I have to store it – and I have very limited storage for Biology, so it is sort of a hardship. I figured with the storage problems we have here and the fact we do not need to operate the

> instruments and they were just used with off-the-shelf, in almost every case – a Dell desktop computer. I mean maybe there is not one in the collection, but there easily could be. So, if we ever wanted to set something up on display in a laboratory setting and we needed a computer, we have one in mine already, so we could substitute it. It just did not seem reasonable to collect. We, in fact, asked the donors not to send the computers and in every case they sent them anyway, because they have the same problems of storage that we do. It's a real problem![43]

Seeger's process of thought – from first considering how best to exhibit these objects, then thinking about practical storage issues to deciding that ultimately the associated desktop computer was not essential to the story of the DNA analyzer– demonstrates adaptable expertise with how a curator is able to circumvent the hardware/software dilemma by being clear what is central and peripheral to the story being recorded. Seeger's concerns as collection manager for the Computers Collection about storage and maintenance for the software that Eklund collected have been previously examined. However, in this instance, the story of the accession was not about software, but the analyzer. It is clear from the accession file that there was never a question of operating the instrument which would make its value in that capacity negligible nor was there any focus on the software itself in its own right.[44] Therefore, computer technology in this instance as being similar to the role electrification has in the computer itself; the technology would not be possible without it, to the point that it is so integral that it ceases to be noteworthy. This in turn shows us how accepted computer-based technology has become in our lives.

The examples from of computer-based technology in the Electricity, Photographic History, Music, and Health Services collections illustrate Allison's position that no one collection at the Smithsonian can reasonably claim exclusivity over computer-based technology – not even the National Museum of American History's Computers Collection. By studying these other collections, similar patterns of collecting behavior emerge, such as collecting software via its representational container, for similar reasons. One can understand how many curators might judge a representational object to be the most appropriate format to record computer software. However, as technology has progressed, creating scenarios both where it is possible to collect digital-based objects and even necessary, more curators are not only willing to challenge that model, but even finding it to be essential to do so.

The Digitally Born

In Chapter 2, Photographic History Curators Michelle Delaney and Shannon Perich both noted that one of the challenges computer-based technology poses to museums is its rapid development and the perception that the museum will be always behind the curve. Yet, as our computer technology advances, so too does our ability to record computer technology. Perich reflects that:

> My career here has witnessed the change from analogue to digital, and that has been a significant professional experience as well as a significant curatorial experience. Photography, as it turns out, is actually a really interesting subject to watch, because it is the harbinger of how the rest of the world is going to change digitally. So, September 11 was really the moment in which we were able to see the impact of this transition from analogue to digital and what it really meant. It meant a number of things. It meant the rapid sharing of images. We did not have to wait for things to go to the drug-store and come back from the amateur point of view. From the professional point of view, we did not have to have films sent down to the dark room at the newspaper and have it printed. Those things were coming rapidly. It was not just the professional; it was actually also the amateur. Everybody's pictures, no matter what their skill level was, no matter what their professional status was, those photographs mattered.[45]

Perich's words reveal how digital photography played such an import part of the tragic events of September 11. As has been seen, it is the story that so often drives museum collecting.

However, unlike so many of our previous examples, the "software media" solution does not solve the challenges posed by computer-based technology in the Photographic History Collection. With digital photography, the photographic image is, essentially, comprised of computer code. To collect only the container to represent this software (whether it would be the device that created the image, such as a digital camera, or the storage container, such as a CD or DVD) would be analogous to collecting a roll of undeveloped film. While interesting from a technological sense, neither would accurately represent those digital images and the stories that they tell. In contrast, David Allison acquired for the Computers Collection a BlackBerry communicator (an early texting device) used by a lawyer who worked at the World Trade Center to locate every person who worked in his office and ensure that they were safe.[46] While a paper-based printout of the actual texts was preserved, the early PDA and how it was used, like the Caponigro iPhone and the Hancock instruments, is the focus of this principally social history story.

As has been previously examined, born-digital photographs represented a completely new technological process for the Museum and for the field of photography in practice. At the start of the twenty-first century, there was no precedent to follow and practitioners were only beginning to test the limits of this new technology. It is, therefore, understandable why the curators in Photographic History had delayed engaging with these changes until circumstances arose that they could not ignore. Delaney notes:

> I probably was a little slow to collect. It probably should have been happening for Photography earlier than that catastrophic event of September 11, but it proceeded that way. I think it was partly because of my uneasiness with accepting the changes that were coming to photography after one hundred years of the Eastman method. How do you then begin to think that the medium that you study and collect is undergoing a major shift as it did 120 years before? How do you learn enough about the new technology or the new format or medium to become that expert in a new area of collecting and display?[47]

With the events of September 11, Delaney and Perich believed they could no longer delay collecting this new method of photography. In Chapter 2, Delaney described the drive she felt to record the events as they were occurring. Over ten years after that interview, she reflects on that period of time:

> Shannon Perich, my colleague and curator also at photography history, we were together in Los Angeles about to attend a conference that was cancelled because of the events. But we started to talk right away, between us about professional point of view and what was happening with September 11. I do not think Shannon had a cell phone. I did, but she did not… I had a laptop. She did not even have a laptop with her. I was carrying all the technology and I was watching people with their new digital cameras, their small digital cameras, take images, share images quickly, and America Online and other services, Reuters and the Associated Press, they were all putting their images up online, but showing people. The news was talking about the significance of the digital response that was happening with September 11 – internationally, but very much focused on New York and Washington and a little bit from the Pennsylvania site. So, I knew pretty much within 24 to 48 hours of the events that happened on September 11 that we should be collecting.[48]

Delaney paints a vivid illustration of how computer technology helped shape their very understanding of the events. Computer-based technology objects served as a conduit through which she and Perich received their information of events that were happening on the other side of the country. It must not be forgotten that one of the three sites – Washington D.C. – is their home and home to the museum where they worked. It is therefore understandable why the two curators might have been so personally motivated to engage with this unknown process. Delaney notes that the learning curve was steep and the pace was relentless:

> Right away within that first year of really being a curator of digital collections, we went right into exhibit mode. So, within those twelve months, I went from really not even specializing in any way for collecting digital, really only building my knowledge, to go forth and collect to then thinking about printing and curating the pieces selected.[49]

It is striking how both Perich and Delaney were faced with practical concerns with engaging with this new technology and both felt that they lacked the skill set needed to meet this challenge.

The solution was two-fold: first, consultation with expert practitioners (distributive expertise); and, second, searching for examples from photographic history that could serve as models (transmitted expertise). Delaney notes that "I did consult. I consulted with the photographers. Our Smithsonian photographers, down in the basement of American History, were in the middle of converting [to born digital photography] when September 11 happened."[50] The timing was fortuitous because the photographers were already exploring answers to the same questions that Delaney might have had in regard to storage and accessibility. Delaney explains that:

> I talked to the people at the Smithsonian who I thought were actually the ones working the majority or working harder at thinking about how they were themselves transforming as professional photographers and transforming the Smithsonian system of capturing the photography of events and exhibits. So how would they recommend doing this?[51]

Perich echoes Delaney's observations:

> In terms of collecting for the history of digital photography, we do have a relationship with the people who are using it, with our own Smithsonian photographers. We learn from them. We are not technologists. We are not in the trenches learning the day to day latest. We depend on their expertise on that.[52]

Perich and Delaney's words reveal distributive expertise in that, while neither curator felt that she had the technical understanding to meet the demands of digital-format objects, they sought the assistance of experts who would be able to guide them through the process.

In addition to contemporary experts, using their own transmitted expertise, Delaney and Perich drew insight and understanding from their predecessors who, as Delaney noted earlier, faced a radical technological shift over a century earlier. Perich explain:

> It became very clear that "Oh, we've done this before." This is not a new transition. When we went from the daguerreotype to negatives, it was radical. It was equally as radical as the transition from analogue

> to digital. It required technological differences. They are not the same, chemically, physically. They look differently, work differently. You have to adjust your aesthetics. You have to change the way that you preconceive working in that mode and how the functionality changes. With the daguerreotype, it is this beautiful cased individual object. When we transitioned to the negative, it is all about distribution. Maybe we lose a little quality, but what do we gain? So, there is a paradigm shift that is in the field itself, in the culture itself. Socially, financially, all of those things shift. And that is exactly that same thing that was happening before.[53]

In fact, Delaney and Perich were able to see many similarities between their modern-day dilemmas and the struggles of their predecessors. Perich notes:

> We had a historical model. We could look back and go "Oh, we know how to do this, we've done it before. What did they do?" They had the same issues. How do you collect negatives? Do you collect negatives? Is it only the positive that matters or is it the process? How do you collect for the process? How do you collect chemicals, how do you collect the ephemeral? How do you collect mistakes? Is the print the "be all end all" or is the negative the "be all end all"? Does it matter if it's the most recent print or the one that was printed the closest to when the negative was? All of these things, all of that was discussed before. Then we could take all of those conversations and see how they applied to the digital, and that's what we did.[54]

Recalling the accession of John Paul Caponigro's "digital darkroom" and how Perich was able to frame the acquisition in terms of previous collecting efforts, it is not clear how Perich's initial questions concerning how to collect born-digital photography likely influenced how she has continued to approach the recording of the history of digital photography.

In Chapter 2, this research examined how the museum regularly encounters instances of collecting with no precedent to follow and how that then in turn creates a precedent for the future. It is now evident how this occurs with the Photographic History Collection's efforts to engage with computer-based technology and born-digital photography. Even when faced with a collecting task of unprecedented proportions, Perich and Delaney used their curatorial expertise to find a method to make the task accessible within the framework of their own collections, by consulting with others and by turning to the past to find previous examples of when photographic history curators were faced with an unprecedented technological change.

The same concern in collecting the digital can be seen at the Cooper Hewitt, Smithsonian Design Museum when they first collected computer code as an accessioned museum object with the 2013 acquisition of the iPad application "Planetary." While the Cooper Hewitt has previous examples of computer technology among its holdings, the majority of those accessions were focused the hardware alone, similar to the collecting practices at the American History Museum. As Matilda McQuaid, the Cooper Hewitt's Deputy Curatorial Director, notes: "It is different, because we were collecting the hardware, and now this is the software."[55] Significantly, this accession was of software without affiliated hardware. Such an undertaking did not happen without examination of its long-term significance. McQuaid explains:

> Our first digital collecting – at least digitally born – was the "Planetary" acquisition. I think this is a sign of things to come. We are not giving up on three-dimensional objects by any means… We are also looking at this other format, which I think is important for us to do. Just as we look at any kind of new technology coming out, it is important for us as a design museum to look at and understand new formats for collecting.[56]

The museum's mission is "to advance the public understanding of design across the thirty centuries of human creativity represented by the Museum's collection."[57] The current understanding of how best to achieve this goal is through collecting and documenting the process of design. McQuaid explains:

> We are very much process driven so we want to collect everything behind it – behind what you see. We have been doing that kind of sporadically and with a certain amount of forthrightness, but I think that as we reopen, as we have been able to take this time to look back on what we have done and what we think we do well and what we want to continue doing well. I think we see process as something very important and something that is not being represented. I think that everything is being driven by that. So, for future acquisitions – whether it is digital or not – we want to collect behind the scenes of how that particular piece or product or textile came to be, whether it was a sketch or whether it was a digital output.[58]

McQuaid offers evidence that the museum's digital holdings, despite their unique challenges, will follow in the tradition established by decades of non-digital collecting, much in the same way that the collecting precedent in the American History Museum's Photographic History Collection serve as a model. However, while Perich and Delany were investigating on how to collect a digital-born object, Cooper Hewitt's focus on the process brought the decision to engage with software directly, with all the challenges that proposition might hold. McQuaid frames these challenges:

> It is trying to determine what is the best way to preserve it, but also keep it active and keep it in the context in which it was collected. Maybe fifty

> years from now, it may seem kind of historic, but I think that we need to make sure that the context in which it was seen and experienced is also somehow preserved. So, I think that some of that also comes with a text explanation. I think also by continuing to collect in this vein you understand the continuum of what is happening. I think once you start, I do not think you can stop because then otherwise it just seems like something that lacks that story. You have to keep collecting. I think it is something that we will certainly do.[59]

What is significant about McQuaid's observation is that it reveals that the "Planetary" acquisition is both following the museum's principles, while establishing a new precedent for the museum's future endeavors in collecting digitally-based objects.

To "preserve the process" of computer application design in a way that would make sense for future generations required technological expertise that the Cooper Hewitt curatorial staff did not necessarily have. McQuaid notes:

> Fortunately, we have a Department of Digital and Emerging Media that will help kind of formulate those parameters of collecting too, because this is something very different for the curators here who are all of [the analogue] age. We were from the analogue age and now we are going into digital. So, I think everyone is certainly on board with it very much, and as I said, being a design museum, we really have to do this. I mean this really is a very important part of contemporary design. So, I think it is really determining kind of the parameters and understanding how to show it in years to come, or even, in two years' time, and then, making sure that we continue to collect in this vein so it is not an anomaly.[60]

For McQuaid, there is a recognition that expertise of how this computer technology works is essential to being able to preserve the technology. You cannot record a process that you do not understand. It is therefore not surprising that, demonstrating the distributive expertise of the Copper Hewitt's Curatorial Division, the collecting initiative was led by Sebastian Chan, the museum's then Director of Digital & Emerging Media and Aaron Cope, who was the Senior Engineer in the same department.[61] As was seen in Chapter 2, both Chan and Cope were well versed in the innate challenges of purely digital objects.

When American History Museum's Photographic History Collection collected born-digital photography, it can be considered purely digital collecting. In this instance, by virtue of being an image, photography – regardless of the process used to create it – is a more static format that an interactive application such as "Planetary." In order to fully understand a given mobile application software, one must understand how it was used. Chan notes:

> I think with a lot of digital culture that meta-data about use is recorded with the object itself and there are ways of revealing that. You know, the Smithsonian has an iPhone and a couple of other cell phones in its collections, yet it has never actually forensically extracted the data from them… Part of the object is what is recorded in it still.[62]

The Cooper Hewitt did not collect the software to be represented by its container. It was for what the software could do. The software itself has meaning, as Cope explains:

> There are interesting aspects in studying the source code as a kind of literature, as a sort of narrative form, but ultimately there is the overarching design of the tool that we are interested in preserving. We have acquired one of the Nest thermostats, the programmable thermostats. And that is great! It is an interesting piece of hardware design, but we have not really done much to collect the software or the actual interactions of the device.[63]

Cope highlights the most significant drawback to the representational model of collecting. With these challenges in mind, in addition to the archival copy stored in a traditional archival box on a cabinet shelf, Chan and Cope's solution was to record the interactions of "Planetary," to open source the code itself and allow full accessibility to anyone who might wish to study or even modify it. On the museum's website, Chan and Cope explain the thought process behind this decision:

> We cannot pretend to have all the answers to these questions but we think it's important to start making the effort to find some of them. We liken this situation to that of a specimen in a zoo. In fact, given that the Smithsonian also runs the National Zoo, consider Planetary as akin to a panda. Planetary and other software like it are living objects. Their acquisition by the museum, does not and should not seal them in carbonite like Han Solo. Instead, their acquisition simply transfers them to a new home environment where they can be cared for out of the wild, and where their continued genetic preservation requires an active breeding program and community engagement and interest. Open sourcing the code is akin to a panda breeding program. If there is enough interest then we believe that Planetary's DNA will live on in other skin on other platforms. Of course, we will preserve the original, but it will be "experienced" through its offspring.[64]

In a later interview, Chan employed a slightly different analogy:

> To make this easy, particularly for journalists, I talk about this like acquiring patents, but you are not acquiring the patent model. You are

> actually just acquiring the patent. You are acquiring the description of the method rather than the implementation of the method. The implementation of the method comes with the acquisition, but it is not what you care about.[65]

In this way, Chan and Cope are shifting the narrative and language from one that is associated with collecting non-digital objects towards a model of understanding that is more accessible to those who are not as well-versed in the specificity of computer technology. This model, in addition to serving the public, allows current curatorial staff at Cooper Hewitt to make the transition from analogue to digital, and in doing so provides curators of the future the tools that will allow them, crucially, to understand the significance of this accession. Their approach, in other words, is illustrative of an expertise that aims to be useful and understandable for future generations. Chan and Cope's reasoning, language and practice, as can be seen in their use of analogy to explain the process and concerns about metadata, also points to a culture of transmitted expertise – where curatorial knowledge and practice aims to preserved in a meaningful way.

Conclusion

Computer technology has posed significant challenges that the curatorial staff of the American History Museum and the Cooper Hewitt were able to meet with both creativity and pragmatism. These museums serve as reflection of the museum sector at large, as computer technology has been incorporated into other fields, curators in related collections have taken up the challenge following the precedents set by their own individual disciplines, an expression of distributive expertise. Some curators find similar solutions to those employed in the Computers Collection, while others employ more suitable answers tailored to the needs of their discipline, demonstrating adaptable expertise. When uncertain of the right way to proceed, curators apply predecessors' experiences to their current situations or look to expert practitioners for guidance, a demonstration of transmitted expertise. In doing so, these curators create a precedent for future computer-based technology collecting.

In short, when confronted with the challenge of the computer-based technology and attempting to collect objects that are not only unprecedented to the museum in many respects, but that also offer the complexities of the duality of hardware and software, the curators of the Smithsonian Institution (and, one might surmise, their counterparts around the world) ultimately found clear and successful strategies for collecting. Significantly, they not only show an agility in their adaptive expertise (willing to challenge convention, adapt their processes, and even their assumptions around object types), as well as working collectively (acknowledging that expertise on that collection may be distributed around the organization), but they also collect with a further acknowledgement that today's expertise of these new objects is only partial, and that it will only be from the vantage point of the future that the significance of these contemporary acts of collecting might become fully apparent. In the next chapter, how that curatorial expertise is expressed when curators are faced with the challenge of presenting computer-based technology in an exhibition will be explored.

Notes

1 Dag Spicer, interview with Petrina Foti, March 28, 2018.
2 Simon J. Knell, "Altered Values: Searching for a New Collecting" in S. Knell, (ed.), *Museums and the Future of Collecting* (Aldershot: Ashgate, 2004) 4.
3 Susan Pearce, *Museums, Objects and Collections: A Cultural Study*. (Leicester: Leicester University Press, 1992) 120.
4 Marc Weber, Smithsonian Institution Archives, Computer Technology and Curation Oral History Interviews, interview with Petrina Foti, March 15, 2017.
5 Ann Seeger, Smithsonian Institution Archives, Computer Technology and Curation Oral History Interviews, interview with Petrina Foti, September 24, 2013.
6 David Allison, Smithsonian Institution Archives, Computer Technology and Curation Oral History Interviews, interview with Petrina Foti, August 12, 2013.
7 Marc Weber, Smithsonian Institution Archives, Computer Technology and Curation Oral History Interviews, interview with Petrina Foti, March 15, 2017.
8 David Allison, Smithsonian Institution Archives, Computer Technology and Curation Oral History Interviews, interview with Petrina Foti, August 12, 2013.
9 National Museum of American History, Accession File 2001.3014, National Museum of American History Computers Collection, Object Records.
10 Alicia Cutler, Smithsonian Institution Archives, Computer Technology and Curation Oral History Interviews, interview with Petrina Foti, June 3, 2013.
11 National Museum of American History, Mimsy XG Database, Object Records (accessed July 2013).
12 Alicia Cutler, Smithsonian Institution Archives, Computer Technology and Curation Oral History Interviews, interview with Petrina Foti, June 3, 2013.
13 Ann Seeger, Smithsonian Institution Archives, Computer Technology and Curation Oral History Interviews, interview with Petrina Foti, September 24, 2013.
14 Ann Seeger, Smithsonian Institution Archives, Computer Technology and Curation Oral History Interviews, interview with Petrina Foti, September 24, 2013.
15 Paul Ceruzzi, *A History of Modern Computing* (Cambridge, MA: MIT Press, 2003) 1.
16 Paul Ceruzzi, Smithsonian Institution Archives, Computer Technology and Curation Oral History Interviews, interview with Petrina Foti, June 1, 2017.
17 Steve Lubar, *InfoCulture: The Smithsonian Book of Information Age Inventions* (New York: Houghton Mifflin, 1993).
18 It should be noted that there is a separate field of study that looks at the computerization of information science, primarily with the digitization of libraries, archives, and, to a lesser extent, museums. Some, like Suzanne Keene's *Digital Collections: Museum and the Information Age* (Oxford: Butterworth–Heinemann,

1998) examine the opportunities that arise with a computer's capabilities and details what current standards and best practices should be. Others, such as Ross Parry's *Recoding the Museum* (London: Routledge, 2007) takes a more historical approach to museum computing, recording what has happened rather than stating what the current standard is or speculating what might happen in the near future.

19 Paul Ceruzzi, *A History of Modern Computing* (Cambridge, MA: MIT Press, 2003) x.

20 Paul Ceruzzi, Smithsonian Institution Archives, Computer Technology and Curation Oral History Interviews, interview with Petrina Foti, June 1, 2017.

21 David Allison, Smithsonian Institution Archives, Computer Technology and Curation Oral History Interviews, interview with Petrina Foti, August 12, 2013.

22 Harold Wallace, Smithsonian Institution Archives, Computer Technology and Curation Oral History Interviews, interview with Petrina Foti, August 14, 2013.

23 Harold Wallace, Smithsonian Institution Archives, Computer Technology and Curation Oral History Interviews, interview with Petrina Foti, August 14, 2013.

24 Shannon Perich, Smithsonian Institution Archives, Computer Technology and Curation Oral History Interviews, interview with Petrina Foti, September 26, 2013.

25 Simon J. Knell, "Altered Values: Searching for a New Collecting" in S. Knell, (ed.), *Museums and the Future of Collecting* (Aldershot: Ashgate, 2004) 4.

26 Lisa Hostetler, Smithsonian Institution Archives, Computer Technology and Curation Oral History Interviews, interview with Petrina Foti, September 4, 2013.

27 Shannon Perich, Smithsonian Institution Archives, Computer Technology and Curation Oral History Interviews, interview with Petrina Foti, September 26, 2013.

28 Shannon Perich, Smithsonian Institution Archives, Computer Technology and Curation Oral History Interviews, interview with Petrina Foti, September 26, 2013.

29 Shannon Perich, Smithsonian Institution Archives, Computer Technology and Curation Oral History Interviews, interview with Petrina Foti, September 26, 2013.

30 Shannon Perich, Smithsonian Institution Archives, Computer Technology and Curation Oral History Interviews, interview with Petrina Foti, September 26, 2013.

31 Stacy Kluck, Smithsonian Institution Archives, Computer Technology and Curation Oral History Interviews, interview with Petrina Foti, August 21, 2013.

32 Stacy Kluck, Smithsonian Institution Archives, Computer Technology and Curation Oral History Interviews, interview with Petrina Foti, August 21, 2013.

33 Stacy Kluck, Smithsonian Institution Archives, Computer Technology and Curation Oral History Interviews, interview with Petrina Foti, August 21, 2013.

34 Stacy Kluck, Smithsonian Institution Archives, Computer Technology and Curation Oral History Interviews, interview with Petrina Foti, August 21, 2013.

35 National Museum of American History, Accession File 2004.0055, National Museum of American History Office of the Registrar, Registration Services Records.

36 Stacy Kluck, Smithsonian Institution Archives, Computer Technology and Curation Oral History Interviews, interview with Petrina Foti, August 21, 2013.

37 Stacy Kluck, Smithsonian Institution Archives, Computer Technology and Curation Oral History Interviews, interview with Petrina Foti, August 21, 2013.
38 Stacy Kluck, Smithsonian Institution Archives, Computer Technology and Curation Oral History Interviews, interview with Petrina Foti, August 21, 2013.
39 See for example: National Museum of American History, Accession File 1985.0118, National Museum of American History Computers Collection, Object Records.
40 Shannon Perich, Smithsonian Institution Archives, Computer Technology and Curation Oral History Interviews, interview with Petrina Foti, September 26, 2013.
41 Accession Record 2004.0226, National Museum of American History Health Services Collection, Object Files.
42 Memo, National Museum of American History, Accession Record 2004.0226, National Museum of American History Health Services Collection, Object Files.
43 Ann Seeger, Smithsonian Institution Archives, Computer Technology and Curation Oral History Interviews, interview with Petrina Foti, September 24, 2013.
44 National Museum of American History, Accession Record 2004.0226, National Museum of American History Health Services Collection, Object Files.
45 Shannon Perich, Smithsonian Institution Archives, Computer Technology and Curation Oral History Interviews, interview with Petrina Foti, September 26, 2013.
46 Accession File 2002.0355, National Museum of American History Computers Collection, Object Records.
47 Michelle Delaney, Smithsonian Institution Archives, Computer Technology and Curation Oral History Interviews, interview with Petrina Foti, September 5, 2013.
48 Michelle Delaney, Smithsonian Institution Archives, Computer Technology and Curation Oral History Interviews, interview with Petrina Foti, September 5, 2013.
49 Michelle Delaney, Smithsonian Institution Archives, Computer Technology and Curation Oral History Interviews, interview with Petrina Foti, September 5, 2013.
50 Michelle Delaney, Smithsonian Institution Archives, Computer Technology and Curation Oral History Interviews, interview with Petrina Foti, September 5, 2013.
51 Michelle Delaney, Smithsonian Institution Archives, Computer Technology and Curation Oral History Interviews, interview with Petrina Foti, September 5, 2013.
52 Shannon Perich, Smithsonian Institution Archives, Computer Technology and Curation Oral History Interviews, interview with Petrina Foti, September 26, 2013.
53 Shannon Perich, Smithsonian Institution Archives, Computer Technology and Curation Oral History Interviews, interview with Petrina Foti, September 26, 2013
54 Shannon Perich, Smithsonian Institution Archives, Computer Technology and Curation Oral History Interviews, interview with Petrina Foti, September 26, 2013.
55 Matilda McQuaid, Smithsonian Institution Archives, Computer Technology and Curation Oral History Interviews, interview with Petrina Foti, September 26, 2013.

56 Matilda McQuaid, Smithsonian Institution Archives, Computer Technology and Curation Oral History Interviews, interview with Petrina Foti, September 26, 2013.
57 Cooper Hewitt National Design Museum, "About Cooper Hewitt," Smithsonian Institution, accessed March 14, 2015, http://www.cooperhewitt.org/about/.
58 Matilda McQuaid, Smithsonian Institution Archives, Computer Technology and Curation Oral History Interviews, interview with Petrina Foti, September 26, 2013.
59 Matilda McQuaid, Smithsonian Institution Archives, Computer Technology and Curation Oral History Interviews, interview with Petrina Foti, September 26, 2013.
60 Matilda McQuaid, Smithsonian Institution Archives, Computer Technology and Curation Oral History Interviews, interview with Petrina Foti, September 26, 2013.
61 Chan and Cope both left the Smithsonian in 2015.
62 Sebastian Chan and Aaron Straup Cope, Smithsonian Institution Archives, Computer Technology and Curation Oral History Interviews, interview with Petrina Foti, September 26, 2013.
63 Sebastian Chan and Aaron Straup Cope, Smithsonian Institution Archives, Computer Technology and Curation Oral History Interviews, interview with Petrina Foti, September 26, 2013.
64 Cooper Hewitt National Design Museum, "Planetary: Collecting and Preserving Code as a Living Object," Smithsonian Institution, accessed March 14, 2015, http://www.cooperhewitt.org/2013/08/26/planetary-collecting-and-preserving-code-as-a-living-object/.
65 Sebastian Chan and Aaron Straup Cope, Smithsonian Institution Archives, Computer Technology and Curation Oral History Interviews, interview with Petrina Foti, September 26, 2013.

5 "The black box conundrum"

Computer technology on exhibit

Introduction

In Chapter 4, the challenges and issues associated with formally accepting computer-based technology objects into a permanent collection were examined. This chapter will further explore the formation of a museum object's narrative and examine the challenges and opportunities that arise when, subsequently, those now-accessioned objects are placed on exhibition.[1] While loans to the museum in question mean that exhibition objects do not necessarily have to be formally part of that museum's collection, in this chapter, we will examine instances of fully accessioned objects on display. As was seen in Chapter 2, there are difficulties in recording history as it is occurring and there are specific challenges that arise when a museum displays computer-based technology. Many curators at the Smithsonian Institution considered the computer to be what they termed a "black box," which does not overtly reveal its function to the viewer. This chapter now follows this inquiry further, by considering how these same curators deal with the display of the "black box" to audiences within the public space of the exhibition – with the added complexity of visitors' own narratives around those objects. David Allison, lead curator on multiple exhibits that featured, at least partly, the history of computer technology, notes:

> During a time of the major PC history when everything looked like a generic black box and there were lots of things that were different but looked all the same, exhibiting those in meaningful ways can be quite challenging. What is interesting in recent years, as form factors have once again become extremely important, you can collect and exhibit them in ways that are compelling to people and smaller tends to be easier to exhibit. Early, large machines were hard to exhibit, because you could not exhibit the whole thing. Generally, you could only exhibit part of it. For example, with the early UNIVAC we exhibited just the control panel and not all the tape drives and the printers and all the things that went along with it, because we simply did not have the space. But I would say that our overarching challenge is helping people see

> through looking at the three-dimensional object, its significance historically and socially and making it relevant to them.[2]

Allison's words echo many of the same concerns expressed by Paul Ceruzzi in Chapter 2. Ceruzzi noted that he had to "grapple with issues of how to present the story of computing, using artifacts" that "revealed little of their function" in exhibition form and how this process was made even more difficult with the growing focus on the digital, "which by definition has no tangible nature to it."[3] As was seen in Chapter 3 with the challenges that computer-based technology poses when curators seek to collect objects that contain or exist because of this technology, we can understand from these two computer curators that the same challenges are found when attempting to exhibit computer-based technology.

In this chapter, three Smithsonian exhibitions that have addressed these challenges will be examined: the National Museum of American History's *DigiLab* (November 10, 1999–January 2, 2003), which examined both the process of digitization at the Smithsonian and the impact of computer-based technology on traditional printing methods; the American History Museum's *American Stories* (opened April 12, 2012),[4] which presents American social history through iconic objects in the museum's holdings ;and the National Air and Space Museum's *Time and Navigation: The Untold Story of Getting from Here to There* (opened April 12, 2013), a joint collaboration between the American History Museum and the Air and Space Museum to present the technological advances from the nineteenth-century navigation equipment to modern GPS devices. All three exhibitions, though differing in subject matter and approaches to history, are examples of computer-based technology being presented as part of a main narrative, rather than a separate and distinct category, providing ways that computer technology is being integrated into general society. For each of these exhibits, specific instances whene curators answered challenges associated with the "black box" of their computer-based technology objects will be explored. In doing so, the patterns of our adaptive, transmitted, and distributed models of curatorial expertise will be explored. More importantly, combined with the pattern of curatorial behavior that was observed in Chapter 4, curatorial methods specifically developed using that expertise to respond to the challenge of computer-based technology are presented in Chapter 6.

At the cutting edge of technology

As Chapter 2 asserts, computer-based technology, as it merges into a new discipline, creates a dual heritage, as can be seen in the *Information Age* exhibition (1990–2006). With *DigiLab*, Curators Helena Wright and Joan Boudreau undertook to record the same process with printing history. Wright and Boudreau were well aware of the challenges that computer technology might offer, even if they had not dealt with it directly in their own fields before. Wright, one of the many curators in Chapter 2 who spoke of the "black box" with Wright, specifically referred to the "black box conundrum."[5] Though computer technology itself was not an area of study for either, both curators were prepared to discuss how the application of computers had begun to shape the field of printing.

In many ways, *DigiLab* can be viewed as two separate exhibits combined into one. While connected by the common element of computer-based technology, there were two separate narratives: how the Smithsonian had begun the process of digitizing its collections and how the computer-based technology had been folded into the processes of printing and graphic arts. The rectangular space was essentially divided in half in a way that the two narratives were separated, though this could be a limitation imposed by the physical constraints of the space and the unusual conditions that gave rise to the exhibition. Helena Wright explains how the problems with the layout in an existing exhibition served as an impetus for *DigiLab*:

> We had an existing Hall of Printing and Graphic Arts. Within that hall there were four "job shops," where we did demonstrations of printing, eighteenth- and nineteenth-century printing… When the Hall of News Reporting was closed, the newspaper shop lost one of its entrance-exit doors and it was a little bit of a beached whale in the rest of the hall. So, there was a discussion about what are we going to do with that space. There was also talk about closing the Printing Hall. David Allison came up with the idea that we could energize it and bring the story of printing more up to date with what was going on in the digital world. I do not honestly remember the arrangement as to how the Photo Lab brought the scanners up there and put the scanners in what had been the newspaper shop. The corner where the DigiLab was installed in the Graphic Arts Hall had originally been a slide show of street typography. There was a wonderful series of posters and billboards and street signs and all kinds of what we would now call the public face of printing. Some of them were really wonderful, graphically and socially-contextually. But the slide projector had never quite worked. It was a technical problem as well as a cul-de-sac in the rest of the hall, so that was the space that was designated to be jazzed up with the addition of the *DigiLab* story.[6]

As can be gathered from Wright's explanation, *DigiLab* was created in part to solve spatial difficulties and, in the process, to bring new relevance to an aging exhibition. What can be seen here is a small-scale variation of what William Walker had identified as a major institutionwide trend:

> Although exhibition controversies continue to crop up from time to time, the main constant of the Smithsonian's history continues to be the expansion of physical space and the resulting organizational and epistemological decisions that emanate from these special considerations.[7]

Walker is referring to the Smithsonian's expansion of its number of museums, but his words remind us that physical considerations are often the motivation for change. In this instance, a problematic space in an existing exhibition provided a set of opportunities and constraints that shaped the new exhibit in ways that it might not have developed otherwise. For example, a potential exhibition about digitization did not necessarily need to delve into this history of printing. *DigiLab*'s location in the Graphic Arts Hall allowed Wright and Boudreau to meditate on the changes that were occurring within their area of expertise.

DigiLab in many ways echoed the themes and approaches used by its parent exhibition. The American History Museum's Hall of Graphic Arts followed in the tradition of placing objects on exhibition through both static display and live demonstration. The Digitizing Laboratory section of the exhibition can be seen as the computer technology equivalent to the "job shops." As Wright explained, these "job shops" were based on historical printing shops and workspaces of the eighteenth and nineteenth centuries and often were the setting for printing demonstrations by costumed interpreters. Consequently, like these earlier counterparts, the process of digitization is explained in the Digitizing Laboratory section of *DigiLab* through demonstration. This half of the exhibition, in turn, can be seen as a narrative that records how computerization has been adopted into the field. Wright explains that "what we did in the *DigiLab* space was to try to tell the story of the change of what used to go on with traditional printing and how that was changed by what we knew about digital operations at that point."[8] Wright's motivations are explicitly stated in one of the main text panels, entitled "Look – I'm Digital":

> Display on computer screens is only one form of digital output. Most books, magazines, and newspapers are now composed as digital files. All the text panels in this exhibition were printed directly on the digital printers in this room [the Digitizing Laboratory].[9]

With their exhibition script, Wright and Boudreau are reconciling modern printing's dual heritage of both being an example of mechanical printing and being computer-based technology. In Chapter 2, Knell framed all museum collecting as contemporary collecting, in regard to the way that the current historical narrative is being shaped by the actions of the curator.[10] This can also be extended to exhibitions that display contemporary history. By presenting computerization as the next major technological advancement in the field of printing, Wright and Boudreau are consciously and deliberately choosing this narrative over one that presents computer technology as replacement. In doing so, the curators are shaping the narrative of what we understand computer-based technology to be and how it has shaped our lives.

In much the same way, the Digitization Laboratory was shaping how we understand the processes and value of digitization. This is reflected in the main text of the "Introduction panel," which read:

> In Digilab and other facilities around the Mall, the Smithsonian is creating electronic information about its artifacts. Digitizing gives the staff new ways to carry out research and to share the results with audiences old and new. It also helps staff preserve the objects you come here to see.[11]

What can be seen here is that the Smithsonian was not only explaining what digitization is, but why it is important. The exhibit framed the Smithsonian's digitization efforts in terms of outreach and forming a tradition that continues to this day.

As has been seen in Chapter 4, David Allison in his role as Curator of the Computers Collections responded to the challenge of the "black box" and the specific challenge posed by software with a simple and clear solution – to collect the container. It is therefore understandable that the technique that he and his fellow curators had employed in *Information Age* to display software was to place the software container in the exhibit case. However, the *DigiLab* exhibition offered a different set of circumstances that presented the opportunity for Allison – who was responsible for all interactive displays for the exhibition – to find a different solution. Allison explains:

> *DigiLab* was an opportunity to exhibit the process of digitizing collections, particularly images, where the people that were doing the work were part of the exhibition itself. So, we had a space in which we had people actually doing digitization, but contextual imagery around it. And the goal was to help the public understand what this process was like, while they were reading about the history and the context and the role of this... We wanted to show how digitization was part of a long process of capturing and sharing information. We used it as an opportunity to have a living piece of the most recent time within the context of the history of printing and information communication.[12]

With *DigiLab*, Allison was able to demonstrate how a software process worked through live demonstration, rather than static objects. Similarly, a section of *Information Age* – an exhibit where Allison was lead curator – did allow visitors to access the internet at a time when very few would have had the opportunity. As with *DigiLab*, this section of the exhibit was meant to display the latest technology, rather than a historical process (as exemplified with the approach of using printing "job shops"). However, as was seen in Chapter 2, computer technology's rapid development cycle means that new technology becomes more readily available to the public in a shorter period. As was seen in Chapter 3, with distributive expertise, museum visitors' own experiences soon catch up and, even in some cases, bypass the technology that is being displayed. Curator for the Electricity Collection Harold Wallace recalled that

> when *Information Age* opened in 1990, it was one of the very few places the ordinary person could sit down and get onto the Internet using the last couple of workstations in the *Information Age*. It got to the point by the time the exhibit closed in 2006, where that was just passé: "Yeah, of course you can get onto the internet. So?" It had lost its technical panache, you know?[13]

This loss of "technical panache" was also true with *DigiLab*, as an increasing number of visitors either owned or had access to scanners for their own personal use by the time the exhibition closed in 2003. For example, Kodak Picture Kiosks, which offered self-service photograph printing and scanning, were introduced in the late 1990s, and were easily found at most pharmacies in the United States during the 2000s. This again shows the difficulty for museums when attempting to present the latest computer technology. Another issue that *DigiLab* faced was more personal in nature: those who had the required technical expertise were uncomfortable being observed as they worked. Wright recalled that "the folks in the Photo Lab did not want to sit on public view doing scanning. They were not very happy with that. So, they put their interns in there."[14] Allison concurs:

> The most difficult part was that a lot of people who worked in *DigiLab* really were behind-the-scenes people and did not want to be seen working. They were not museum explanators or public programs people. They were real technicians and so it was not seen as being a particularly desirable place to work. So, we did have some trouble keeping it staffed, and we staffed it with more people whose job was to be explainers to the public.[15]

This serves as reminder that even the most seemingly straightforward solutions can have unforeseen complications. Since those who had the technical digitization expertise were, quite reasonably, uninterested in performing their ordinary work commitments in front of an audience, the computer stations were then staffed with museum volunteers and educators who learned the skills specifically to demonstrate the process to museum visitors, emulating the model previously established by the "job shops."

In a different capacity, technical knowledge also served as the main challenge of the other side of the exhibition as the Graphic Arts Curators attempted to familiarize themselves with the latest computer technology developments in printing and graphic display. Wright notes that

> that was a real learning curve for us, I must say. Personally, my field is the nineteenth century, so even twentieth-century topics were a little [out of range], and this is the very end of the twentieth century. So, getting into what was really new material was a challenge.[16]

Wright's candid observations reveal a curator who is willing to engage with unknown subjects and actively seeks to learn more. Within the Smithsonian, there were Allison and Ceruzzi[17] available for consultation. However, Wright and Boudreau soon realized that they would need a more specialized area of expertise: people who were familiar with computer-based technology as it related to Graphic Art. Wright explains:

> David [Allison] was certainly there as a resource, but he was not really terribly involved with computer applications for printing. So, we turned to industry contacts and the internet, primarily, but also talking with local printers. There was a studio right on 7th Street, David Adamson's Studio; he was the printer for Amy Lamb. Amy Lamb was a local photographer who was issuing her work digitally and she was also doing it in print. She was a perfect figure for this transition mode. It got us to be able to tell the story of the fact – and it is still true today, twenty years later – that digital output has not completely replaced ink on paper. For longer runs and certain kinds of products, you do computer-to-press and they are still printing. That was an important part of the story that we learned and that we definitely wanted to tell in what was, essentially, a printing hall.[18]

What Wright shows us here is that knowledge comes from a variety of sources and inspirations. When looking to explain a given subject, Wright and Boudreau turned to practitioners in the field, much the same way that curators in years past had. In terms of our reflection on the strategies used by curators to display the challenging "black box" computer-based technology, an important illustration of distributive expertise can be seen in this example of consultation with Amy Lamb. Here, when confronted with the opaque and the unfamiliar, the staff of the Smithsonian are seen to turn to precedent and examples of previous curatorial practice to serve as guidance for navigating through unfamiliar territory. The objects themselves on display may have been unprecedented and unfamiliar, and yet the strategies for dealing with such a challenge came, in fact, with familiar precedent.

We might pause here to recall from Chapter 2 that Wright, as a collecting curator for objects associated with September 11, expressed concerns about collecting without having a period of reflection to evaluate.[19] It is important to note that these concerns were still paramount to her, despite the success of *DigiLab* only a few years before. One of the main differences between the two instances is that there was a lack of precedent. Since, historically, the Graphic Arts Collection has not engaged with a social history narrative, there were, therefore, no previous collecting efforts that Wright and Boudreau could then apply to the September 11 collecting efforts. In contrast, the historical narrative of *DigiLab* was firmly rooted in the history of the technology associated with Graphic Arts, even if that particular technology happened to be computer technology. This is similar to the approach that the Music Collection took in regard to musical instruments that employed computer technology, as was seen with the Herbie Hancock accession in Chapter 4. In that case, curators in the Music Collection were so familiar with new technologies being incorporated into familiar instruments that they were able to respond to collecting computerized instruments in a similar manner. Again, curators are responding to computer-based technology in the same way that they would respond to any new technology by using transmitted expertise.

The result of this familiar framework for dealing with the unfamiliar was that the curators were able to engage with this unfamiliar subject matter and identify potential trends. Though their intention was not to predict the future, they did so in the case of the Rocket e-book. Rather than a loan, it was added to the Museum's permanent collection at a time when the technology was just emerging and its impact on society was still unknown. Wright explains:

> That [e-reader] was brand new, right off the shelf. We dealt directly with the company on that. It did not have a history of use. It was a very new technology at the time. I am not sure how easy it would have been to find people who were actually using them. There was a lot of literature in traditional sources like newspapers and magazines about whether these electronic readers were going to actually be accepted or whether they going to wipe out traditional books. There was a lot of hot air being spilled on this topic. So, it was something that we really thought about. We felt we should include it, because it seemed to be a direction for the future. And this again was before the Kindle, before the Nook, before the brands of readers that have actually taken off and become commercially successful. I think the poor old [Rocket] e-book did not do very well in real life. I am not sure what its technical problems were, but it did not survive.[20]

Wright's notation of the object's lack of "history of use" – a concern of social history – allows us to conclude that this acquisition was considered for its contribution to the history of technology, and that in turn offered guidance as to what to collect. The e-book reader can therefore be considered an example of an object that was collected due to the impact or contribution it has made to a field. As has been seen in Chapter 2, this decreases the chance that the object will be viewed as irrelevant by future generations, since marketing failures, which as Wright indicates, the Rocket e-book ultimately proved to be, do not preclude technological significance.

In the same section of the exhibition was a hand-printed book that was sold on the internet. The individual letterpress book is not remarkable in itself. It is a way to represent the otherwise intangible, uncollectable internet. Wright explains:

> I was looking for some way to relate the story of late twentieth-century resurgence in the book arts and the great interest in hand printing by letterpress and these Book Arts programs in universities that seemed to start bubbling up in the 1980s and 1990s, and how do we relate that to what was going on with the new digital world. The answer seemed to lie in a hand-printed book on the subject of typography that was being advertised and sold over the internet.[21]

What is significant in this example is Wright identifying an unknown structure and finding an object to represent the whole. In this case, representing the system that computer technology created, rather than describing how the technology itself worked, is the focus of the exhibition, in much the same way that *DigiLab* was explaining how computer-based technology was adapted to the field of Graphic Arts printing, rather than how computer-based technology was developed. There was little need to do so as *Information Age* was still on view. Indeed, one of *DigiLab*'s exhibit panels directs visitors down to that exhibition to learn more about how the internet was developed.[22]

On the whole, *DigiLab* can be seen as an example of merging dual heritages; in other words, it represents both computer and printing history. Importantly, the *DigiLab* exhibit design does this by following precedented strategies of previous displays, namely, those set by the *Information Age* exhibition, which was itself an exhibit representing the dual heritages of computer technology and communication devices. The *DigiLab* exhibit became an opportunity for the Museum's Graphic Arts curators to learn more from experts in the field to think creatively when presented with unknown challenges. In doing so, they created a dynamic and, at times, prophetic exhibit as new applications to computer-based technology were occurring. However, much has changed in the decades since *DigiLab* was developed. Technology has become more commonplace and museum visitors have become more technologically adept. Rather than presenting new technology, Museum staff found themselves learning at the same rate as their visitors. It is in this climate that our next two exhibits were developed. In these examples, the challenge for the curators was not in how to explain the unfamiliar, but rather to provide a meaningful and relevant context, while the story is still actively unfolding and occurring.

Recording history as it occurs

The central example (and computer-based object) for our next discussion, for all intents and purposes, appears to be a car. In reality, it is a driverless vehicle, commonly referred to as "Stanley,"[23] famous for winning the 2005 Defense Advanced Research Projects Agency (DARPA) Grand Challenge, a contest held by the United States Defense Department to promote invention and innovation, generally in the area of robotics and autonomous vehicles.

Collecting Curator Carlene Stephens, in a memo to the American History Museum's Collection Committee written that same year, explained that

> "Stanley" is the complex robotic offspring from the marriage of the computer and a very early, much more simple robot already in the NMAH collection – the 1948 "tortoise" that, with the aid of sensors, moves across the floor and around obstacles. Earlier breakthroughs in artificial intelligence related mostly to the development of computing power and machine logic. This is best illustrated in our collections by "Deep Blue," the computer now on display in *Information Age* that played chess at the grand master level to beat champion Garry Kasparov. The most recent and promising advances in artificial intelligence are, as "Stanley" has demonstrated, in areas pertaining to perception and sensing, in contrast to earlier breakthroughs in machine logic.[24]

What can be seen from the formal description is that the Museum was most interested in "Stanley"'s technological advances, comparing it to Deep Blue.[25] Rather than a merging of a dual heritage of computer history and the Graphic Arts as was the case with *DigiLab*, the Museum had firmly classified "Stanley" as "computer history." This reminds us that computer-based technology can be enclosed in surprising, even misleading containers. It can be challenging for exhibit teams to ensure that museum visitors, when encountering computer technology in an unfamiliar format, are still able to easily grasp what narrative the museum is trying to express.

In fact, the Museum itself must often first identify how best to classify the object in question. This was certainly the case with "Stanley" when the lead developer Sebastian Thrun first offered it to the Museum. Stephens notes:

> When we get an offer like that – that it is not immediately obvious what the article is – we have a discussion; a group gets together. So, we had Peter Liebhold as representing Production Engineering, where most of our robots fit. We have industrial robot arms, mostly. There was me, because I am the robot curator now and we have them in a line with our Renaissance automatons and eighteenth-century, nineteenth-century walking dolls and so forth. We had someone from Military History because of the DARPA sponsorship of the robot race and Roger White, who represented the car collection. Roger reminded me the other day that we decided as a group that this was a robot, that it was not particularly military – even though it was sponsored by the Defense Department – and that, because it was not carrying people, it was not a car. So, that is why it ended up being collected as a robot. Of course, DARPA had billed all of this as a robot race; DARPA was trying to get autonomous vehicles fielded. The Defense Department had been putting money into autonomous vehicles for 20 years, but they needed them right now, in two wars in the Middle East, so they wanted to see what

> was going to bubble up. And they represented it as a robot race, so that's how it was conceived, and that's how we collected it. And because I was the Robot Curator, I was standing too close to the fire and here I am.[26]

Stephens' words reveal how a curatorial team works together to understand and classify the unfamiliar. In this case, Stephens found herself in discussion with colleagues from different collections and divisions: Engineering, Automotive, Military History, and Stephens' own Mechanisms Collection. For "Stanley" to be finally classified as a "robot" required the involvement of many different viewpoints in dialogue. Chapter 4 examined how curators such as Stacy Kluck and Shannon Perich incorporated computer-based technology-related objects within the existing structure of their collections. Yet, with "Stanley," museum staff were instead confronted with an object that did not clearly fall into existing collection classifications because it shared identifying traits with multiple existing collections. This once again recalls Ceruzzi's observations in Chapter 2 on how computer-based technology, with its ever-growing capabilities and versatility posed specific challenges for museum collections that are subject based, since computer-based technology crosses those academic barriers.[27] However, while curators might have been initially uncertain to which collection they should assign "Stanley," this would not be the first time they had encountered circumstances such as these. Chapter 2 examined how curators are meeting the challenge of collecting objects that have no previous precedent to follow, by following the example set by previous instances of unprecedented collecting. With the team formed to discuss who should take the lead in collecting "Stanley," the methods curatorial staff employ to accomplish this are illustrated.

Like the e-book reader that Wright and Boudreau collected for *DigiLab*, "Stanley" was collected at a moment when its full legacy was unknown. Chapter 2 identified one particular form of unprecedented collecting – collecting without the benefit of an existing historical narrative – as the major challenge that contemporary collecting poses for curators. Stephens experienced similar concerns when collecting "Stanley":

> We are not always as explicit as we might be about contemporary collecting. If there were no limits, if there were no limits to space, if there were no limits to resources, we would be collecting much more to document the world we live in now. I went out on a limb, I think, on "Stanley." It could have gone either way. It could have been that all this DARPA stuff might have just been a "flash in the pan," so to speak, and that autonomous vehicles would have gone nowhere. That turned out not to be true. It is now possible to buy automobiles with autonomous systems already in place. It was already on the horizon when "Stanley" did the race. There are cars that can park themselves. There are cars that have warning systems about lane drift; they have front and back collision sensors if not correctors, depending upon how much of this

> people are willing to pay for at this point – at this point it is really expensive. But there are predictions that this is five years down the road, ten years down the road. Now Tesla [Motors, Inc.] says we are three years away from it. When I read these things, I watch with great interest because I do not want to have made an incorrect decision. We do it all the time; we make decisions about contemporary collecting and lots of things just do not pan out. But with a big blue thing like "Stanley," it would be very costly to the museum in terms of space and so forth not to be right about this. So, I am hoping I am somewhat right, because it is a bigger question about contemporary collecting.[28]

In Chapter 2, curators expressed similar worries of making "incorrect" collecting decisions or overlooking something important. This might begin to serve as testament to the care that curators take when considering collecting an object contemporaneously. The frequency with which "Stanley" has been exhibited since its accession might serve as evidence that Stephens was justified in collecting. However, as was seen with the example of the 1847 "life car" invented by Joseph Francis discussed in Chapter 2, an object might not always be considered as significant by later generations as a contemporary audience might have found it to be. Despite current growing interest in self-driving cars, the same might easily hold true for "Stanley" in the future, hence Stephens' worries. This example also illustrates that transmitted expertise not only is expressed in a concern of what to collect, but also in terms of the possible burden a future accession might have for the curator's successors.

It is important to note that in the ten years since the 2005 memo to the Collection Committee, "Stanley" had been on display in three separate exhibitions, which could be considered as evidence of the interest that "Stanley" has generated and highlights the flexibility that comes with having a particular object available in a museum collection. This also presents us with the opportunity to examine the different narratives of each exhibition. Stephens notes that

> each time, it was different. The first time, it was really a stripped down, sparse "Here's the winner of the DARPA 2005 Grand Challenge, isn't it cool?" It had no other context except explaining what the DARPA Grand Challenge was and explaining what Stanley was. That took some doing because there is nothing like Stanley. Then we collected a bunch of other stuff around the DARPA Grand Challenges. So, in *Robots on the Road* we could tell more of the Grand Challenge story, but we could put it in the context of other wheeled robots. There were two story-lines in there. We have wheeled robots that go back to the Renaissance… Then the third context is the larger story of time and navigation. The computer software story kind of gets soft-pedalled there because we have it as a navigation problem, with GPS integrated with all kinds of other information and the computer is implied. I mean, it is the computer that

> is doing all the integrating. So yes, three different contexts each time. I would imagine each time it goes on display that will happen. It is so versatile. Stanley is so versatile.[29]

It is interesting to note that Stephens is able to declare a specific-purpose object such as "Stanley" as versatile. As discussed in Chapter 3, this is an illustration of the creativity and open-mindedness of the adaptive expertise that curators regularly employ in the course of their work. Further examination of the ways in which "Stanley" has been exhibited serves as evidence as to what Stephens might mean.

The first time that "Stanley" was on exhibit, it was solely to highlight the Museum's recent acquisition. Therefore, the display, much as Stephens suggests, was very simply executed in front of the ground floor escalators of the West Wing.[30] In contrast, the second time "Stanley" was exhibited, the focus was to display the scientific research and innovation that made the vehicle possible and therefore required more interpretation. Like *DigiLab*, *Robots on the Road* (November 21, 2008–January 8, 2012) was meant to update an existing exhibition – *Science in American Life* (April 27, 1994–November 27, 2011) and therefore its goals and objectives were attuned to those of its parent exhibition. A draft of the exhibit proposal states these intentions explicitly:

> The main message of the proposed exhibition falls under the main message of "Science in American Life": robotics, like all American science and technology, is embedded in American society and culture. Visitors will learn that although "Stanley" emerged from research sponsored for military purposes, the impact of the race is likely to be felt in other areas of American life, especially automotive safety. This follows the pattern of the integrated circuit, the internet and other technologies with strong military connections.[31]

As was seen with the letterpress book in *DigiLab*, "Stanley" was being used to tell a complex story; in this case of this exhibition, it was one about military invention and innovation that is then applied to civilian life. More than simply presenting "Stanley" as the winner of the DARPA Grand Challenge, the exhibit went further to present the reasons why this was an important technological development.

To do so, it was necessary for Stephens to engage with "Stanley" as an example of computer-based technology. While it may not resemble the conventional image of a computer, "Stanley" presented the same "black box" challenges as an IBM PC or an Apple Mac might: a museum visitor typically may not be able to see how the machine worked merely by viewing it. However, Stephens understood that the computer code that made "Stanley" possible was the key part of the story and made that explicit in *Robots on the Road*:

> A little piece of the navigation code was on the barrier in *Robots on the Road*. I really wanted that there. By that time, I had enough contact with the Stanford Racing Team, I could go right to the fellow who could send me a disk and it was no problem. Mike Montemerlo's computer is in the collection now and it is a little laptop... There was a famous off-road place in the Nevada desert close to California. They would go there and, at a biker bar there, Mike would sit there and reprogram things on the fly, because that is where they were practicing with 'Stanley' out there in the desert. It wasn't just that they showed up one day with all this stuff fully formed. They had to practice, experiment and so forth. So, there was lots of programming on the fly.[32]

Stephens' words provide evidence that she views "Stanley" as a tangible representative of the computer code that the Stanford Racing Team worked so hard to perfect. As seen in Chapter 4, there are numerous examples in the Computers Collection of computer code being represented by its container. It is now apparent how that model might work in an exhibition setting. Yet it was not museum precedent that led Stephens to take this representational approach. In regard to viewing "Stanley" as a computer code story, she explains:

> I learned that from Sebastian and the racing team. All of them pretty much decided that. They looked at the problem. DARPA said "You must have a vehicle that can travel off-road on really terrible terrain, go 130 or so miles with no human driver." So, they thought about it and *they* decided that they did not have to reinvent the car. Now other people in the races tried to reinvent the car. But Sebastian and company thought, "You know, the car is a mature technology; it does just fine. So, what we're going to do is we're going to focus on the things that help the car drive itself." And that became their definition of all of that was a software problem. "The race is going to be a software problem" is probably a quote from Sebastian. I think we had it on the wall in the exhibition... The more advanced people understood that it was a problem integrating different kinds of information – sensors and GPS and inertial measurement units and cameras or video color pictures. All that information had to be processed and then the car had to decide on its own: "Is this road or not road? Is this safe or not safe? What is that and can I go around it or can I go over it?" Stanley had trouble with that. Stanley could not tell the difference between a tumble-weed and a rock, so it would always go around a tumble-weed when it could just have gone right through it.[33]

If the Stanford Racing Team had thought the answer to the problem was a mechanical solution, it is likely that would have been the focus of *Robots on the Road*. Since computer code was the central focus of the team's development process, Stephens made that story explicit with quotes and with a visual reproduction of the actual code. As with Wright and Boudreau with digital printing and, from Chapter 4, Delaney and Perich with digital photography, Stephens provides yet another example of distributive expertise with a curator looking to the specialists beyond the museum for guidance on a subject area that is unfamiliar to the curator.

Since 2013, "Stanley" has been on display in the *Time and Navigation* exhibit at the Air and Space Museum. The exhibit is a joint collaboration between the National Air and Space Museum and the National Museum of American History, with the exhibit team made up of staff from both. Though physically located at the Air and Space Museum, the exhibit featured objects from the two museums' collections. *Time and Navigation* can be considered a history of technology exhibition, as it is a chronological exhibition explaining the development of a certain category of technology, in this particular instance navigation and timekeeping technology. As with *Information Age*, computer-based technology enters the exhibit's narrative with the invention of the electronic computer, as navigation and timekeeping calculation were among the earliest applications of computer technology development.

"Stanley" is located in the section at the end of the exhibit that actively engages with current technology that affects museum visitors' daily life, specifically with the prevalence of GPS. It is interesting to note that, in this particular exhibit, "Stanley" is more closely identified with being a "car" compared to the internal object documentation for the American History Museum, which made a much clearer distinction for classification purposes. For instance, by looking at the collection record in the Museum's electronic cataloge Mimsy XG, one can see that the American History Museum classifies "Stanley" as an "autonomous/robotic vehicle."[34] Though the text on the object rail – likely written by Stephens – refers to "Stanley" as an adapted Volkswagen and does not use the term "car," the introductory label to the section states:

> Researchers around the world are beginning to craft a future where drivers with electronically enhanced cars, buses, and trucks will navigate automated highways. Transportation planners hope to create a highly efficient road system and to foster the technologies to make it happen. Will your next car drive itself?[35]

Aligning "Stanley" with automobiles once more is likely done as a method to further connect the museum visitor to an otherwise confusing example of technology. Paul Ceruzzi, Curator at the Air and Space Museum and member of the exhibit team, notes that museum visitors will likely recognize an object such as "Stanley" as a car much like one they might own, and that presents an opportunity to allow those visitors to consider a familiar aspect of their lives in a new way:

> Everybody has a car and everybody assumed that a car must have a driver. Somebody came along and said "Well, what if we don't have a driver? What would that be like?" It is interesting in that we do not have elevator operators anymore, except for a few places. You can get on these people-movers that are like subways without a driver, but obviously they are restricted by rails to a very specific track. So, the question is can we do it with an automobile? People really enjoy that one too, because a lot of people drive a Volkswagen and it is a Volkswagen that's been modified. So, it is familiar.[36]

What can be seen from Ceruzzi's observations is that the visitors use familiarity as a point of connection and that allows them to speculate further about future technological advances. However, as shall now be examined, visitors' familiarity with a contemporary object can also offer challenges as well as opportunities.

Reintroducing the familiar

In the *Time and Navigation* exhibit, in the same section as "Stanley" and in one of the last cases in the exhibit is an iPhone, opened to reveal its circuitry. The iPhone would be a familiar object to many museum visitors, being an everyday mode through which GPS is commonly used. However, unlike "Stanley," the iPhone is a multifunctional object, which means that it serves a great number of purposes beyond its GPS capabilities. The challenge for the exhibition would actually be how to let visitors clearly understand, like *DigiLab*'s letterpress, why this particular iPhone – or the GPS chip within the iPhone, to be more precise – was included as part of the exhibition.

The curator for this section was Paul Ceruzzi, who has been mainly referred to in this study thus far as the computer historian. Yet, here Ceruzzi is acting as museum practitioner, putting his familiarity with computer-based technology into practice. For example, when reflecting on how he first decided to display a disassembled iPhone, Ceruzzi responded:

> I guess it was when I first realized that they had an accelerometer on board. I collect accelerometers, which are very large and expensive handmade devices, and I just could not believe they had one in the phone. I did some research and I found out how they got them so small. Then I realized that it was worth an exhibit about it. I mean it was not just an accelerometer, but a GPS receiver as well that they have. They have a lot of things in them.[37]

Ceruzzi was able to translate his enthusiasm for computer technology into a dynamic display. By disassembling an iPhone as prototype, Ceruzzi was able to judge whether this display technique would be visually interesting to a general public. This chapter began by recalling Ceruzzi's concerns in displaying computer technology that "revealed little of their function." This provides insight into Ceruzzi's solution in this exhibition to the "black box" conundrum. In a stunning example of adaptive expertise, he has, quite literally, opened a small black box to reveal its inner workings, so that an interested public might better understand its function.

While "Stanley" was an example of how the familiar will offer the visitor a way to understand the unknown and complex, the disassembled iPhone takes the familiar and offers a different visual experience of an object that they might already be holding in their hand. Removing the outer case to display the circuitry was a repeatedly employed display feature for all computer technology in *Time and Navigation*. However, with the iPhone, the familiar outer case remains on display with the GPS chip to make it still instantly recognizable. Rather than a complication, Ceruzzi viewed the iPhone's familiarity as an advantage:

> We were fortunate in that almost half the people who come into the museum have those phones; so they could recognize the shape of it when they saw it. It was sort of fun, I think. It has worked out pretty well that we have it right next to a submarine guidance system and we say, "Everything on that submarine is in your phone – except for the nuclear tipped missiles!" Everything else is there. The gyroscopes, accelerometers, radio satellite navigation, computer, keyboard, everything is there. People get a kick out of that.[38]

Ceruzzi displays his distributive expertise by understanding that visitors to the exhibition would likely have a certain level of technical savvy, which in turn speaks to how much that same technology had been adopted into society. The knowledge that Ceruzzi and the rest of the *Time and Navigation* exhibition team provided is not meant to enlighten museum visitors to an unknown subject, but rather to augment their already existing knowledge on a given subject.

As exemplified in his analysis of "Stanley," Paul Ceruzzi was aware of the power of the familiar as a point of entry for complex technical topics. In this instance, he applies the same principles in response to the multifunctionality of an iPhone, using its familiarity not only to understand modern GPS navigation, but as a lens to view the entire gallery:

> The good news is everyone knows what a smartphone is so we do not have to explain what an iPhone is. The rest of the gallery tells people what is inside. We have examples of gyroscopes and satellites and

> everything else there in the gallery. So, if they have gone through the gallery in the proper order they will have this in their heads: "Oh, this is what I just saw over there, there's the satellite and this is picking up that satellite signal, or this is the radio and it's picking up that radio signal." I do not know how many people will understand that it has an accelerometer on it or gyroscope on it, but we have those things and it is all in one piece, which is why it is such a revolutionary product.[39]

As familiar as an iPhone is to a contemporary audience, most people have not seen them disassembled. *Time and Navigation* allows the visitors to peer within their arguably most familiar "black box" to see part of what makes it function.

This speaks to a larger challenge in exhibiting computer technology. Computer chips are very difficult to exhibit, not only for their "black box" qualities, but because they are very small, which offers a whole different set of display issues, which the display of the iPhone GPS chip successfully navigates. Across the National Mall, the American History Museum's *American Stories* exhibition offers a different, yet not less successful approach. Described as "a chronological look at the people, inventions, issues, and events that shape the American story,"[40] the exhibit has two chips on display in a case dedicated to computer technology. The case contains the first integrated circuit and an integrated circuit from the SEGA game system that featured "chip art" – microscopic artwork built into the microchip as a signature. Stevan Fisher, Lead Designer for the exhibition, explains:

> Small things get lost, especially if they are in a case that you cannot really get close to… In this case you can, but something we did with that specifically is do a photograph of it as well to give a better view, part of it is for those who cannot see so well anyway – entering that demographic – and others to say "this is what you're looking at. Get a better view of it." The integrated circuit there, from the SEGA game system is actually part of an additional strategy in the gallery, where we take one object from each of the five clusters, each of the areas we are representing and do a "What does this object tell us?" label that is mounted on the wall that includes a very close view of the object on display. So, in that case you can see the chip, you can see a photograph of the chip, and then on the wall you can see Godzilla from that chip, showing a photo of the chip in close up and then an electron scanning microscope view of the Godzilla at the top.[41]

Fisher emphasizes that the image cannot be seen by the naked eye and that trait can be a point of entry to introduce a different way to consider a familiar object:

> It is on the molecular level, which also says something about the people who work in the industry and what you cannot see that might be there.

> We do the same with the ruby slippers [from the movie *The Wizard of Oz*] in that same area. We show that the pair we have on display were used in the long-shots and the dancing scenes under microphone, because they have felt on the [bottom of the] shoes so they do not make noise on the set. So that when Dorothy Gale is walking, she is not stepping on her lines, as it were.[42]

Whether it is a computer chip or a famous pair of shoes, Fisher demonstrates the same practice of offering augmented knowledge that Ceruzzi utilized with the disassembled iPhone. One can begin to see a pattern of trust and creativity that binds current Smithsonian curators and exhibit teams in creating exhibitions that present contemporary history, whether social or technical, to an audience that should already be familiar with the subject matter, as can be seen with another case in *American Stories* where a 2004 Apple iPod[43] was on display from 2012 until 2015.[44]

The American History Museum's *American Stories* exhibition might, at first glance, appear to be a "highlights" show – an exhibition meant to represent the entire Museum and/or collection. However, its inception served a greater purpose for the Museum. Since 2006, the American History Museum has been in the midst of a phased-plan renovation of its building on the National Mall; the phase during the time of the exhibition's development called for the closing of the wing on the west side of the building, where many long-term, popular exhibits had been on view.[45] Curator Bonnie Campbell Lilienfeld, Assistant Director for the Museum's Office of Curatorial Affairs and former Chair for the Department of Home and Community Life, was Lead Curator for *American Stories*. She describes the motivations for the exhibit's development:

> It was basically a museum initiative to put things on the floor that were not going to be exhibited anymore, partly because of the closing of all the exhibits in the West Wing. So, *Information Age*, *Communities in a Changing Nation* and *Popular Culture*. There was the fear that not only would the objects not be on display, but the ideas and the themes that were represented in the exhibits would not be on the floor. That was the initial initiative, I think, for doing that exhibit.[46]

As can be seen from Campbell Lilienfeld, the exhibit was created within a specific timeframe. *American Stories* opened within weeks of the closing and deinstallation of the west side of the building. The precedent for this was set during a previous phase of renovation. While the museum was closed as its central section was renovated, the *Treasures of American History* exhibition (November 17, 2006–April 13, 2008) at the Air and Space Museum displayed key objects from the American History Museum's collection. Both exhibits serve as evidence that the Museum holds certain subjects and even objects so important to its mission that it will always ensure that they are represented "on the floor." However, more than a straight recycling of objects that were on display, curators from both exhibitions viewed this as an opportunity to also highlight high-priority topics and objects that, for whatever reason, were not currently being exhibited. For Campbell Lilienfeld, computer-based technology was one of these high-priority topics.

Information Age had been permanently closed and partially deinstalled when the Museum closed for renovation in 2006. However, from the time that the American History Museum had reopened two years later, computer technology had only been represented in small, temporary displays. Campbell Lilienfeld saw this new exhibition as a way to rectify that:

> Once *Information Age* closed, there really was not any computer presence that I can think of... So, in *American Stories*, I was interested in talking about technology in different ways, in part because it was not really represented. Not very much. We do have a [computer] technology case in there, but the iPod is actually in the case about economy.[47]

By looking for additional opportunities to present computer-based technology, Campbell Lilienfeld is demonstrating that the computer has an important value to society, one that is not to be relegated and made peripheral within the museum. This forces the curator to think outside the "black box," so to speak, in new and different ways. The end result is that what is displayed on the floor is actually a truer representation of the impact of computer-based technology on people's lives.

It is important to recognize that Campbell Lilienfeld is not a computer historian or indeed a History of Technology Curator at all. Campbell Lilienfeld, in addition to her administrative role, was Curator for the Ceramics and Glass Collection and has worked in recent years to bring more social history perspective to a previously decorative arts-based collection. It is noteworthy to see that computer-based technology has become so commonplace that a nonspecialized historian would have both the knowledge and the ability to interpret these objects. Partly this comes with expert curation and what might be classified as a more universal curatorial skill set. With *American Stories*, Campbell Lilienfeld is using these same principles to present and interpret computer-based technology as she did to reshape the Ceramics Collection, allowing for another narrative to take prominence. Campbell Lilienfeld explained:

> Clearly, it is a technology story, but it also seemed to me to be an interesting story about economics and manufacturing in this country... That if you looked at the record player which is from 1949, it just struck me that that was made in America and then it is a portable turntable, so not a big table top model. And then, the Walkman made in the 1980s,

> also another portable music technology, but made in Japan, because that was really indicative of what was going on throughout different manufacturing industries in the United States. I thought that was really interesting. And a portable music player. Things are getting more portable. It is a whole different type of infrastructure. You have to buy the tapes rather than the records. And then you look at the Apple. It was maybe the mark on the back of the Apple that actually made me start thinking about this: "Designed in America. Made in China." I thought that was really fascinating. I thought it was a really, really interesting arch, that manufacturing and economic story in the US and also that was tied to technology. It was interesting because it was music. Trying to tell the story of manufacturing could be sort of dry, but if you can get people to think about the thing they have in their pocket and the history of how we have listened to music.[48]

As demonstrated through Campbell Lilienfeld's adaptive expertise, computer-based technology can be used to tell multiple stories beyond the invention and innovation narrative. In some ways, this can be seen as the complement to the letterpress book in *DigiLab*. In that particular case, Wright expertly used a familiar object to explain a complex system based on computer technology, whereas in the case of the iPod, Campbell Lilienfeld employed a familiar computer-based technology object to explain a complex economic system. This particular design and manufacturing story could be told through a number of mass-produced objects, but by choosing a company as familiar as Apple, the exhibit engages the visitor's interest.

As was seen in Chapter 3, there is a difficulty in collecting contemporary objects while their history is still being recorded, and, as exemplified with *DigiLab* and "Stanley," those same challenges apply to the exhibition of these objects. However, as with "Stanley" and the iPhone, visitors' familiarity and personal connection to the technology are viewed as an asset and is reflected in the design of the exhibition case. Fisher notes that

> it was popular culture, but it was taken from a technological standpoint. So, from 1945 until at the time the exhibit opened in 2012, we had a 1945 45 RPM turntable, we had a 1970s Walkman and we had an iPod showing the change in accessing music. And the way the labels were written were "This is what people listened to, this is where it was made, and this is how the technology changed." Those three components along with an iTunes gift card are on display in one case. It is not a very large case. It is maybe three feet by two feet and [the objects] are arranged in a walk around case that you can read each of the labels for those... The whole concept of the gallery was that things mean something and they mean different things to different people – that was one of the backgrounds to the development of the center section, which was not tied into any period, but the idea was that this object represents

> something, and it was taken to represent changes in technology and manufacture, in personal listening devices.[49]

To Fisher, the exhibit's format is meant to create a narrative flow where the objects are in dialogue, which, in turn, fosters a dialogue among its viewers. This brings to mind Rhys' words from Chapter 2: "Contemporary collecting helps to fill those gaps [in collections], but can also create a dialogue between past and present objects."[50] Contemporary objects can foster a quite literal conversation between Museum visitors. Fisher further explains that

> a tweener [a preadolescent] would be able to recognize the iPod, but wouldn't necessarily know what a 45 RPM record player was and may have missed entirely the technology that is represented by a Walkman. Likewise, the person they are probably here with (because usually a tweener is not travelling alone) will recognize the older thing and recognize the newer thing and will make their own connections about why these things are grouped together.[51]

Fisher's observations indicate that the exhibit was designed intentionally for a technologically savvy audience. The exhibition team, demonstrating distributive expertise, felt safe to assume that the majority of their visitors could be expected to have used one, if not all, of the examples of technology on display; that assumption serves as an example of how commonplace these items had become and highlights that this entire case is made up of contemporary collecting objects. In doing so, the exhibit team was able to create a more complex narrative. Campbell Lilienfeld explains:

> What we decided to do in this exhibit was to use the object as kind of a starting point to tell a bigger story. We were using the iPod and these other musical things to tell a bigger story about economy and manufacturing. We were hoping that at least some people would get the idea that you can use these objects as a gateway to a bigger story that helps you understand the American Experience and the experience of lots of different people in the country and throughout the world. And it seems to me that they would get that with more contemporary things that they can recognize.[52]

Both Fisher and Campbell Lilienfeld's statements reveal the trust that the exhibition team has in their audience to be able to make the connections on their own. The case does not explicitly state the development of technology, since it does so visually. Campbell Lilienfeld's exhibit text offers information that augments Museum visitors' existing knowledge, allowing visitors to consider an aspect of a familiar object that they might not have previously considered. In both the *American Stories* and *Time and Navigation* exhibits, distributive expertise is at work, with Smithsonian curatorial staff trusting that their visitors would bring a level of computer literacy to the display. With both the iPhone and the iPod, exhibits' labels reflect this, offering to augment the visitor's existing knowledge rather than assuming that everything relating to computer-based technology needs to be explained.

The label for the portable music player case discusses the ramifications of digitization without explaining the process as *DigiLab* had. In the decade between the two exhibitions, the general population had become more digitally literate and the case in *American Stories* has been designed accordingly. Each music player is paired with the means to play that music: a record for the record player, a cassette tape for the Walkman, and an iTunes gift card with the iPod. A careful observer will note that the iTunes gift card is not actually a container for the music. It is the means to procure the music. However, as can be seen from Fisher's comments and the exhibit label (which noted that the iPod changed how music was purchased) the exhibit team was aware of the distinction. The label had been written for an audience that would already be familiar with iTunes and the process of acquiring digital music. Once again, curators trust that Museum visitors will understand how computer technology works. This, in turn, allowed Campbell Lilienfeld to tell a more dynamic story:

> [That] is why I ended up getting into the story about the economy, since it is just as much about buying the music as it is buying the hardware. It is really interesting. I think something like the iPod is so interesting because you can tell so many different stories.[53]

Since the purpose of the case is not to describe how the technology works, the result of this is that the "black box conundrum" is completely circumvented. Campbell Lilienfeld's words about how many stories can be told from one object are also an echo of Fisher's and Stephens', as well as aligning in practice with Wright and Boudreau. This is adaptive expertise in action. Therefore, one might begin to identify this expertise as a trait that is shared among the staff at the American History Museum and perhaps even across the Smithsonian in general. This, in turn, serves as another illustration as to how curators were prepared to meet the challenge of the unknown represented by computer-based technology using their expertise in curation.

Conclusion

As can be seen in this chapter, curators at the Smithsonian Institution have met the challenge of exhibiting computer-based technology with agility by using museum techniques and strategies that, in fact, already existed within the organization. As the examination of the *DigiLab* exhibit showed us, Graphic Arts Curators are as capable of telling the story of digitization as a curator of Computer History. As can be seen across the museum sector worldwide, the curatorial teams choose to exhibit computer-based technology regardless of their academic specialties, such as Bonnie Campbell Lilienfeld's engaging with the display of the iPod in *American Stories*. In these examples, when confronted with the "black box" of the computer, especially in an unfamiliar and sometimes unprecedented format, these curators looked circumspectly to colleagues and other expert practitioners in the organization from whom they could learn and draw guidance. Yet, crucially, these curators also in some cases trusted the technical savvy of their audience – and in doing so, conceptualized an extended network and body of expertise. This distributive expertise was seen in the way the *American Stories* exhibit team presented the iPod in a manner that acknowledged their visitors' technological savvy and familiarity with the device, as well as in the recognition that the Curators of the Graphic Arts Collection gave to expert practitioners in the field when confronted with the challenge of digital printing.

Curators in the Smithsonian utilize these types of curatorial expertise to meet the difficulties posed by the "black box." Both here and in Chapter 4, curators have risen to the challenge of collecting computer technology, in terms of both collecting and exhibition. This then creates a precedent for other curators, now and in the future, at the Smithsonian and beyond, to follow. Indeed, with such wealth of examples of curating computer technology, this study might, in turn, be able to trace patterns that inform a wider model of curatorial expertise specifically tailored to computer-based technology. The ramifications of this will be examined more closely in the next chapter.

Notes

1 It is important to note that exhibition development is a highly collaborative process between curators, museum educators, exhibit designers, and others. To focus in this chapter on the role that the curator plays is not meant in any way to diminish the significance of the exhibition team. For an example of a closer examination of this dynamic, please see: Sharon Macdonald, *Behind the Scenes at the Science Museum* (Oxford: Berg, 2002).

2 David Allison, Smithsonian Institution Archives, Computer Technology and Curation Oral History Interviews, interview with Petrina Foti, August 12, 2013.

3 Paul Ceruzzi, *A History of Modern Computing* (Cambridge, MA: MIT Press, 2003), x.

4 It should be noted that both *American Stories* and *Time and Navigation* currently have no closing dates. *American Stories* was originally scheduled to be opened during the Museum's ongoing West Wing renovation, while *Time and Navigation* was developed to be a "permanent" exhibition.

5 Helena Wright, Smithsonian Institution Archives, Computer Technology and Curation Oral History Interviews, interview with Petrina Foti, August 5, 2013.

6 Helena Wright, Smithsonian Institution Archives, Computer Technology and Curation Oral History Interviews, interview with Petrina Foti, August 5, 2013.

7 William S. Walker, *A Living Exhibition* (Boston: University of Massachusetts Press, 2013) 227.

8 Helena Wright, Smithsonian Institution Archives, Computer Technology and Curation Oral History Interviews, interview with Petrina Foti, August 5, 2013.
9 Helena Wright, "DigiLab: Final Script" (July 8, 1999), National Museum of American History Graphic Arts Collection, Exhibit Files, DigiLab.
10 Simon J. Knell, *Museums and the Future of Collecting* (Aldershot: Ashgate, 2004) 33–34.
11 Helena Wright, "DigiLab: Final Script" (July 8, 1999), National Museum of American History Graphic Arts Collection, Exhibit Files, DigiLab.
12 David Allison, Smithsonian Institution Archives, Computer Technology and Curation Oral History Interviews, interview with Petrina Foti, August 12, 2013.
13 Harold Wallace, Smithsonian Institution Archives, Computer Technology and Curation Oral History Interviews, interview with Petrina Foti, August 14, 2013.
14 Helena Wright, Smithsonian Institution Archives, Computer Technology and Curation Oral History Interviews, interview with Petrina Foti, August 5, 2013.
15 David Allison, Smithsonian Institution Archives, Computer Technology and Curation Oral History Interviews, interview with Petrina Foti, August 12, 2013.
16 Helena Wright, Smithsonian Institution Archives, Computer Technology and Curation Oral History Interviews, interview with Petrina Foti, August 5, 2013.
17 Ceruzzi was asked to formally review the exhibition script. See: National Museum of American History Graphic Arts Collection, Exhibit Files, DigiLab.
18 Helena Wright, Smithsonian Institution Archives, Computer Technology and Curation Oral History Interviews, interview with Petrina Foti, August 5, 2013.
19 National Museum of American History. "September 11: Bearing Witness to History," Smithsonian Institution, accessed June 5, 2012, http://americanhistory.si.edu/september11/collen/curatctioors.asp
20 Helena Wright, Smithsonian Institution Archives, Computer Technology and Curation Oral History Interviews, interview with Petrina Foti, August 5, 2013.
21 Helena Wright, Smithsonian Institution Archives, Computer Technology and Curation Oral History Interviews, interview with Petrina Foti, August 5, 2013.
22 Helena Wright, "DigiLab: Final Script" (July 8, 1999), National Museum of American History Graphic Arts Collection, Exhibit Files, DigiLab.
23 National Museum of American History. Accession Record 2008.0185, National Museum of American History, Office of the Registrar, Registration Services Records.
24 "Collections Committee Memorandum" (December 1, 2005), National Museum of American History. Accession Record 2008.0185, National Museum of American History, Office of the Registrar, Registration Services Records.
25 National Museum of American History, Accession File 2002.0251, National Museum of American History Computers Collection.
26 Carlene Stephens, Smithsonian Institution Archives, Computer Technology and Curation Oral History Interviews, interview with Petrina Foti, September 23, 2013.
27 Paul Ceruzzi, Smithsonian Institution Archives, Computer Technology and Curation Oral History Interviews, interview with Petrina Foti, June 1, 2017.
28 Carlene Stephens, Smithsonian Institution Archives, Computer Technology and Curation Oral History Interviews, interview with Petrina Foti, September 23, 2013.

29 Carlene Stephens, Smithsonian Institution Archives, Computer Technology and Curation Oral History Interviews, interview with Petrina Foti, September 23, 2013.
30 Part of this simple approach was due to time constraints, to ensure that "Stanley" would be exhibited before the museum closed for renovations in 2006.
31 "Draft IPAC/IPRC Proposal" (February 1, 2006). Accession Record 2008.0185, National Museum of American History Office of the Registrar, Registration Services Records.
32 Carlene Stephens, Smithsonian Institution Archives, Computer Technology and Curation Oral History Interviews, interview with Petrina Foti, September 23, 2013.
33 Carlene Stephens, Smithsonian Institution Archives, Computer Technology and Curation Oral History Interviews, interview with Petrina Foti, September 23, 2013.
34 National Museum of American History, Mimsy XG Database, Object Records (accessed July 2013).
35 Text Panel, *Time and Navigation*, visited May 20, 2014.
36 Paul Ceruzzi, Smithsonian Institution Archives, Computer Technology and Curation Oral History Interviews, interview with Petrina Foti, July 24, 2013.
37 Paul Ceruzzi, Smithsonian Institution Archives, Computer Technology and Curation Oral History Interviews, interview with Petrina Foti, July 24, 2013.
38 Paul Ceruzzi, Smithsonian Institution Archives, Computer Technology and Curation Oral History Interviews, interview with Petrina Foti, July 24, 2013.
39 Paul Ceruzzi, Smithsonian Institution Archives, Computer Technology and Curation Oral History Interviews, interview with Petrina Foti, July 24, 2013.
40 Smithsonian Institution, "Exhibitions: American Stories," Smithsonian Institution, accessed July 1, 2014, www.si.edu/Exhibitions/Details/American-Stories-244.
41 Stevan Fisher, Smithsonian Institution Archives, Computer Technology and Curation Oral History Interviews, interview with Petrina Foti, August 5, 2013.
42 Stevan Fisher, Smithsonian Institution Archives, Computer Technology and Curation Oral History Interviews, interview with Petrina Foti, August 5, 2013.
43 This is the same iPod that we discussed in Chapter 1. However, I did not play any role in the development of the *American Stories* exhibition, though Campbell Lilienfeld was my supervisor at the time.
44 The iPod remains on view in a different exhibition, located in the newly renovated West Wing. This emphasizes that the purpose of *American Stories* to represented objects and stories that would not be available during the renovation.
45 The National Museum of American History began a phased reopening of the West Wing of the museum starting in 2015.
46 Bonnie Campbell Lilienfeld, Smithsonian Institution Archives, Computer Technology and Curation Oral History Interviews, interview with Petrina Foti, April 26, 2013.
47 Bonnie Campbell Lilienfeld, Smithsonian Institution Archives, Computer Technology and Curation Oral History Interviews, interview with Petrina Foti, April 26, 2013.
48 Bonnie Campbell Lilienfeld, Smithsonian Institution Archives, Computer Technology and Curation Oral History Interviews, interview with Petrina Foti, April 26, 2013.

49 Stevan Fisher, Smithsonian Institution Archives, Computer Technology and Curation Oral History Interviews, interview with Petrina Foti, August 5, 2013.
50 Owain Rhys, *Contemporary Collecting: Theory and Practice* (Edinburgh: Museums Etc, 2011) 17.
51 Stevan Fisher, Smithsonian Institution Archives, Computer Technology and Curation Oral History Interviews, interview with Petrina Foti, August 5, 2013.
52 Bonnie Campbell Lilienfeld, Smithsonian Institution Archives, Computer Technology and Curation Oral History Interviews, interview with Petrina Foti, April 26, 2013.
53 Bonnie Campbell Lilienfeld, Smithsonian Institution Archives, Computer Technology and Curation Oral History Interviews, interview with Petrina Foti, April 26, 2013.

6 Internal processing

The methods of curating computer-based technology

Introduction

As seen in Chapter 2, Tilly Blyth, Head of Collections and Principal Curator for the Science Museum (London), in her edited volume *Information Age: Six Networks That Changed Our World*, explained that

> museums acquire material culture as evidence, as tangible proof of technological change. But information – the bits and data – is insubstantial. When the machines are turned off, the messages cease to flow, information disappears. It is the machines, the hardware, that lives on, providing the only proof of the form of change and the lives previously touched through information and communication technology. The material culture of information – floppy discs, CDs, Morse tapes, punched tap – can all be displayed, but the information they contain is invisible, sometimes undecodable, lost to history like momentary thought.[1]

From digital music to born-digital photographs, from computer code to internet communication, through the course of this study, the "insubstantial" digital aspect computer-based technology and the information contained therein have played a large role. Ross Parry, as part of a larger discussion about the adoption of the computer by the museum sector as an information management system and as a communication device, notes that

> Digital Media (like any media) is anything but a neutral vessel. Instead of passively and objectively carrying and migrating content, digital technology contributes its own set of connotations and inferences for the user. Consequently, to decide to convey an idea using a computer is also to decide (implicitly) to cast this idea within another set of meanings associated with computing. In short – *if it is not too evident to say so* – digital media becomes part of the message.[2]

Parry reminds us that when a museum opts to use computer technology as a means for communication, such as a museum interactive, that choice might prompt a different response from museum visitors than a familiar manual interactive might. Parry's observations can be expanded beyond the use of computer technology in museums to include the history of computer-based technology being recorded by museums. In Chapter 2, Simon Knell reminded us that all collecting can be considered as contemporary collecting since what the museum has deemed significant enough to preserve is a reflection of the values and perspectives of the curatorial staff who completed the acquisitioning. The contemporary collected objects in a museum's holdings serve as both barometer and mirror to measure and reflect a culture's response. By observing how these Smithsonian museums have chosen to respond to computing, a deeper perspective on how society currently views and values this technology is gained.

In particular, the number of curators who were driven to record the impact of computer-based technology as part of their disciplines' individual narrative suggests how pervasive computer technology has become. From DNA analyzers to music synthesizers, from solid-state electronic ballasts to born-digital photographs, from the laptop used during the filming of the television show *Sex and the City* to "Stanley" the autonomous robot vehicle, the sheer diversity of the many forms of computer-based technology objects is evidence of this. It is now clear precisely what Robert Leopold meant in Chapter 2 when he said: "I believe that it is not only easy to collect computer-based technology, I think [museums] do it all the time. I think that there is no way to stop museums from collecting."[3] A precedent has now been formed, where none previously existed. Through expert curation, the challenge of computer-based technology has been met by the curatorial staff at the Smithsonian with solutions that are adaptive, distributive, and transmitted. These methods of curatorial practices, a number of which have been examined closely, cover a range of disciplines as broad as the Smithsonian itself, but, whether in terms of exhibiting or collecting, most, if not all, can be seen to fall into three primary curatorial methods: *documenting*, *operating*, and *representing*. While these methods should be familiar concepts to museum staff worldwide, as they have long been established as part of general museum practice, these methods take on new dimensions when applied to computer-based technology. The documenting method, as the name implies, is the act of recording the technological development of the machine that we call a "computer." The operating method allows software to perform in a way that emulates the user experience (usually by running on a historic machine). The representing method goes beyond simple cases where hardware is substituted for software to engage with computer-based technology in metaphoric terms.

These curatorial methods should not be considered exclusionary. Indeed, all three methods can be seen in the Computer History Museum's "Make Software: Change the World!" exhibition (opened January 28, 2017). The exhibition presents a wide range of computer hardware – from early cell phones to MRIs – that document the history of software development. As a practical demonstration, working computers have been placed throughout the exhibition allowing visitors to do such things as learn to code, edit a Wikipedia article, or engage with an early example of Photoshop software. In the section devoted to the video game *World of Warcraft* where a such interactivity would require too steep a learning curve, a large screen shows a video of recorded game play, allowing visitors who may never have played the game to visually experience it, which, as will be explored, is also a type of operating method. Finally, as will be examined more closely with the representing method, the curatorial team employed a series of creative and, at times, unexpected objects to serve as metaphor for complex concepts. These three methods are tools that the curator employs depending on the circumstances, not an uncompromising system of structures to which practice must rigidly adhere.

Taken together, what these methods indicate is that, more than merely a precedent, this is perhaps the establishment of a curatorial tradition for computer-based technology in History Collections at the Smithsonian museum. By extending our study to include curatorial practices at the Science Museum in London and the Computer History Museum in California, there is evidence that this curatorial tradition has universal application wherever and whenever a museum might choose to curate computer-based technology.

Documenting method

With the documenting method, in terms of both collecting and exhibiting, museum artifacts relating to computer-based technology serve as evidence within a specific framework of history of pioneering developments, inventions, and breakthroughs. As examined in Chapter 2, the majority of museums are focused on their collection and are driven to collect "because of the belief that objects are important and evocative survivals of human civilization worthy of careful study" in order to "preserve their holdings so as to transmit important information to the present generation and to posterity."[4] Curators, while more comfortable collecting with the distance of time, often choose to collect contemporaneously out of concern that materials that are so readily available now will be difficult for their successors to secure. This drive, at least partially, is likely motivated by the need to document – to provide evidence for the future – of these historic events. With this framework, the National Museum of American History's Ralph Baer video games prototypes seen in Chapter 3 and the museum's Microsoft Windows NT OS/2 Design Workbook from Chapter 4 are both examples of the documenting method. These objects give testament to historic milestones and achievements.

Many computer history exhibitions, both past and present, trace the roots of computer-based technology to early mechanical computers, such as Charles Babbage's difference engine, or as far back as forms of calculation such as abaci. Tilly Blyth notes in her article "Exhibiting Information: Developing the Information Age Gallery at the Science Museum" that "most exhibitions on computing created during the 1970s responded to the euphoria and excitement surrounding the new computational machines of the day. Often they were developed as marketing and promotional tools, commissioned by the computing companies themselves."[5] Many of the early computer exhibitions at the Smithsonian follow such a celebratory narrative as well, presenting computers that represent significant technological innovations, such as the Atlas Computer, the IAS Machine, or ENIAC, as iconic objects and technological marvels. This sense of importance can often be highlighted by either the exhibit's transitory nature or, in the other extreme, its permanent display. This is illustrated with the loan of the Atlas Computer to the Smithsonian for temporary exhibition. Here the Atlas became a physical representation of a moment of technological progress and the limited time in which to view the Atlas only reinforced the significance of that moment. Likewise, the fact that portions of ENIAC have been on display at the National Museum of American History for the majority of the time since the Museum first opened evidences the object's change from technological milestone to museum treasure. In terms of exhibiting using the documenting method, display techniques can offer complex, interpretive labeling, but they also can be quite simple, with the artifacts standing as mute evidence, as was the case with the Computer History Museum's *Visible Storage* exhibition, as examined in Chapter 2. Hansen Hsu, Curator for the Computer History Museum's Center for Software History, notes that

> There are ways to exhibit computer technology that are not that difficult. One way, as we do in our museum, in our main exhibit is just to exhibit them as artifacts, as just dead items sitting on a shelf. That is the traditional museum way. That is fairly easy, I think... Putting a box on a self is the easiest thing that people can do and it is probably the least resource intensive.[6]

This echoes the words of Harold Wallace in Chapter 2, when he explained that exhibiting computer-based technology was easy "in some respects" because there are physical objects "that you can put in a showcase that people can look at and relate to." But, as was also seen, he then went on to note that computer technology was not intuitive in that "you cannot see the electrons running around and the ones and zeroes flopping back and forth."[7] In order for the documenting method to work effectively on exhibition, there must be some way of presenting the software. Marc Weber, the Curatorial Director for the Internet History Program at the Computer History, notes that

> a weakness of all computers, is that, if they are turned off, it can get very dull to look at a lot of gray screens, particularly with mobile [technology]. Look at an iPhone. As we have gone to the full screen format,

> there is not a whole lot going on if [mobile device] switched off. So, one of the things that we did in "Mobile" was to find a balance. You go to the phone store. They used to fake it up with a sticker that would show you a screenshot. We are not going to do that, because it is so obviously fake. So, the compromise is, behind a lot of those PDAs and various hand-held and portable computers, there is some picture frames with rotating images of the screenshots. So at least it gives you a taste of what these things would do when they were alive. But it is that borderline between you do not want to mock up something that is fake. On the other hand, you do not want to show [something] completely dead.[8]

Weber applies his adaptive expertise as he evaluates the various options to present the software on exhibit, settling on the one that made the most sense in context. In keeping with the documenting method, Weber's solution uses "screenshots" of the mobile technology in operation as evidence of what the software could do.

It is important to note Weber's concern in presenting "something that is fake." While museums are concerned with the authenticity of their objects, when the artifact in question is an example of a historical technology, there an increased responsibility to maintains the object's integrity. As previously seen, Tilly Blyth has stated that "museums acquire material culture as evidence."[9] She further explains:

> I think when you have an original artifact, it is actually really important to try to maintain that as an original artifact for visitors so it can be used as a historical record in the future. Because I may be here, for the next ten years, twenty years, but in a hundred years who is going to know what the changes were that were made? In 200 years, are people going to be looking at that wondering "well, what does it really represent?"[10]

With the documenting method, the object is evidence and therefore, as Blyth clarifies, the object must be physically preserved. Blyth also reveals a strong sense of transmitted expertise in her concern about what will be preserved for her successors. Reflecting on her own experience at the Science Museum, she explains:

> I have enormous respect for my predecessors. Not least for the incredible collections that they have left us with and the wonderful objects that we have to work with. It never ceases to amaze me when I think "Oh, I really would like an object that would help me tell this story. I wonder if we have one of those." And then you look up and go "Oh, my god! Of course, we have!" It is incredible that they knew what we were trying to think about. I have incredible respect for the work of my processors. Going forward? Will I leave the legacy that they have left me

> with? I will be very, very proud if I even leave it with half the legacy that they have left us with.[11]

Blyth's words emphasize the importance in continuing the strong curatorial legacy that she inherited from her predecessors. This transmitted expertise has shaped how she views the objects in her collection, since they exist not only for the needs of the present, but also for the possible needs of the future.

Another striking example of transmitted expertise can be seen in the American History Museum's Electricity Collection. In the late 1990s, Curator Harold Wallace led a collecting initiative from the American company General Electric. Among the items he acquired were examples of lighting design software. Wallace explains:

> I collected a bunch of archival material and one of the set of pieces that I brought back were these several examples of lighting design software from the early 1990s, where General Electric is putting together the software packages so that specifiers and lighting designers can use their product and get the most out of the technical designs of their products. So, we have floppy discs and we have some paper describing the programs and so forth. But is it really an object? ... Because by themselves they are just cute little pieces of plastic with magnetic recording medium. But there is data on those disks that is important to the history of lighting design, this transition from the pure drafting table version of lighting design into the CADCAM world of automation. And so, potentially this is a set of really good objects. But how do we get that information off of there in a meaningful way?[12]

Interestingly, in this instance, a curator is using the documenting method to preserve software. Wallace understands that while he might not currently have a way of accessing the information, future technological developments might provide the means to record the computer code in a way that is more understandable, or "meaningful" to use Wallace's term. And so, he collected these artifacts in anticipation of such a time. Wallace likened it to the work of fellow curator Carlene Stevens into the 1880s glass disc recordings of Alexander Graham Bell.[13] These recordings were created as test experiments for a new emerging technology, and, therefore, there was no way, at the time, to be able to play back what was recorded. However, in 2011, in collaboration with the Library of Congress and the Lawrence Berkeley National Laboratory, the National Museum of American History was able to recover the sound.[14] This research led to the exhibit *"Hear My Voice": Alexander Graham Bell and the Origins of Recorded Sound* (January 26, 2015 to October 25, 2015). This technological triumph illustrates the potential benefits to Wallace's collecting for future use. Unlike with the Computer Collection's emphasis on the "software media," as seen in Chapter 4, for the Electricity Collection, the importance of the lighting software acquisition is in the software itself. In this instance, for this institution, for this curator, within the specific frame of reference and value set in this context, the outside container of the objects appears as less important. This is a striking example of transmitted expertise, with a curator thinking about the future and capabilities that might someday be possible and that expertise driving the curatorial approach to documenting that object. It is also important to note how different curators with different collection needs might find different solutions even within the same museum.

At the Computer History Museum, a similar transmitted expertise is at work in service of the Museum's mission. Dag Spicer, Senior Curator for the Computer History Museum, explains:

> A big part of what the museum does is what I call the "Noah's Ark" mission, which is to send an ark full of our culture's computing legacy into the future. We deal with 500-year timelines at the museum, whereby we hope that someone 500 years from now can piece together the intellectual and material legacy of the computer age. So, in a way, we are doing it on faith.[15]

The Museum's mission to document "our culture's computing legacy" has resulted in a large collection of both hardware and software. The software is of particular note, since, as previously examined in Chapter 4, it is often difficult to collect in a way that is meaningful. David Brock, Director of the Center for Software History at the Computer History Museum, notes that

> it is in every single form that software takes. There is two big categories: source code and executable code. Source code is code that a person wrote, or at least co-wrote with some other sort of system, and executable code is a transformation of that into code that a machine can more directly understand and perform. Those genres of software take myriad forms. So, source code can be printouts, also sometimes called listings or dumps. That can be of paper of any sort of variety you can imagine. That source code can also be encoded onto different media: punched paper cards, punched paper tape, all forms of magnetic media, hard disks, floppy disks of all shapes and sizes, magnetic tape, semiconductor devices like ROMs or PROMs, cartridges. In our collection, we have every form of data storage medium.[16]

It might be helpful to pause here to appreciate the many forms that a software "container" might take. This serves as a reminder of the sheer amount of digital technology that exists. For every example of computer hardware, there are multiple examples of related software. Brock confirms that "there is just a lot out there" and adds "there is no way that we could ever hope to be completionist, because it is fractal. You are never going to get there."[17] In many respects, the variety of software formats is similar to those found in the National Museum of American History, primarily in the Computers Collection. However, the Computer History Museum takes an extra precaution in its documentation. Spicer explains the collection management process for a newly accessioned piece of software:

> If it is shrink-wrapped or comes in a box, we will leave it in the box. We will keep the disks. They will be physically removed from the box, though, for preservation reasons and be moved into our media archive, which is a very cold refrigerated room where all our magnetic media, not just video, but software is kept. And photographed as well… For software distributed on floppy disk, for example, we use a thing called a KryoFlux, which is a device that makes a perfect bit-for-bit copy of the medium. We then take that disk image and store it.[18]

Just as the physical software disks are removed from their retail boxes for conservation reasons, by creating a digital copy of the donated software, the Computer History Museum has taken the precaution that effectively removes the software from its container – usually plastic – that might become compromised in the future, corrupting the software in the process.

The key concern for curators who collect software using the documenting method is how to make the information that is contained in a digital format accessible in a way that is useful and comprehensible for the future. Robert Leopold, Deputy Director of the Smithsonian Center for Folklife, notes:

> While born digital collections are easier to search, they are not "eye legible." It is not like you if you find a floppy disk in a folder, you can know what that is. File naming conventions present other obstacles. Sometime a file is named something that is obscure or does not indicate – or sometimes falsifies – what it is, because people write over things and change their minds. There is both transparency and obscurity in digital media that presents different challenges to archivists, but then it presents different opportunities to archivists as well.[19]

Leopold's understanding is based on his experience as an Archivist and former Director of the Smithsonian's National Anthropological Archives and Human Studies Film Archives. He explains:

> My own experience is as an archivist and is as a director to an anthropological archive and, in our case, we were collecting the research product of anthropologists and others that conducted research that would be of interest to anthropologists. Obviously, that material was produced digitally after a certain point. So that, at one point in our archives' history, a large percentage of the collections that we acquired were born digital or hybrid collections, including born-digital material and analog material as well… The very first time I acquired [born digital materials],

> I recognize that the archive that I was working in – that [was based on a collection that] was founded in the nineteenth century – had no guidelines or procedures for the acquisition of digital materials and I recognized that I was going to need to write those myself.[20]

Leopold's first experience was with a donation that contained digital files, which was challenging both in preservation and in accessibility.

> [The anthropologist] had conducted all of his research using a Mac. This was circa 1990. So, none of the word processing applications he had used to produce his field notes were in existence. If you called them up into a latter-day word processing program, you got a lot of machine code looking stuff. They were not formatted the way that he had format them. You saw printing instructions embedded in them and things like that. So, I recognized that these need to be both preserved in their original form – that is what archivists do – and migrated to another application… I had questions in my mind about the fidelity to the original and whether the translation program was actually making a translation that was true to what the original looked like.[21]

Leopold's experience demonstrates the difficulty that born-digital media present from an archival standpoint and how this might relate to the museum field. Though museum and archival collections differ in many ways, their concerns for the structural integrity of their holdings are the same.

In the documenting method curators approach computer-based technology as an object. The software is seen as inseparable from the hardware. Like the intact filament of a working lightbulb, the software is an integral part of the object, but it is rendered inaccessible without electricity. But, as has been previously noted, software plays a critical role both in terms of computer history and in our own daily lives. So, curators seek other means to preserve software in collection storage and present it on the exhibition floor. The question then becomes one of how to represent the software on exhibition or in collections, when there is no affiliated hardware or in cases when the hardware does not convey all that computers encompass. This will be explored more closely with the operating method.

Operating method

It is impossible not to see the evidence of how software has shaped modern society from the overtly obvious, such as the regularly updated operating system software in our handheld devices, to the easily overlooked such as the humble yet ubiquitous word processing program. The operating method is based on the belief that the software must be experienced in order for a museum visitor to truly be able to comprehend it. More than just a static object, computer-based technology requires interactivity. Hansen Hsu,

Curator for the Computer History Museum's Center for Software History, notes that

> there are cases where we do want to provide some form of access or try to get some software running on either emulation or vintage machine. And that is because we have a large collection of software. We can collect the physical media or we can collect can collect the source code and just sit it on a shelf or read the code, [but] it does not really convey the experience of using the software. The software needs to be run. It needs to be performed in order for it to come alive. In order for any sort of cultural understand of the software. And a lot of software is a medium of some form, especially nowadays, that needs to be experienced. So, it has to be run, in order to be experienced.[22]

Demonstrating how computer technology is used can offer a dynamic way of presenting software and for museums such as the Living Computers Museum[23] in Seattle, Washington, or the National Museum of Computing[24] in Bletchley Park, United Kingdom, it is their primary means of display. Working computer-based technology on a museum exhibition floor might take many forms. The National Museum of Emerging Science and Innovation, more commonly known as the Miraikan, in Tokyo, Japan, has daily robot demonstrations and working androids on permanent exhibition.[25] Museums such as the Living Computers Museum or the Centre for Computing History[26] in Cambridge, United Kingdom, offer visitors "hands-on" experiences allowing them to use historic machines. However, this level of interactivity is not always a feasible solution for large museums. At the National Museum of American History, for example, the number of visitors in one day can range in the thousands. To cater to such large numbers, exhibits must at least be partially dependent on visual display. In these cases, a popular approach would be to present a video of the software in use, similar to the screenshots that Weber used in the Mobile Gallery at the Computer History Museum. In a more dramatic method a working computer is demonstrated on the floor of the museum by trained museum docents.[27] Examples of the latter can be seen with the Computer History Museum's "Demo Labs" for the collection's IBM 1401 computer and DEC PDP-1 minicomputer. *DigiLab*, as examined in Chapter 5, also contained an element of the operating method with the Digitization Lab, though the rest of the exhibition more closely adhered to the documenting method. Live demonstrations have the additional benefit of featuring not just the computers, but knowledge and skills of the trained museum docents. Weber explains:

> Yes, you can put people in front of a live working IMB Mainframe. And what does that tell them? They do not know how to use it. Like our 1401 which is not quite a mainframe but similar kind of uses or similar

user interface, meaning it is not ready for the general public. That we have docents who run through it and explain it.[28]

Weber's words highlight how distributive expertise plays a vital role in operating method. Computer technology before the age of personal computing was not what a visitor today would understand to be "user friendly," nor are these computers that might be easily operated alone. A modern visitor would not to be able to navigate these computers without training. The computer interface would be unfamiliar and the techniques required to operate such a computer would be too dissimilar to those that are required today for visitors to grasp intuitively. Therefore, it is the expertise of the gallery docents – an expertise that the curator may not necessarily have – that allows the computer to operate.

Another interesting example of a working computer on exhibit would be the Ferranti Pegasus computer that was on display at the Science Museum in London. The Ferranti Pegasus (usually referred to simply as Pegasus) was an early commercial British computer. According to the object records available on the museum's website, Pegasus computers were utilized "in banks, universities, and engineering and research establishments. For most of these organisations and their staff Pegasus was their first computer, and therefore the herald of a new age."[29] The University College London donated their Pegasus to the Science Museum in 1983. Tilly Blyth explains:

> We had a project from the early 1990s to get that machine running with the Computer Conservation Society. They were very keep on demonstrating the machines and running machines. The Pegasus seemed like a very good contender for that because it is from that early stage of 1950s digital electronic machines. There was still a strong cohort of engineers who understood it. They loved running it and working with it. And they liked the opportunity to do that for visitors and demonstrate that for visitors. So again, that was on display during the 1990s and through to early 2000s, until it became, we felt, unsafe for it to be continued to be demonstrated and displayed in that way.[30]

The Science Museum's use of expert volunteers to run the computer is similar to the demonstrations at the Computer History Museum, where the computer technicians also serve as gallery interpreters. The majority of the volunteers were retired computer engineers who worked on similar machines during the course of their careers. Operating the Ferranti Pegasus computer gave them an opportunity once again to do something that they had enjoyed and to be able to discuss it with others who were interested. One such volunteer, Rodney Brown, in a video about Pegasus produced by the Science Museum, notes:

> It is very, very easy, in this day and age, to forget these first-generation computers. Computers of this type have very specific lessons that can be learnt by younger generations. This machine has been not only fun to maintain, but it's been fun to demonstrate.[31]

Brown's words convey both the enjoyment and value that working computers provided both museum staff and visitors alike.[32] Blyth concurs:

> There is something about a computer that is working that explains itself in a way that a non-working or dead machine does not. For me, it was always wonderful to have the Pegasus machine when it was running. Visitors were really interested. Not just for the "what's it doing?" but for the physical experience. What does it sound like? What does it smell like? What is it that people do around it? What are these men and women doing when they are programming this computer? Seeing the punch tape go in and come out. All of those things were a great experience for visitors to really help them understand that kind of fledgling industry and the birth of digital electronic machines in the 1950s. It was a wonderful thing that we could do that. However, electronics get old. Capacitors leak and valves expire.[33]

Blyth's observations highlight how distributive expertise plays an important role in the demonstration method. The working computers, especially mainframes and minicomputers, require expert knowledge on how to operate and care for these large machines, expertise that the Museum would not have on staff. So, curators turn to the men and women who would have that knowledge to share in the Museum's goal to help their visitors understand the history of computer technology.

Yet Blyth also identifies the major detriment to the operating method. Machines are not able to run forever. Eventually, they will break. As Hansen Hsu notes:

> It gets more complicated when you want to exhibit say software or you want to exhibit a running computer, because then, if the computer is running, it will break down and it will require maintenance, which changes the artifact itself. So, you have to be very careful about that, what changes you make. Computers do not have an infinite life.[34]

Curators who wish to follow the operating model must evaluate the benefits of the demonstration method against the possible collection management concerns. For some, the risk is too great. As seen in Chapter 4, allowing the objects the National Museum of American History's Computers Collection to be operated, as a general rule, was not deemed practical or sustainable by the collection's curatorial staff. David Allison notes that historic machines, we tend not to run. We have occasionally turned them on if we know for sure that the circuits are trustworthy and we are supervised, but by and large we do not have that technical expertise on staff – we do not have electrical engineers that can check the wiring and all that kind of thing, so it is rare that we actually operate something.[35]

Again, there is a focus on distributive expertise. The National Museum of American History will not run historic computers without the expert knowledge of former and current computer engineers. These concerns were further reinforced by the Museum's own history. In 1970, while the Museum was closed, a working computer terminal on exhibit sparked a fire that caused smoke and water damage to the surrounding exhibitions. The computer terminal itself was destroyed before the fire could be contained.[36] While modern fire abatement would certainly mitigate such a risk, this dramatic point of history shows the hazards that come with running electricity-powered museum objects such as computers. In fact, it was the threat of fire that ultimately forced the Science Museum to reconsider the operating method. Blyth recollects:

One day [in 2009], we had a group of volunteers who were there running the machine. We [had] fitted it with smoke detectors. And so, there was a very slight smoldering and one of the smoke detectors picked that up straight away and we shut down the machine. Our control room picked that up and said "there's a problem, close down the machine."[37]

Unlike with the fire at the American History Museum, the Science Museum was able to prevent any damage to human and machine alike through good collection care procedures, but the ramifications of the narrowly avoided disaster could not be ignored. Blyth explains:

We looked at if we could run it again and we worked very closely with the volunteers to see whether it would be possible to do that safely. But it was our belief that actually it was just too risky. First of all, too risky for the machine, because actually you are dealing with a lot of old wiring and a lot of old components. That presents some problems. And then it is too risky for the building and the public. So, I think we did come to the right decision.[38]

While the safety of visitors and staff is paramount, there was also a philosophical rationale, one that shows Blyth demonstrating her transmitted expertise. Reflecting on the decision, she elaborates:

It actually came back to the kind of fundamentals of why as a curator you acquire historical artifacts and to me they are a type of evidence. They are historical evidence. And actually, yes, we could have kept that

> machine running. We could have taken out some of the wiring and put in new wiring and replace some components with new components. But then at what point are you just displaying a replica, really? At what point is it the original historic machine that you are showing to visitors or at what point are you showing something that is a weird hybrid.[39]

Blyth's words echo Hsu's observations that "if the computer is running, it will break down and it will require maintenance, which changes the artifact itself."[40] Blyth further notes that if Pegasus had been repaired in order to keep operating, then the computer "represents something that has been completely, internally changed and, the tacit knowledge that exists with those volunteers, it will not be there in the future, but the artifact still will."[41] Earlier, Blyth stated that importance of preserving original artifacts in order for them to be "used as a historical record in the future."[42] One can now see the practical implications of that belief. It is also significant how the Science Museum shifted its curatorial approach from the demonstration method to the documentation method, as the needs of the object changed.

Before Pegasus was officially retired from use, the Science Museum filmed the computer and the expert volunteers who operated it. Tilly Blyth notes:

> We did a short film with [the expert volunteers], because we wanted to mark the moment and mark the considerable time and their experience and knowledge that they had with the object. So, we made a film with them. We put that up on the internet and made a bit of a thing about it, because it was a passing of that moment and it was slightly sad not to be able to demonstrate it.[43]

This recording means that a document demonstrating how the computer operated has been preserved for the future, even if the computer will never run again. In many ways, the decision that Blyth faced with Pegasus is similar to how curators at the American History Museum approach the instruments in the Museum's Music Collection. Like computer hardware, musical instruments can be displayed easily in an exhibit case. However, as with computer software, museum visitors would not be able to get a sense of how the instrument might sound. For that, the instrument must be played and this is one of the reasons the American History Museum's Music Collection will occasionally invite musicians to play the instruments in their collection. Stacy Kluck, one of the Music Collection Curators as well as Chair for the Culture and the Arts Division, explains the criteria used to decide which instruments will be played:

> It really depends on the condition of the object. Same thing with whether it is electrified or non-electrified. We have to look at the condition of the object. How stable is it? Can it withstand being played? Once we make that assessment, we determine how often we want to

> use these instruments. Not only be putting into playing condition, but maintaining it, because musical instruments are meant to be played. Do we just want to do one a one-off thing and then never play it again? If that is the case, especially given the fragility of the object, as long as it is stable, I think we can make it work for a short period of time.[44]

Kluck frames a system for assessing whether or not the objects in his collection should be played. Yet, such a performance is transitory in nature. This trait is somewhat at odds with the museum's need to preserve for the future. Kluck acknowledges this, noting:

> At the same time, we need to document that somehow. Certainly, recorded audio tape, videotape, photography, that sort of thing, so we can document what has been going on, what is happening, and to be able to tell that story. But it is really long-term maintenance of collections. Is it something that it is interesting right now or is this something that maybe future generations will still be interested in? Certainly, the violin is still around. The harpsichord and pianos are still around. It is hard to say with newer instruments, with electronic instruments, how stable are they for future use. Do we need to record them? Do we need to somehow take the object and save what we can for future generations?[45]

Kluck identifies many of the same concerns expressed by both Blyth and Allison in regard to running computer technology in their collections. Like their counterparts in the Music Collection, curatorial staff in the Computers Collection at American History have evaluated the risk of running their artifacts and, in this instance, have determined that operating the computer artifacts would not be the best use of resources, and so static "software media" remain the preferred form of collecting software. With the Pegasus computer, the Science Museum ultimately decided to preserve the artifact as evidence to transmit to the future. But understanding that the ability to see the computer in operation would also be, as Kluck frames, "something that future generation will still be interested in," the museum also chose to record the computer while it was still operating.

Hansen Hsu noted earlier that software "needs to be performed in order for it to come alive."[46] After a comparison to the Curators in the Music Collection at the National Museum of American History, it is clear how this is an apt description. Curator David Brock wrote in an article about the Computer History Museum's Center for Software History:

> Computer programs are inherently performative. People create code so that a computer might run it. The fullest meaning of software can be found in its performance, which presents great challenges and opportunities for software history. At the Center for Software History, we are simultaneously exploring the pursuit of these people-centered stories

and filming software in action to preserve and present software history and its implications to diverse publics.[47]

With this in mind, the operating method perhaps might be better defined as being based on a view that software is, by nature, more like a cultural performance or event than a tangible object. Curators at the Computer History Museum with this view therefore have borrowed from the field of ethnography rather than adapt material culture techniques. Brock explains:

> I came up with this idea that we should do an archival video documentation of the historical software running on the restored equipment with the knowledgeable person showing us around, evoking the dynamic artifact. That archival documentary video footage would itself become a kind of preservation. It is documentation of this thing, because the hardware is going to break eventually, presumably. It could be the only opportunity we have to have that software running on the original equipment. It might not happen again. But this documentation and digital video might survive.[48]

In these videos, the user – often one of the original software engineers – demonstrates how to operate the software using a restored historic machine. In a later interview, Brock noted, "The focus of it has been creating these things as an act of preservation in hope that this capture of that dynamic artifact will find use for interpretation and exhibit."[49] As with the recording of Pegasus, the curators at the Computer History's Center for Software History demonstrate their transmitted expertise in providing a recording of that would benefit future curators and researchers alike. Hsu concurs, noting that, even after the computer has returned to its nonoperational state, video ethnography "will be the artifact [that] will continue to live on."[50] It is also important to note the distributive expertise at work as computer engineers are trusted by the Museum as the authorities on the software that they developed. Brock explains:

> We have talk about doing video ethnographies where we have a curator running a program and speaking about what they are doing, which may be important in cases, which may be necessary in some cases. But to date, we have had access to either people who made [the software] or were significant users for one reason or another. It seemed much more interesting and potentially valuable to have them help create the dynamic artifact and talk about what is going on.[51]

At the Computer History Museum, Curators are using their adaptive expertise by adopting the video ethnography approach to recording software as it is performed. Their distributive expertise is at work as the Curators turn to the software's creators to provide their expert knowledge. Finally, their transmitted expertise has led them to preserve the video ethnographies with the understanding that these will be valuable resources in the future for curators and researchers alike.

The operating method allows computer-based technology to come alive. In Chapter 4, Matilda McQuaid, the Cooper Hewitt's Deputy Curatorial Director, framed the challenges of collecting computer code as "trying to determine what is the best way to preserve [the computer app 'Planetary'], but also keep it active and keep it in the context in which it was collected."[52] Therefore, Cooper Hewitt's decision to open the source code might be considered a variation of the operating method, one that allows the experience of coding to be preserved, albeit outside the museum walls. However, McQuaid also stated that the Cooper Hewitt is "very much process driven so we want to collect everything behind it – behind what you see" and that the Museum's curatorial staff "see process as something very important" and therefore "everything is being driven by that."[53] With this larger context, "Planetary" serves a role much larger role for the museum by representing the process of design. This leads to our third method.

Representing method

The representing method – when a physical object is used as a physical substitute for a complex concept – is perhaps the most common tool that museums employ when faced with the intangible. From the campaign button collected to represent a political movement to a famous pair of red shoes worn by the actress Judy Garland to represent the film industry's adoption of color motion picture processes, the museum has a long tradition of collecting a tangible object as a physical method of representing a concept, event, or school of thought, a representational approach overtly encountered in Chapter 4, with Curators from the National Museum of American History collecting hardware in place of software. However, upon further reflection, it is clear that, in reality, this curatorial approach is more closely aligned with the documenting method. The software in the Computers Collection is historical evidence of both technological milestones in computational history and of the physical object that were used during that particular period. Contrast that with Herbie Hancock's synthesizer and other computerized musical instruments in the Music Collection or the Computer History Museum's BlackBerry used during the September 11 attacks and a different pattern emerges. The early PDA was used by a lawyer who worked at the World Trade Center to contact via text messages all sixteen of his coworkers and confirm that they were safe. While the device certainly could be seen as evidence of increasing adoption of text messaging as a form of communication, this is overshadowed by the role that the computer technology played during September 11. This small, black palm-sized device represents the fear and anxiety of New Yorkers, especially the ones who actually worked at the World Trade Center, as they tried to find information about their missing friends and loved ones. Here, in this instance, computer-based technology is the medium used to convey a deeper insight into a tragic historical event.

With the representing method, museum objects are more than just the testaments to technological progress; they are metaphors to better understand complex social developments. Computer History Museum Curator Dag Spicer explains:

> With, what I call average people, normal, non-technically trained people, you have to appeal to them using stories. The technology itself, while hardly incidental, is merely a catalyst for social change. And that is really what we are trying to get at. Social, political, and economic change. That is what a more mature display of artifacts would comprise. There is some history of technology issues too that you want to address, such as maybe the nature of invention or simultaneous invention. That goes on all the time in computing.[54]

These words are echoed by Tilly Blyth. She explains that in the Science Museum's *Information Age* exhibition, "we tried to do things like tell the stories of the engineers that were developing them" and adds "these things were created by people! It is not just about this abstract thing of the technology."[55] Providing a human connection is an effective way for visitors to relate to a much more complex subject matter. This type of narrative naturally lends itself topics such as "the nature of invention," as Spicer noted. The concept of the "genius inventor" is one that is already familiar to most museum visitors due to stories about people like Thomas Edison or Alexander Graham Bell. Ralph Baer's early video game prototypes, which were first examined in Chapter 3, fit this narrative as well. Since November 2008, the National Museum of American History has featured "large, iconic artifacts in the main corridor of each wing [of the American History Museum] [that] highlight the wing's key exhibition themes"[56] called landmark objects. In 2015, when the Museum reopened the first floor of the recently renovated West Wing, a new landmark object was chosen to represent the wing's theme of invention and innovation – or rather a set of objects were chosen. For this exhibition, entitled *Ralph Baer's Inventor's Workshop* (opened July 1, 2015),[57] the main focus is not the prototypes themselves, but the workshop that Baer used in the basement of his home in Manchester, New Hampshire, which had been reinstalled in the museum. The workshop is not evidence of a moment in time, but rather a visual metaphor for the complex and oftentimes difficult process of invention and creation.

This narrative of invention and innovation of computer-based technology can also be traced in fields more closely associated with the arts. For example, in Chapter 4, Curator Stacy Kluck noted that the accession of Herbie Hancock's synthesizers "captures his changing style of music [and] experimenting with different sounds and different things," which allowed the noted jazz musician to gain new audience by "taking advantage of this new technology and turning around and doing something different with it."[58] Kluck also observed that

> one interesting thing with Herbie Hancock is the fact that MTV was also a really important part of the story, because not only taking this new music, but also having a video of it. It opened Herbie to a completely new audience who probably would never have heard of Herbie Hancock had it not been for MTV and "Rockit."[59]

Kluck's words reveal that Hancock's synthesizers represent a multitude of stories beyond those that are related to the technology's development, such as the power that the cable television music channel MTV had in the 1980s popular music scene. In contrast, the donor of the Apple Mac synthesizer, which was also examined in Chapter 4, was an artist who, like Hancock, experimented with new technology during the process of composing music. In this instance, computer-based technology represents a more localized music community that often gets overshadowed by mainstream narratives.

The representing method is often an opportunity for curators to employ their adaptive expertise to find creative ways to make the esoteric accessible. In Chapter 5, Curator Carlene Stephens framed each of the three separate exhibitions where "Stanley" the autonomous vehicle was displayed. The first, a "stripped down, sparse"[60] exhibition, was an example of the documenting method, as, Stephens noted, the exhibit "had no other context except explaining what the DARPA Grand Challenge was and explaining what Stanley was."[61] The second and third exhibitions, however, were examples representing method at work as "Stanley" was used to present the concepts of technological innovation in computer coding and the practical applications of GPS in their respective exhibitions. Adaptive expertise is also at work at the Computer History Museum's *Make Software: Change the World!* exhibition. In the seven sections (MP3, Photoshop, MRI, Car Crash Simulation, Wikipedia, Texting, and World of Warcraft), the exhibition will often present the analog counterpoint to the software in question. As Curator Marc Weber explains:

> In a sense, we always do that. It can be visually interesting. It mixes it up. But, also, because all these things do come out of some analog predecessor, for the most part… There are two legitimate ways to look at it, though the function or through the technology. So, we are trying to do both.[62]

While many are straightforward examples, such as a copy of the *Encyclopedia Britannica* in the section about Wikipedia or an assortment of vinyl records in the section devoted to MP3s, the section on Photoshop has a much more surprising object on display. A subsection of the exhibition titled "A New Normal" examines how the software's photograph editing capabilities can change perceptions of reality. The exhibit label posed the question "What happens when perfection becomes the norm?" and presented cases of how the media could use Photoshop to do everything from removing skin blemishes to changing the appearance of fashion models to the point of unnatural thinness, creating a false standard of beauty. The related exhibition case contains makeup from the 1950s and a corset from the early 1900s. While it is unexpected to find an example of turn-of-the-century undergarments in a computer-history exhibition, this article of clothing represents far more than an outdated form of dress. As Weber notes, "There are many ways to shape your impression of reality without a computer," though he also acknowledges that "Photoshop does not usually hurt."[63] This is an example of an artifact, seemingly unrelated to computer technology, that serves as metaphor for a complex issue about the application of a commonly used software, demonstrating the flexibility and creativity that the representing method offers.

In Chapter 3, we examined a number of examples where the representing method similarly employed when the curators in the Entertainment Collection used adaptive expertise to record the impact that computer-based technology has had on American popular culture in the twenty-first century. As previously noted, the props, scripts, and costumes from long-form narrative television programs could represent the types of computer-based technology that made this type of storytelling possible. Deputy Chair of the Division of Art and Culture Eric Jentsch had used his adaptive expertise to reinterpret the *Sex and the City* laptop when he explained that there is "a way to explain [Carrie Bradshaw, the main character] as being this modern woman that people can relate to, especially in the use of her technology."[64] No longer just representing the television show that it appeared on, the *Sex and the City* laptop could be seen as a metaphor for internet communication in late twentieth and early twenty-first centuries, with Carrie Bradshaw's blog about her personal life representing the ways that we use social media to document our own lives. The way that the internet has transformed our interpersonal connections is of great interest to Joshua Bell, Curator of Globalization at the Smithsonian's National Museum of Natural History. In Chapter 3, Bell discussed his motivations for the Natural History Museum's computer-based technology exhibition on mobile technology, which he described as trying "to push people to think that technology is not outside of us, but it is part of what we conceive of as our nature."[65] This is reflected in the exhibition's working title of *Unseen Connections: A Natural History of Cell Phones*. Bell adds:

> For me, the goal of the exhibit is to get people to realize how interconnected we are through technology. Not, of course, how we use it to Skype around the world, but then also, more importantly in some ways, the ways in which our device connects us to places and people in the world we do not think about. So, the laborers in Foxconn [contract

> electronics manufacturing company], for one example, or Brazil in factories who manufacture cell phones, the people that actually extract the minerals that go into the device, the designers, etc. The hope there is to get people to realize that their consumption and use of things actually have impacts. And then I am hoping that that will get them to think more cautiously about their activities.[66]

In this exhibition, much like the communicating pager used during September 11, computer-based technology is a physical representative for the way human beings are connected to one another. What can be seen here are three different examples of computer-based technology – an early PDA, a late 1990s laptop computer, and a yet-to-be-determined smartphone – that interest curators for very different reasons. One is associated with a tragic event. The second was collected because it had been a prop on a popular television show. The third will be an example of commonly used technology. And yet, in all three cases, the curator is deliberately using these objects to say something meaningful about the human condition and how we function as a society, both locally and globally. It might even be argued that as we better understand computer-based technology, we better understand ourselves.

The established tradition of computer curation

To turn our attention away from the Smithsonian for a different example of the representing method, the Victoria and Albert Museum in London in their architecture design exhibition *Engineering the World: Ove Arup and the Philosophy of Total Design* (June 18, 2016–November 6, 2016) presented structural engineer Ove Arup's adoption and use of computer technology in the 1950s for structural analysis calculations as an example of his innovation. Zofia Trafas White, Cocurator of the exhibition, writes that "Arup's pioneering application of computers on the Sydney Opera project pushed the limits of contemporary technology and revolutionised engineering practice," adding that this "is particularly meaningful in the context of the ubiquity of computers in design processes today."[67] The use of computer calculation in the process of designing the Sydney Opera House is not in and of itself a significant technological development. In this instance, the computer is an example of innovative practice. In a surprising coincidence, directly across the street, the Science Museum had in its holdings the very kind of computer that was used on the Sydney Opera House project: the Ferranti Pegasus. This is even more remarkable since, as noted on the Science Museum's website, only "thirty-eight Pegasus Is and IIs were sold."[68] Since the Science Museum's Pegasus was no longer in operation, it could be lent to the Victoria and Albert for the Museum's exhibition, representing how computer technology was adopted as a new tool to be used during the design process. With this one computer, all three methods – documenting, operating, and representing – have been utilized in a stunning display of adaptive expertise as curators find new ways to present this early example of computer-based technology.

Pegasus was first examined in terms of the operating method, when it was regularly demonstrated on the floor of the Science Museum in London. Those demonstrations were eventually called to a halt over safety concerns, both for the visitors and for the computer itself. It was determined that continuous operation would eventually compromise the object's structural integrity, destroying valuable historical evidence. And so, the computer was then understood to be a historical record to be preserved, as called for with the documenting method. Finally, curators at the Victoria and Albert Museum, using the representing method, interpreted the computer as a metaphor for the concept of innovation in architectural design. This illustrates how curators, as they use their adaptive expertise, are able to choose the methodology that best fits the circumstances. In Chapter 4, the American History Museum's acquisition of a DNA analyzer used by the National Cancer Institute's Lab of Pathology, significant for the fact that Curator Ann Seeger chose not to collect the desktop computer used with the analyzer, was first examined. Seeger explained her thought process:

> I figured with the storage problems we have here and the fact we do not need to operate the instruments and they were just used with off-the-shelf, in almost every case – a Dell desktop computer. I mean maybe there is not one in the collection, but there easily could be. So, if we ever wanted to set something up on display in a laboratory setting and we needed a computer, we have one in mine already, so we could substitute it. It just did not seem reasonable to collect.[69]

What curators choose not to collect is often as revealing as what they decide to accession. Therefore, it is interesting to note how the three curatorial methods apply to Seeger's decision not to collect the desktop computer. First, it is clear that Seeger, in keeping with general practice at the American History Museum, had decided against the operating method as a viable option for the national museum, since there was no need for the software to be performed. Next, Seeger found no justification to keep the desktop computer under the documenting method, as the "off-the-shelf" computer could provide no direct evidence itself and could be easily substituted with a similar computer on display. Finally, using the representing method, it can be understood that Seeger identified the DNA analyzer itself as a stronger object to illustrate the concept of molecular biology. With the DNA analyzer, as with the Ferranti Pegasus, the methodology that is employed by the curator is based on how the computer-based technology is viewed. If the computer-based technology machine is seen as evidence and has been collected or exhibited for its physical traits, then the curator will likely choose an approach that can be classified as the documenting method. If the machine is seen to be the most meaningful when in action, the operating method will provide the means for a demonstration. Finally, if the most important aspect of the computer-based technology in question is an intangible, complex concept, then the machine has been collected or exhibited as a metaphor with the representing method. This, in turn, reveals our own evolving understanding of computer-based technology.

Chapter 5 examined the iPod that had been on display in the American History Museum's *American Stories* and it was noted that there were two different narratives in the exhibition case: progress of portable music technology, which is told visually, and a story of manufacturing and economics that was told through the exhibit labels. However, by applying an understanding of computer-based technology curation methods, something more complex is revealed to be at work. It is not just two separate narratives displayed, but two different expert curatorial methods employed. As was seen in Chapter 5, Campbell Lilienfeld noted that the exhibition team "were using the iPod and these other musical things to tell a bigger story about economy and manufacturing."[70] These objects, by virtue of where they were manufactured, were able to serve as a metaphor for a larger story about globalization and market economies in a way that visitors would be able to understand. However, visually, the exhibition team was presenting a technological development story using a documenting method approach that requires little to no interpretive information. In Chapter 2, Curator Dag Spicer noted that when the Computer History Museum still had a visible storage exhibition the visitors who had a technical background had a "built in understanding, most of them did not even read the labels."[71] With the iPod's music technology case, Campbell Lilienfeld and the *American Stories* exhibition team recognized that, in this instance, for this example of computer-based technology, their visitors would have the technical background to provide the "built in understanding" that would not require exhibit labels. The distributive expertise in this instance was not shared between the museum staff and a specialized group of expert practitioners. With this example of computer-based technology, we could all be trusted to be computer technology experts because portable electronic music technology had become that ubiquitous.

Conclusion

Early on, computer-based technology was framed as an unprecedented type of object for the museum to collect and exhibit. What is now proposed is that a curatorial tradition is in the process of being established. This tradition has, so far, been expressed in three methodologies: *documenting*, *operating*, and *representing*. As previously demonstrated, these methods allow curators to find creative solutions to exhibition challenges and to provide guidance as to what to collect and preserve. There is evidence both in this chapter and in those previous that computer-based technology has begun to take on an amorphous quality as computer software has become less dependent on computer hardware. It is therefore worth considering what the possible ramification the rise of the digital might have for the balance between hardware-dependent software and software-dependent hardware. Current museum precedent indicates that the museum will continue to engage with these protean objects, facing new unknown challenges even as curatorial methods are being established for the current challenges. We might today understand computer-based technology to be an object, an action, and a concept, but future technological developments might provide new insights into the nature and capabilities of computers. Should that happen – and it likely will – this classification system will then grow to contain more methodological categories. As computer-based technology evolves, so too will its associated tradition of expert curation.

Notes

1 Tilly Blyth, ed., *Information Age: Six Networks That Changed Our World* (London: Scala Arts, 2014) 15.
2 Ross Parry, "Introduction to Part Four," in R. Parry (ed.), *Museums in a Digital Age* (London: Routledge, 2010) 228.
3 Robert Leopold, Smithsonian Institution Archives, Computer Technology and Curation Oral History Interviews, interview with Petrina Foti, May 17, 2013.
4 Edward P. Alexander et al., *Museums in Motion: An Introduction to the History and Functions of Museums* (Lanham, MD: AltaMira Press, 2008) 188.
5 Tilly Blyth, "Exhibiting Information: Developing the Information Age Gallery at the Science Museum," *Information & Culture: A Journal of History*, 51, no. 1 (2016), 4.
6 Hansen Hsu, Smithsonian Institution Archives, Computer Technology and Curation Oral History Interviews, interview with Petrina Foti, March 16, 2018.
7 Harold Wallace, Smithsonian Institution Archives, Computer Technology and Curation Oral History Interviews, interview with Petrina Foti, August 14, 2013.
8 Marc Weber, Smithsonian Institution Archives, Computer Technology and Curation Oral History Interviews, interview with Petrina Foti, March 15, 2017.
9 Tilly Blyth, ed., *Information Age: Six Networks That Changed Our World* (London: Scala Arts, 2014) 15.
10 Tilly Blyth, Smithsonian Institution Archives, Computer Technology and Curation Oral History Interviews, interview with Petrina Foti, December 7, 2017.
11 Tilly Blyth, Smithsonian Institution Archives, Computer Technology and Curation Oral History Interviews, interview with Petrina Foti, December 7, 2017.
12 Harold Wallace, Smithsonian Institution Archives, Computer Technology and Curation Oral History Interviews, interview with Petrina Foti, August 14, 2013.
13 Harold Wallace, Smithsonian Institution Archives, Computer Technology and Curation Oral History Interviews, interview with Petrina Foti, August 14, 2013.
14 National Museum of American History, "'Hear My Voice': Smithsonian Identifies 130-Year-Old Recording as Alexander Graham Bell's Voice," Smithsonian Institution, accessed February 2, 2015.
15 Dag Spicer, interview with Petrina Foti, March 28, 2018.

16 David Brock, Smithsonian Institution Archives, Computer Technology and Curation Oral History Interviews, interview with Petrina Foti, March 16, 2018.
17 David Brock, Smithsonian Institution Archives, Computer Technology and Curation Oral History Interviews, interview with Petrina Foti, March 16, 2018.
18 Dag Spicer, interview with Petrina Foti, March 28, 2018.
19 Robert Leopold, Smithsonian Institution Archives, Computer Technology and Curation Oral History Interviews, interview with Petrina Foti, May 17, 2013.
20 Robert Leopold, Smithsonian Institution Archives, Computer Technology and Curation Oral History Interviews, interview with Petrina Foti, May 17, 2013.
21 Robert Leopold, Smithsonian Institution Archives, Computer Technology and Curation Oral History Interviews, interview with Petrina Foti, May 17, 2013.
22 Hansen Hsu, Smithsonian Institution Archives, Computer Technology and Curation Oral History Interviews, interview with Petrina Foti, March 16, 2018.
23 Living Computers, "About," Living Computers: Museum + Labs, accessed June 19, 2018, https://livingcomputers.org/Join/About.aspx.
24 National Museum of Computing, "About Us," National Museum of Computing, accessed June 29, 2018, www.tnmoc.org/about-us.
25 National Museum of Emerging Science and Innovation, "Robots in Your Life," Miraikan, accessed June 29, 2018, http://www.miraikan.jst.go.jp/en/exhibition/future/robot/robotworld.html.
26 Centre for Computing History, "Visiting," Centre for Computing History, accessed June 29, 2018, http://www.computinghistory.org.uk/pages/28568/Visiting/.
27 This study will examine working computers operated by museum volunteers, as that was the primary method employed at the Smithsonian, Science Museum, and Computer History Museum. There are other methods that allow visitors to use the software itself, on both historic artifacts and emulations. For a more detailed examination of visitor interactive software exhibitions, please see: Marc Weber, "Exhibiting the Online World: A Case Study," in A. Tatnall, T. Blyth, and R. Johnson (eds.), *Making the History of Computing Relevant*, IFIP Advances in Information and Communication Technology, vol. 416 (Berlin: Springer, 2013).
28 Marc Weber, Smithsonian Institution Archives, Computer Technology and Curation Oral History Interviews, interview with Petrina Foti, March 15, 2017.
29 Science Museum Group, "Ferranti Pegasus computer, 1956. 1983-1440," Science Museum Group Collection Online, accessed March 30, 2018, https://collection.sciencemuseum.org.uk/objects/co62559.http://collection.sciencemuseum.org.uk/objects/co62559/ferranti-pegasus-computer-1956-mainframes-computers.
30 Tilly Blyth, Smithsonian Institution Archives, Computer Technology and Curation Oral History Interviews, interview with Petrina Foti, December 7, 2017.
31 Science Museum, "The Pegasus Computer," Filmed 2014, (YouTube video, 5:08), Posted May 13, 2015, https://youtu.be/L0YQk3a24pE.
32 As seen in Chapter 5, this is a contrast to the Digitizing Laboratory in the *DigiLab*,where museum technicians did not enjoy this public aspect of working in front of the public. It might reasonably be assumed that this is due to the fact that the technicians at the American History Museum were museum staff who were accustomed to working in the privacy of offices away from the public. It is understandable that they would not like it when they were suddenly forced to work under constant observation and possible interruption from inquisitive visitors. The primary purpose of gallery assistants, in contrast, is to work with

the public and answer their questions. Indeed, the reason that these historic computers were running at all was for the sake of the visitors.

33 Tilly Blyth, Smithsonian Institution Archives, Computer Technology and Curation Oral History Interviews, interview with Petrina Foti, December 7, 2017.

34 Hansen Hsu, Smithsonian Institution Archives, Computer Technology and Curation Oral History Interviews, interview with Petrina Foti, March 16, 2018.

35 David Allison, Smithsonian Institution Archives, Computer Technology and Curation Oral History Interviews, interview with Petrina Foti, August 12, 2013.

36 Alfred E. Lewis, "Fire at Smithsonian Museum Destroys Computer Exhibit," *The Washington Post*, October 1, 1970, C4.

37 Tilly Blyth, Smithsonian Institution Archives, Computer Technology and Curation Oral History Interviews, interview with Petrina Foti, December 7, 2017.

38 Tilly Blyth, Smithsonian Institution Archives, Computer Technology and Curation Oral History Interviews, interview with Petrina Foti, December 7, 2017.

39 Tilly Blyth, Smithsonian Institution Archives, Computer Technology and Curation Oral History Interviews, interview with Petrina Foti, December 7, 2017.

40 Hansen Hsu, Smithsonian Institution Archives, Computer Technology and Curation Oral History Interviews, interview with Petrina Foti, March 16, 2018.

41 Tilly Blyth, Smithsonian Institution Archives, Computer Technology and Curation Oral History Interviews, interview with Petrina Foti, December 7, 2017.

42 Tilly Blyth, Smithsonian Institution Archives, Computer Technology and Curation Oral History Interviews, interview with Petrina Foti, 7 December 2017.

43 Tilly Blyth, Smithsonian Institution Archives, Computer Technology and Curation Oral History Interviews, interview with Petrina Foti, December 7, 2017.

44 Stacy Kluck, Smithsonian Institution Archives, Computer Technology and Curation Oral History Interviews, interview with Petrina Foti, August 21, 2013.

45 Stacy Kluck, Smithsonian Institution Archives, Computer Technology and Curation Oral History Interviews, interview with Petrina Foti, August 21, 2013.

46 Hansen Hsu, Smithsonian Institution Archives, Computer Technology and Curation Oral History Interviews, interview with Petrina Foti, March 16, 2018.

47 David C. Brock, "Introducing the Center for Software History," *CORE* (2017): 13.

48 David Brock, Smithsonian Institution Archives, Computer Technology and Curation Oral History Interviews, interview with Petrina Foti, March 16, 2018.

49 David Brock, Smithsonian Institution Archives, Computer Technology and Curation Oral History Interviews, interview with Petrina Foti, March 16, 2018.

50 Hansen Hsu, Smithsonian Institution Archives, Computer Technology and Curation Oral History Interviews, interview with Petrina Foti, March 16, 2018.

51 David Brock, Smithsonian Institution Archives, Computer Technology and Curation Oral History Interviews, interview with Petrina Foti, March 16, 2018.

52 Matilda McQuaid, Smithsonian Institution Archives, Computer Technology and Curation Oral History Interviews, interview with Petrina Foti, September 26, 2013.

53 Matilda McQuaid, Smithsonian Institution Archives, Computer Technology and Curation Oral History Interviews, interview with Petrina Foti, September 26, 2013.

54 Dag Spicer, interview with Petrina Foti, March 28, 2018.

55 Tilly Blyth, Smithsonian Institution Archives, Computer Technology and Curation Oral History Interviews, interview with Petrina Foti, December 7, 2017.

56 Smithsonian Institution, "Landmark Objects," Smithsonian Institution, accessed March 14, 2018, https://www.si.edu/exhibitions/landmark-objects-307.
57 I was not affiliated with this as exhibition development occurred after I had left the National Museum of American History.
58 Stacy Kluck, Smithsonian Institution Archives, Computer Technology and Curation Oral History Interviews, interview with Petrina Foti, August 21, 2013.
59 Stacy Kluck, Smithsonian Institution Archives, Computer Technology and Curation Oral History Interviews, interview with Petrina Foti, August 21, 2013.
60 Carlene Stephens, Smithsonian Institution Archives, Computer Technology and Curation Oral History Interviews, interview with Petrina Foti, September 23, 2013.
61 Carlene Stephens, Smithsonian Institution Archives, Computer Technology and Curation Oral History Interviews, interview with Petrina Foti, September 23, 2013.
62 Marc Weber, Smithsonian Institution Archives, Computer Technology and Curation Oral History Interviews, interview with Petrina Foti, March 15, 2017.
63 Marc Weber, Smithsonian Institution Archives, Computer Technology and Curation Oral History Interviews, interview with Petrina Foti, March 15, 2017.
64 Eric Jentsch, Smithsonian Institution Archives, Computer Technology and Curation Oral History Interviews, interview with Petrina Foti, September 10, 2013.
65 Joshua Bell, Smithsonian Institution Archives, Computer Technology and Curation Oral History Interviews, interview with Petrina Foti, November 2, 2017.
66 Joshua Bell, Smithsonian Institution Archives, Computer Technology and Curation Oral History Interviews, interview with Petrina Foti, November 2, 2017.
67 Zofia Trafas White, "Computers and the Sydney Opera House," Victoria and Albert Museum, accessed March 30, 2018, https://www.vam.ac.uk/articles/computers-and-the-sydney-opera-house.
68 Zofia Trafas White, "Computers and the Sydney Opera House," Victoria and Albert Museum, accessed March 30, 2018, https://www.vam.ac.uk/articles/computers-and-the-sydney-opera-house.
69 Ann Seeger, Smithsonian Institution Archives, Computer Technology and Curation Oral History Interviews, interview with Petrina Foti, September 24, 2013.
70 Bonnie Campbell Lilienfeld, Smithsonian Institution Archives, Computer Technology and Curation Oral History Interviews, interview with Petrina Foti, April 26, 2013.
71 Dag Spicer, interview with Petrina Foti, March 28, 2018.

7 The ever-evolving future

This book has attempted to show the complexity of curatorial practice and the thought and care that go into decisions relating to collections stewardship. This is brought into vivid relief by examining instances when curatorial staff are confronted with objects for which there is no previous museum precedent, as is the case with complex and rapidly evolving computer-based technology. As has previously been explored, computer-based technology is a specific example of museums not just collecting the contemporary – and all the challenges that that might bring – but collecting objects that have no direct parallel in terms of structure or capabilities. The interesting and revealing addition to this area of museology is that the museum practitioners considered in this study were able to create precedents by connecting previous examples of curatorial responses to new technology and to employ that as a model of behavior to serve as a guide. This agility of thought and practice serves as evidence that expert curatorial methodology has evolved and continues to evolve, moving away from a model of practice defined by rigid process and fixed standards toward one that is more responsive and distributive. This is an outcome of this research that speaks very directly to Eilean Hooper-Greenhill's observations that "the closed and private space of the early public museums have begun to open, and the division between private and public has begun to close"[1] as it establishes how this process has been occurring. Similarly, this research is perhaps a fully evidenced exemplar of the type of transformative practice noted by Simon Knell that allows "museums to remain those object-centered oases in a world of change,"[2] demonstrating how curatorial staff achieve this change.

This study began first by assembling a model of "expert curation." Three categories of behavior – adaptive expertise, distributive expertise, and transmitted expertise – were presented in terms of curatorial practice at the Smithsonian museums. Adaptive curation was evidenced in curators' ability to meet the unfamiliar with creativity and flexibility. This was seen this with Paul Ceruzzi's use of a disassembled iPod to convey the story of GPS in the *Time and Navigation* exhibition and in the how Curator Eric Jentsch reinterpreted an existing museum object – the *Sex and the City* laptop – to tell the story of how Americans in the early part of the twenty-first century communicated using the internet. Distributed curation could be seen in the sharing between museum professionals, field experts, and museum visitors. This ranged from curators such as Helena Wright's consulting with expert practitioners in the field of Graphic Arts about digital printing to Bonnie Campbell Lilienfeld's recognizing the computer expertise of her visitors in the object label for the iPod on exhibition in *American Stories*. Finally, transmitted curation was seen in the processes and actions that preserve knowledge in a way that is beneficial for the next generation of collection stewards, as was seen with Harold Wallace's preserving lighting software with the hopes that his successors would have better tools and technology than he had available now. Together, these types of expertise were framed as defining traits of a wider pattern and characteristic of expertise in the museum practice of curation, which was then further evidenced in subsequent chapters.

However, in the course of the study into museum practice, a second pattern of curation has emerged relating to the methodologies that the curators employ when they collect and exhibit computer-based technology. A curator might view computer-based technology as an object to be recorded and will therefore use the documenting process to present and preserve the object as evidence. That same curator might also believe that computer-based technology has a function that is only revealed while it is working and that performance must be preserved and might then choose to employ the operating method, if conditions allow. Finally, the curator might turn to the representing method to use computer-based technology as metaphor for complex concepts. Together these methods seem to offer evidence that a museological tradition for curating computer-based technology has begun to form. A natural extension of this study of how curatorial staff has collected and curated computer-based technology would be to broaden the scope to include other types of museums and archives worldwide to see whether similar patterns of curatorial behavior emerged there. Additionally, since these methods of expert curation reveal how we have come to understand computer-based technology as a society, a tantalizing question forms: Can these methods be "reverse engineered"? In other words, if the documenting method is based on the view of computer-based technology as an object and the operating method is based on the view that computer-based technology is an action that must be performed, then could we form methodology to collect and exhibit cloud computing, for example, if curators can identify how we have come to understand this particular type of computer-based technology?

Perhaps our interest in preserving these topics would be revealing enough for the future. What we, as curators and collection managers (and as museum educators, interpreters, exhibit designers, project managers, and all the other valuable people who help make a museum a museum), chose to bring into our museum collections and put out for the public on our exhibition floors and websites reflects on who we are as human beings in the early twenty-first century. Once again, Simon Knell's thoughts in *Museums and the Future of Collecting*, which were first presented in Chapter 2 and have often been revisited through the course of this study, are brought to mind. Knell explained:

> So while some museum workers have been at pains to distinguish contemporary collecting from history collecting, the fact is that all collecting is inevitably contemporary collecting, even if we are collecting things which are valued because of their association with the past. Contemporary collecting is one of the most difficult of practices because of its overwhelming and multifaceted nature, and because we are collecting things that reflect our own society, which we know to be complex. Collecting historical material only seems easier because there is less of it, we know it less well, and because historians have constructed narratives which value one thing above another.[3]

These words resonate as computer-based technology has developed and continues to develop exponentially. What technological advances might have once occurred over many generations, are happening within the lifetime of one curator, often in a matter of years, not decades. In his article "The End of the Beginning: Normativity in the Postdigital Museum," Ross Parry examines the changing role that digital media have played in strategic plans and organizational structures at several national museums in the United Kingdom. He explains that

> to say that the digital is being treated normatively in the museums in question here means (in philosophical terms) much more than just implying the digital is accepted or assimilated. Rather, it is to signal that the normative digital is knowingly (in this local context) an agent to something good. Or, to follow Barham's formation, the presence of digital media (the norm) connects the museum's goals (the ends) to the museum's activity (the means). The presence of digital as a norm furthers the actualization of the museum's ends. In essence, arguing that the digital has become normative (and specifically to use that word) in the museum is not to say that it is widespread or accepted (even though both of these may or may not be true); it is rather to say that digital has become logically wired into the reasoning of the museum.[4]

It is not surprising that the curatorial staff in museums would begin to view the digital, not as "new media," but as a normative tool, since that reflects the presence of digital technology in our own lives. To borrow Parry's framework, digital technology is the norm that helps us accomplish our daily activities, whether it would be to book a trip, access our bank statements, or listen to music.

This study began with the National Museum of American History's acquisition of an iPod as the technology's history was still being written. As of July 27, 2017, less than twenty years after the first iPod was introduced, the American History Museum's 2004 iPod had become a museum piece in truth.[5] Where once we used dedicated hardware devices to listen to music, they have now been replaced with applications on our smartphones. No longer sold by its manufacture, the iPod, like all MP3 players, has been rendered obsolete by computer-based technology. If the museum is increasingly confronted by a lack of material culture relating to computer-based technology, it is only because our own lives have increasingly moved toward the digital. As I typed these words in 2018 on my hybrid tablet (a black box with a keyboard attached) with my smartphone (a pocket-size black box in a black plastic case) playing music beside me, I understood that many of the technologies that I presented in this book – and indeed the very tools I used to write this book – will shortly be as obsolete as the iPod became over the course of my research. We cannot predict how computer-based technology might develop in the future. But we can predict, that no matter what the future might hold, the museum will be there to record it. The question then becomes what new methods of computer-based technology curation will evolve from these technological advances and what that will say about us.

During the course of this book, I used the analogy of the "black box" to describe how these plastic (and generally dark-hued) boxes do not reveal their internal processes and how this quality is particularly challenging for museums in general as one of their primary functions is to display and explain. Yet through this investigation, we have seen that it is not just computer-based technology that is a "black box." With museum curation, we can see the new acquisitions that go in and the exhibits that come out, but only rarely do we see the internal processes that make these things possible. This research seeks to record a moment in time when curators at the Smithsonian Institution are actively working to dismantle the "black box" of computer-based technology, forming new curatorial traditions as they do so. And so, in attempting to see beyond the walls of the quite-often-boxlike museum buildings to examine the thoughts and beliefs of the curatorial staff working inside, this research perhaps allows the "black box" of museum curation to become slightly less opaque.

Notes

1 Eilean Hooper-Greenhill, *Museums and the Shaping of Knowledge* (London: Routledge, 1992) 200.
2 Simon J. Knell, *Museums and the Future of Collecting* (Aldershot: Ashgate, 2004) 46.
3 Simon J. Knell, "Altered Values: Searching for a New Collecting," in S. Knell (ed.), *Museums and the Future of Collecting* (Aldershot: Ashgate, 2004) 33–34.
4 Ross Parry, "The End of the Beginning: Normativity in the Postdigital Museum," *Museum Worlds*, 1, no. 1 (2013), 27.
5 David Pierce, "Goodbye iPod, and Thanks for All the Tunes." Gear, *Wired*, July 27, 2017, https://www.wired.com/story/goodbye-ipod-and-thanks-for-all-the-tunes/.

Bibliography

Alexander, Edward P., and Mary Alexander. *Museums in Motion: An Introduction to the History and Functions of Museums.* 2nd ed. New York: AltaMira Press, 2008.

Allison, David. Smithsonian Institution Archives. Computer Technology and Curation Oral History Interviews. Interview with Petrina Foti. August 12, 2013.

Altshuler, Bruce, ed. *Collecting the New: Museums and Contemporary Art.* Princeton, NJ: Princeton University Press, 2005.

American Alliance of Museums. "Collections Stewardship." American Alliance of Museums. www.aam-us.org/resources/ethics-standards-and-best-practices/collections-stewardship (accessed March 10, 2015).

Aspray, William, and Paul E. Ceruzzi. *The Internet and American Business.* History of Computing. Cambridge, MA: MIT Press, 2010.

Barber, James. Smithsonian Institution Archives. Computer Technology and Curation Oral History Interviews. Interview with Petrina Foti. April 3, 2012.

Bedi, Joyce. Smithsonian Institution Archives. Computer Technology and Curation Oral History Interviews. Interview with Petrina Foti. September 13, 2013.

Bell, Joshua. Smithsonian Institution Archives. Computer Technology and Curation Oral History Interviews. Interview with Petrina Foti. November 2, 2017.

Bell, Joshua, and Joel Kuipers, eds. *Linguistic and Material Intimacies of Cell Phones.* London: Routledge Press, 2018.

Bello, Mark, William Schulz, and Smithsonian Institution. *The Smithsonian Institution: A World of Discovery: An Exploration of Behind-the-Scenes Research in the Arts, Sciences, and Humanities.* Washington, DC: Smithsonian Institution, 1993.

Berners-Lee, Tim, and Mark Fischetti. *Weaving the Web: The Past, Present and Future of the World Wide Web by Its Inventor.* London: Texere, 2000.

Bird, William L., and Faith Bradford. *America's Doll House: The Miniature World of Faith Bradford.* New York: Princeton Architectural Press, 2010.

Bird, William L., and National Museum of American History (U.S.). Division of Political History. *Souvenir Nation: Relics, Keepsakes, and Curios from the Smithsonian's National Museum of American History.* New York: Princeton Architectural Press, 2013.

Blyth, Tilly, ed. *Information Age: Six Networks That Changed Our World.* London: Scala Arts, 2014.

Blyth, Tilly. "Information Age? The Challenges of Displaying Information and Communication Technologies." *Science Museum Group Journal* 3, no. 3 (2015).

Blyth, Tilly. "Exhibiting Information: Developing the Information Age Gallery at the Science Museum." *Information & Culture: A Journal of History* 51, no. 1 (2016): 1–28.

Blyth, Tilly. Smithsonian Institution Archives. Computer Technology and Curation Oral History Interviews. Interview with Petrina Foti. December 7, 2017.

Brock, David C. "Introducing the Center for Software History," *CORE* (2017): 13–16.

Brock, David C. Smithsonian Institution Archives. Computer Technology and Curation Oral History Interviews. Interview with Petrina Foti. March 16, 2018.

Burton, Chris. "The Pegasus Computer." Science Museum. https://blog.sciencemuseum.org.uk/the-pegasus-computer/ (accessed March 30, 2018).

Campbell-Kelly, Martin, and William Aspray. *Computer: A History of the Information Machine*. Boulder, CO: Westview Press, 2004.

Campbell Lilienfeld, Bonnie. Smithsonian Institution Archives. Computer Technology and Curation Oral History Interviews. Interview with Petrina Foti. April 26, 2013.

Castells, Manuel. *Communication Power*. 2nd ed. Oxford: Oxford University Press, 2013.

Centre for Computing History. "Visiting." Centre for Computing History. www.computinghistory.org.uk/pages/28568/Visiting/ (accessed June 29, 2018).

Ceruzzi, Paul E. "Non-Standard Models of Innovation." *Knowledge, Technology & Policy* 11, no. 3 (1998): 40–49.

Ceruzzi, Paul E. *History of Modern Computing*. 2nd ed. Cambridge, MA: MIT Press, 2003.

Ceruzzi, Paul E. "Ready or Not, Computers Are Coming to the People: Inventing the PC." *Organization of American Historians Magazine of History* 24, no. 3 (2010): 25–28.

Ceruzzi, Paul E. *Computing: A Concise History*. The MIT Press Essential Knowledge Series. Cambridge, MA: MIT Press, 2012.

Ceruzzi, Paul E. Smithsonian Institution Archives. Computer Technology and Curation Oral History Interviews. Interview with Petrina Foti. July 24, 2013.

Ceruzzi, Paul E. Smithsonian Institution Archives. Computer Technology and Curation Oral History Interviews. Interview with Petrina Foti. June 1, 2017.

Chan, Sebastian, and Aaron Straup Cope. Smithsonian Institution Archives. Computer Technology and Curation Oral History Interviews. Interview with Petrina Foti. September 26, 2013.

Charlton, Thomas L., Lois E. Myers, and Rebecca Sharpless, eds. *History of Oral History: Foundations and Methodology*. Plymouth, UK: Rowman and Littlefield, 2007.

Chi, Michelene T. H., Robert Glaser, and Marshall J. Farr. *The Nature of Expertise*. Hove: Lawrence Erlbaum Associates, 1988.

Conaway, James. *The Smithsonian: 150 Years of Adventure, Discovery, and Wonder*. Washington, DC: Smithsonian Books, 1995.

Cooper Hewitt National Design Museum. Smithsonian Institution. www.cooperhewitt.org/ (accessed March 14, 2015).

Crouch, Tom. Smithsonian Institution Archives. Computer Technology and Curation Oral History Interviews. Interview with Petrina Foti. April 5, 2012.

Cutler, Alicia. Smithsonian Institution Archives. Computer Technology and Curation Oral History Interviews. Interview with Petrina Foti. June 3, 2013

Day, Giskin, and Louise Wilson. *Inside the Science Museum*. London: NMSI Trading, 2001.

De Groot, Jerome. *Consuming History: Historians and Heritage in Contemporary Popular Culture*. London: Routledge, 2009.
Delaney, Michelle. Smithsonian Institution Archives. Computer Technology and Curation Oral History Interviews. Interview with Petrina Foti. September 5, 2013.
Dudley, Sandra. *Museum Objects: Experiencing the Properties of Things*. London: Routledge, 2012.
Dudley, Sandra. *Narrating Objects, Collecting Stories: Essays in Honour of Professor Susan M. Pearce*. London: Routledge, 2012.
Ellis, Carolyn, Tony E. Adams, and Arthur P. Bochner. "Autoethnography: An Overview." *Historical Social Research/Historische Sozialforschung* 36, no. 4 (138) (2011): 273–290.
Ericsson, K. Anders. *Development of Professional Expertise*. Cambridge: Cambridge University Press, 2009.
Ericsson, K. Anders. "Expertise." *Current Biology*: CB 24, no. 11 (2014): R508–R510.
Evans, Richard J. *In Defence of History*. London: Granta Books, 2000.
Ewing, Heather P., and Amy Ballard. *A Guide to Smithsonian Architecture*. Washington, DC: Smithsonian Books, 2009.
Finn, Bernard. Smithsonian Institution Archives. Computer Technology and Curation Oral History Interviews. Interview with Petrina Foti. August 14, 2013.
Fisher, Stevan. Smithsonian Institution Archives. Computer Technology and Curation Oral History Interviews. Interview with Petrina Foti. August 5, 2013.
Freidson, Eliot. *Professional Powers: A Study of the Institutionalization of Formal Knowledge*. Chicago; London: University of Chicago Press, 1986.
Freidson, Eliot. *Professionalism Reborn: Theory, Prophecy, and Policy*. Cambridge: Polity Press, 1994.
Freidson, Eliot. *Professionalism: The Third Logic*. Cambridge: Polity, 2001.
Garcia Canclini, Nestor. "How Digital Convergence Is Changing Cultural Theory." Translated by Margaret Schwartz. *Popular Communication* 7, no. 3 (2009): 140–146.
Gardner, James B., and Sarah M. Henry. "September 11 and the Mourning After: Reflections on Collecting and Interpreting the History of Tragedy." *The Public Historian* 24, no. 3 (2002): 37–52.
Genoways, Hugh H., and Mary Anne Andrei. *Museum Origins: Readings in Early Museum History and Philosophy*. Walnut Creek, CA: Left Coast Press, 2008.
Germain, Marie-Line. "A Chronological Synopsis of the Dimensions of Expertise: Toward the Expert of the Future." *Performance Improvement* 50, no. 7 (2011): 38–46.
Golding, Vivien. *Learning at the Museum Frontiers: Identity, Race and Power*. Farnham: Ashgate, 2009.
Goode, G. Brown. *An Account of the Smithsonian Institution: Its Origin, History, Objects and Achievements*. Washington, DC: Smithsonian, 1895.
Green, Anna, and Kathleen Troup. *The Houses of History: A Critical Reader in Twentieth-Century History and Theory*. Manchester: Manchester University Press, 1999.
Hafertepe, Kenneth, and Smithsonian Institution. *America's Castle: The Evolution of the Smithsonian Building and Its Institution, 1840–1878*. Washington, DC: Smithsonian Institution Press, 1984.
Hashagen, Ulf, Reinhard Keil-Slawik, and Arthur Norberg, eds. *History of Computing: Software Issues*. New York: Springer, 2002.

Hein, George E. *Learning in the Museum*. London: Routledge, 1998.
Higgins, Sarah. "Digital Curation: The Emergence of a New Discipline." *International Journal of Digital Curation* 6, no. 2 (2011): 78–88.
Hobsbawm, E. J. *On History*. London: Abacus, 1997.
Hooper-Greenhill, Eilean. *Museums and the Shaping of Knowledge*. London: Routledge, 1992.
Hostetler, Lisa. Smithsonian Institution Archives. Computer Technology and Curation Oral History Interviews. Interview with Petrina Foti. September 4, 2013.
Hsu, Hansen. Smithsonian Institution Archives. Computer Technology and Curation Oral History Interviews. Interview with Petrina Foti. March 16, 2018.
Hughes, Philip. *Exhibition Design*. London: Laurence King, 2010.
Jentsch, Eric. Smithsonian Institution Archives. Computer Technology and Curation Oral History Interviews. Interview with Petrina Foti. September 10, 2013.
Kavanagh, Gaynor, ed. *History Curatorship*. Leicester: Leicester University Press, 1990.
Kavanagh, Gaynor, ed. *The Museums Profession: Internal and External Relations*. Leicester: Leicester University Press, 1991.
Kavanagh, Gaynor, ed. *Museum Provision and Professionalism*. New York; London: Routledge, 1994.
Kavanagh, Gaynor, ed. *Making Histories in Museums*. London: Leicester University Press, 1996.
Keene, Suzanne. *Digital Collections: Museums and the Information Age*. Oxford: Butterworth–Heinemann, 1998.
Kidwell, Peggy Aldrich, Paul Ceruzzi, and Smithsonian Institution. *Landmarks in Digital Computing: A Smithsonian Pictorial History*. Washington, DC: Smithsonian Institution Press, 1994.
Kiramidas, Kimon. 2015. "Exhibiting the Interface: Curating Computers and Designing Didactic User Experiences." Paper presented at MW2015: Museums and the Web 2015, Chicago, April 8–11, 2015. http://mw2015.museumsandtheweb.com/paper/exhibiting-the-interface-curating-computers-and-designing-didactic-user-experiences/.
Kluck, Stacy. Smithsonian Institution Archives. Computer Technology and Curation Oral History Interviews. Interview with Petrina Foti. August 21, 2013.
Knell, Simon J., ed. *Museums and the Future of Collecting*. 2nd ed. Aldershot: Ashgate, 2004.
Knell, Simon J., Peter Aronsson, and Arne Bugge Amundsen. *National Museums*. London: Routledge, 2010.
Knell, Simon J., Sheila E. R. Watson, and Suzanne MacLeod. *Museum Revolutions: How Museums Change and Are Changed*. New York: Routledge, 2007.
Kurin, Richard, and Smithsonian Institution Center for Folklife Programs and Cultural Studies. *Smithsonian Folklife Festival: Culture of, by, and for the People*. Washington, DC: Center for Folklife Programs and Cultural Studies, Smithsonian Institution, 1998.
Larson, Magali Sarfatti. *The Rise of Professionalism: A Sociological Analysis*. London: University of California Press, 1977.
Lavington, Simon. *Alan Turing and His Contemporaries: Building the World's First Computers*. Swindon, UK: British Informatics Society, 2012.
Leopold, Robert. Smithsonian Institution Archives. Computer Technology and Curation Oral History Interviews. Interview with Petrina Foti. May 17, 2013.

Lewis, Alfred E. "Fire at Smithsonian Museum Destroys Computer Exhibit." *The Washington Post*, October 1, 1970, C4.

Liebhold, Peter, and Harry R. Rubenstein. "Bringing Sweatshops into the Museum." In *Sweatshop USA: The American Sweatshop in Historical and Global Perspective*, edited by R. Greenwald and D. Bender. New York: Routledge, 2003.

Living Computers. "About." Living Computers: Museum + Labs. https://livingcomputers.org/Join/About.aspx (accessed June 19, 2018).

Lubar, Steven. *InfoCulture: The Smithsonian Book of Information Age Inventions*. New York: Houghton Mifflin, 1993.

Lubar, Steven D., and Kathleen M. Kendrick. *Legacies: Collecting America's History at the Smithsonian*. Washington, DC: Smithsonian Institution Press, 2001.

Macdonald, Sharon. *Behind the Scenes at the Science Museum*. Oxford: Berg, 2002.

MacLeod, Suzanne, Jonathan Hale, and Laura Hourston Hanks. *Museum Meanings: Museum Making: Narratives, Architectures, Exhibitions*. Taylor & Francis, 2012.

Malaro, Marie C. *A Legal Primer on Managing Museum Collections*. 2nd ed. Washington, DC: Smithsonian Books, 1998.

Malaro, Marie C. *Museum Governance: Mission, Ethics, Policy*. Washington, DC: Smithsonian Institution Press, 1994.

Marty, Paul F. "An Introduction to Digital Convergence: Libraries, Archives, and Museums in the Information Age." *Museum Management and Curatorship* 24, no. 4 (2009): 295–298.

McQuaid, Matilda. Smithsonian Institution Archives. Computer Technology and Curation Oral History Interviews. Interview with Petrina Foti. September 26, 2013.

Meikle, Graham, and Sherman Young. *Media Convergence: Networked Digital Media in Everyday Life*. Basingstoke: Palgrave Macmillan, 2012.

Melder, Keith. Smithsonian Institution Archives. *American Association of Museums Centennial Interviews*, 2006.

Message, Kylie. *Museums and Social Activism: Engaged Protest*. Hoboken, NJ: Routledge, 2013.

National Air and Space Museum. Smithsonian Institution. http://airandspace.si.edu/ (accessed March 14, 2015).

National Museum of American History. National Museum of American History Computers Collection. Object Records.

National Museum of American History. National Museum of American History Electricity Collection. Object Records.

National Museum of American History. National Museum of American History Entertainment Collection. Object Records.

National Museum of American History. National Museum of American History Graphic Arts Collection. Exhibit Files. DigiLab.

National Museum of American History. National Museum of American History Health Services Collection. Object Records.

National Museum of American History. National Museum of American History Office of the Registrar. Registration Services Records.

National Museum of American History. National Museum of American History Photographic History Collection. Object Records.

National Museum of American History. "September 11: Bearing Witness to History." Smithsonian Institution. http://americanhistory.si.edu/september11/ (accessed June 5, 2012).

National Museum of American History. Mimsy XG Database. Object Records. Accessed July 2013.

National Museum of American History. "'Hear My Voice': Smithsonian Identifies 130-Year-Old Recording as Alexander Graham Bell's Voice." Smithsonian Institution. http://americanhistory.si.edu/press/releases/smithsonian-identifies-graham-bell-recording (accessed February 2, 2015).

National Museum of American History. Smithsonian Institution. http://americanhistory.si.edu/ (accessed March 14, 2015).

National Museum of Computing. "About Us." The National Museum of Computing. www.tnmoc.org/about-us (accessed June 29, 2018).

National Museum of Emerging Science and Innovation. "Robots in Your Life." Miraikan. www.miraikan.jst.go.jp/en/exhibition/future/robot/robotworld.html (accessed June 29, 2018).

Netflix Media Center. "A Brief History of the Company That Revolutionized Watching of Movies and TV Shows." Netflix. https://pr.netflix.com/WebClient/loginPageSalesNetWorksAction.do?contentGroupId=10477. (accessed February 20, 2015).

Parry, Ross. *Recoding the Museum: Digital Heritage and the Technologies of Change.* London: Routledge, 2007.

Parry, Ross. *Museums in a Digital Age.* London: Routledge, 2009.

Parry, Ross. "The End of the Beginning: Normativity in the Postdigital Museum." *Museum Worlds* 1, no. 1 (2013): 24–39.

Pearce, Susan M. *Museums, Objects and Collections: A Cultural Study.* Leicester: Leicester University Press, 1992.

Pearce, Susan M. *Interpreting Objects and Collections.* London: Routledge, 1994.

Pearce, Susan M. *On Collecting: An Investigation into Collecting in the European Tradition.* London: Routledge, 1995.

Pearce, Susan M. *Collecting in Contemporary Practice.* London: Sage, 1998.

Perich, Shannon. Smithsonian Institution Archives. Computer Technology and Curation Oral History Interviews. Interview with Petrina Foti. September 26, 2013.

Pierce, David. "Goodbye iPod, and Thanks for All the Tunes." Gear, *Wired*, July 27, 2017. www.wired.com/story/goodbye-ipod-and-thanks-for-all-the-tunes/.

Post, Robert C. *Who Owns America's Past? The Smithsonian and the Problem of History.* Baltimore: The Johns Hopkins University Press, 2013.

Proctor, Nancy. Smithsonian Institution Archives. Computer Technology and Curation Oral History Interviews. Interview with Petrina Foti. August 15, 2013.

Ray, Joyce. "The Rise of Digital Curation and Cyberinfrastructure: From Experimentation to Implementation and Maybe Integration." *Library Hi Tech* 30, no. 4 (2012): 604–622.

Rhys, Owain. *Contemporary Collecting: Theory and Practice.* Edinburgh: Museums Etc, 2011.

Ronchi, Alfredo M. *ECulture: Cultural Content in the Digital Age.* Berlin; Heidelberg: Springer, 2008.

Rosander, Göran and SAMDOK. *Today for Tomorrow: Museum Documentation of Contemporary Society in Sweden by Acquisition of Objects.* Stockholm: SAMDOK Council, 1980.

Rubenstein, Harry. Smithsonian Institution Archives. Computer Technology and Curation Oral History Interviews. Interview with Petrina Foti. April 12, 2012.

Schlereth, Thomas J. *Artifacts and the American Past*. Nashville, TN: American Association for State and Local History, 1980.

Schlereth, Thomas J. *Cultural History and Material Culture: Everyday Life, Landscapes, Museums*. London: University Press of Virginia, 1992.

Schwarzer, Marjorie, and American Association of Museums. *Riches, Rivals and Radicals: 100 Years of Museums in America*. Washington, DC: American Association of Museums, 2006.

Science Museum Group. Ferranti Pegasus computer, 1956. 1983–1440." Science Museum Group Collection Online. https://collection.sciencemuseum.org.uk/objects/co62559.http://collection.sciencemuseum.org.uk/objects/co62559/ferranti-pegasus-computer-1956-mainframes-computers (accessed March 30, 2018).

Science Museum Group. "The Pegasus Computer." Filmed 2014. YouTube video, 5:08. Posted May 13, 2015. https://youtu.be/L0YQk3a24pE.

Seeger, Ann. Smithsonian Institution Archives. Computer Technology and Curation Oral History Interviews. Interview with Petrina Foti. September 24, 2013.

Shayt, David H. "Artifacts of Disaster: Creating the Smithsonian's Katrina Collection." *Technology and Culture* 47, no. 2 (2006): 357–368.

Shayt, David H. "Collecting Katrina: The Museum Challenge," March 10, 2006 draft.

Smithsonian Institution. *Annual Report of the Board of Regents of the Smithsonian Institution*. Washington, DC: Smithsonian Institution, 1847–1964.

Smithsonian Institution. "Collection Search Center." Smithsonian Object Database. http://collections.si.edu/search/ (accessed March 2014).

Smithsonian Institution. "Landmark Objects." Smithsonian Institution. www.si.edu/exhibitions/landmark-objects-307 (accessed March 14, 2018).

Smithsonian Institution. *Increase and Diffusion: A Brief Introduction to the Smithsonian Institution*. Washington, DC: Smithsonian Institution, 1970.

Smithsonian Institution. Smithsonian Institution. www.si.edu/ (accessed March 14, 2015).

Smithsonian Institution Archives. Record Unit 158. United States National Museum. Curators' Annual Reports.

Spicer, Dag. Interview with Petrina Foti. March 28, 2018.

Stephens, Carlene. Smithsonian Institution Archives. Computer Technology and Curation Oral History Interviews. Interview with Petrina Foti. September 23, 2013.

Tatnall, Arthur, Tilly Blyth, and Roger Johnson, eds. *Making the History of Computing Relevant: IFIP WG 9.7 International Conference, HC 2013, London, UK, June 17–18, 2013, Revised Selected Papers*. Vol. 416. Berlin, Heidelberg: Springer, 2013.

Thomas-Jones, Angela. *The Host in the Machine: Examining the Digital in the Social*. Oxford: Chandos Publishing, 2010.

True, Webster Prentiss. *The First Hundred Years of the Smithsonian Institution, 1846–1946*, Washington, DC: Smithsonian Press, 1946.

Van Dijk, Jan. *The Network Society*. 3rd ed. London: Sage, 2012.

Walker, William S. *A Living Exhibition: The Smithsonian and the Transformation of the Universal Museum*. Amherst: University of Massachusetts Press, 2013.

Wallace, Harold. Smithsonian Institution Archives. Computer Technology and Curation Oral History Interviews. Interview with Petrina Foti. August 14, 2013.

Weber, Marc. "Self-Fulfilling History: How Narrative Shapes Preservation of the Online World." *Information & Culture: A Journal of History* 51, no. 1 (2016): 54–80.

Weber, Marc. Smithsonian Institution Archives. Computer Technology and Curation Oral History Interviews. Interview with Petrina Foti. March 15, 2017.

Weil, Stephen E. *Making Museums Matter*. Washington, DC; London: Smithsonian Institution Press, 2002.

White, Zofia Trafas. "Computers and the Sydney Opera House." Victoria and Albert Museum. www.vam.ac.uk/articles/computers-and-the-sydney-opera-house (accessed March 30, 2018).

Witcomb, Andrea. *Re-Imagining the Museum: Beyond the Mausoleum*. London: Routledge, 2003.

Wright, Helena. "Prints at the Smithsonian: The Origins of a National Collection." *Museum Management and Curatorship* 15, no. 4 (1996): 440–440.

Wright, Helena. Smithsonian Institution Archives. Computer Technology and Curation Oral History Interviews. Interview with Petrina Foti. August 5, 2013.

Yochelson, Ellis Leon, Mary Jarrett, and National Museum of Natural History (United States). *The National Museum of Natural History: 75 Years in the Natural History Building*. Ann Arbor, MI: UMI Books, 1996.

Zick, Greg. "Digital Collections: History and Perspectives." *Journal of Library Administration* 49, no. 7 (2009): 687–693.

Index